TABLE OF CONTENTS

D1370436

CHART OF TABLES AND FIGURES

LIST OF PRIVACY ENFORCEMENT CASE STUDIES (U.S.)

FOREWORD

In the late 1990s, the information economy sparked the expansion of companies' abilities to gather, use, and share personal information. In response, the U.S. Congress—and separately, the E.U. Commission—decided to proactively pass privacy laws in their jurisdictions that required companies to inform individuals as to how they use, share, and protect customer information. Companies were, and still are, compelled to allow individuals to choose how their personal information is used and shared.

Many of us, from legal compliance, risk management and other areas, were thrown into this wilderness to develop a new discipline, a new industry—the privacy profession.

Over many years, we have seen our profession grow from several dozen to several thousand. Some of this growth was helped along by a proliferation of other laws affecting privacy and data security: GLBA, HIPAA, COPPA, CAN-SPAM, FACTA, TSR, TCPA and ECPA to name just a few.

Companies themselves came to realize that privacy just makes good business sense. It engenders trust among customers and helps companies gain a larger share of existing customer business—in addition to helping to attract new customers.

More recently, privacy breaches in dozens of companies are generating another round of state and federal legislative reactions that will get more companies' attention and likely swell our ranks even more.

I am proud to have been a part of the IAPP since its inception in 2001 and am even prouder to have been named President by my peers. The IAPP has quickly grown from a few U.S.-based privacy wonks to a large and diverse network of privacy professionals from around the world.

The IAPP is integral to all of our successes as privacy professionals and will continue to figure prominently in what we do each day. The association's two annual conferences, the Summit and the Academy, are now must-attend events for anyone who is interested or involved in the task of protecting data.

Privacy certification is the capstone to the IAPP's many efforts to date. It is not only one of our largest services to members today—but arguably our most significant contribution to the privacy profession ever.

The Certified Information Privacy Professional (CIPP) officially launched in the fall of 2004. The Certified Information Privacy Professional/Government (CIPP/G) followed in March 2005 and in October 2006 the IAPP unveiled our first international credential, the Certified Information Privacy Professional/Canada (CIPP/C). These are all pillars in the IAPP's future master's program. All are born of an idea to cast a uniform body of knowledge necessary before any group can truly proclaim itself to be a "profession."

The book you now hold is the first real attempt by any organization to document a foundation body of knowledge around the practice of information privacy. It is appropriate that such a considerable work be published by the IAPP, the only international organization devoted to meeting the needs of privacy professionals.

Information Privacy offers the prospective privacy professional a window into the new world that he or she is about to enter. It has been designed to provide each student with the basics to understand and apply information management practices in a variety of regulatory, technical and operational environments.

For current privacy professionals, this book will help to support the knowledge and skills that you have already developed. Most importantly, successful completion of the CIPP program will tell any prospective employer that you have the necessary skills to spot and analyze a wide array of privacy issues.

I want to thank my colleagues on the board of directors of the IAPP who approved privacy certification in concept and found the financial and human resources necessary to get the first program off the ground. I also would like to thank the CIPP advisory board who helped to develop the course curriculum and general outline for this book. I want to thank the Moritz School of Law at the Ohio State University who provided us with the able talents of Professor Peter Swire and his team.

Finally, to Peter Kosmala, I want to say that without your ability to keep a thousand plates spinning at once, I doubt that I'd be writing this foreword today. Thank God that Trevor Hughes had the good fortune to hire you!

Kirk Herath, CIPP/G
President
International Association of Privacy Professionals
Chief Privacy Officer and Associate General Counsel
Nationwide Insurance Company

March 2007

ACKNOWLEDGEMENTS

I joined the IAPP in March of 2004 for the rare opportunity not only to develop the privacy industry's first major credential but to help to define the profession itself through a major educational initiative. I brought with me what I considered to be a decent track record in authoring and managing professional development programs for a number of organizations and private sector companies. And I leveraged my own background in advertising, publishing and Internet media.

But the opportunity demanded so much more. It required the knowledge, insight and perspective of a vast group of talented professionals, many of whom graciously volunteered their time, effort and expertise. I am honored to have worked so closely with these privacy leaders to create what we know and respect today as the CIPP program.

My sincere gratitude begins with the IAPP leadership and staff: President Kirk Herath, Executive Director Trevor Hughes, the board of directors of the IAPP and my colleagues at the association. It has been both a pleasure and a privilege to become a part of your organization and to serve your vision of establishing a recognized educational and testing standard in privacy.

I am also grateful to the founding grantors of the CIPP program: Hewlett-Packard and Microsoft. Very simply, the CIPP would not have been possible were it not for the generous support of both of these organizations—nor would I have had the opportunity to join the IAPP as its first director of certification.

Our collective thanks go to the CIPP advisory board, a distinguished group that first articulated the requirements of the CIPP and which remains today as the guiding force behind the program. The former and current members of the CIPP advisory board are:

Dan Swartwood, CIPP
Privacy Protection Officer, Motorola, and inaugural CIPP advisory Board Chair;

Kirk Herath, CIPP/G
*Chief Privacy Officer and Associate General Counsel, Nationwide Insurance Company,
and IAPP President;*

Sandy Hughes, CIPP
Global Privacy Executive, Procter & Gamble, and IAPP Vice President;

Peter Cullen, CIPP
Chief Privacy Strategist, Microsoft Corporation, and IAPP board member;

Barbara Lawler, CIPP
Chief Privacy Officer, Intuit, and IAPP board member;

Jonathan Avila, CIPP
Vice President-Counsel, Chief Privacy Officer, The Walt Disney Company, and IAPP board member;

Larry Ponemon, CIPP
Founder, The Ponemon Institute;

Peggy Eisenhauer, CIPP
Founder and Principal, Privacy and Information Management Services P.C.;

Jim Jordan, CIPP
Founder, Jordan Legal Counsel P.C.;

Dennis Becktell, CIPP,
Chief Technology Strategist and Distinguished Architect, eBay, Inc.;

Richard Purcell, CIPP
Chief Executive Officer, Corporate Privacy Group;

Scott Taylor
Chief Privacy Officer, Hewlett-Packard Company;

Brendon Lynch, CIPP
Director of Privacy Strategy, Microsoft Corporation; and,

Tammy Oswald, CIPP
Privacy Manager, Nordstrom.

I am both gratified and honored that Professor Peter Swire and Sol Bermann accepted our invitation to write the very first reference text on the CIPP program. Their impressive work now lies before you.

Professor Swire brings a distinguished record of achievement as the very first privacy officer in U.S. government and as the C. William O'Neill Professor of Law at the Moritz College of Law of The Ohio State University. He continues to be a leading speaker, writer and thinker on privacy issues in both the public and private sectors through his work with OSU-Moritz, the Center for American Progress and the Social Science Research Network.

Sol Bermann helped to manage one of the very first event series dedicated to privacy issues, PrivacyCon, (now incorporated into IAPP events). He also teaches privacy law at OSU-Moritz and serves as Managing Editor of a leading quarterly review of privacy issues, *I/S: A Journal of Law and Policy for the Information Society*.

Professor Swire and Mr. Bermann have researched and authored a seminal reference that will serve the needs of both certification candidates and existing certified professionals. We are most appreciative for their fine work.

A number of individuals also contributed to sections of this textbook whether through researching, editing and/or authoring source material. I would like to recognize these contributors by section:

Matt Beirlein
For "Privacy Fundamentals"

Peggy Eisenhauer
For "Privacy Law and Compliance"

Margaret Betzel and Jim Jordan
For "Workplace Privacy"

Josh Deinsen and Dennis Becktell
For "Information Security"

Katy Delaney
For "Online Privacy"

Shannon Rogers and Barbara Lawler
For "Data Sharing and Transfer"

I thank Elise Berkower for her excellent copy editing and Heather Roman and Tammy Sneddon for their exemplary book design and layout work, respectively.

My final thanks go to you, the reader, for purchasing this textbook and for participating in this important industry initiative.

The CIPP program is about much more than the strategic objectives of an association, the collective efforts of a group or even the project leadership of an individual. It is about your involvement in the privacy profession as a valued IAPP member and your ability to strengthen and advance your standing in the industry through a recognized and respected credential, the CIPP.

I trust you will embrace the CIPP program and *Information Privacy*, its reference text, with the same vigor and enthusiasm as all of the individuals who have contributed so much to both of these efforts.

Peter Kosmala, CIPP
Assistant Director
International Association of Privacy Professionals

March 2007

INTRODUCTION

O n a seasonably muggy October morning in New Orleans, 140 brave privacy
professionals gathered together at the 2004 IAPP Privacy Academy to take the
very first CIPP examination.

Some came to validate their privacy knowledge and industry experience. Others came
to earn their entry to a new profession. And still others sought to be a part of a pioneering
moment: the launch of the very first, publicly available credential ever to be offered in
information privacy. But I most remember the day for the remarks that an IAPP member
conveyed to me afterward:

"I think we've just seen the evolution of privacy as a career."

Privacy offers a career that is full of opportunity, and the establishment of a baseline
set of standard knowledge is important in order to demonstrate the credibility of the
profession—to business, to government and to the customers and citizens we serve.

The market dynamics of privacy are constantly evolving. Demonstrating knowledge of
the foundational tenets of privacy is a critical first step in not only understanding how to
approach the responsibilities incumbent on a privacy professional but also in forging a clear
path within the profession.

It is nearly three years since the debut of IAPP privacy certification and our association offers not one but three major credentials—CIPP, CIPP/G and CIPP/C—with more
international and industry-specific certifications on the horizon. We will soon offer a
master's program that is designed specifically for chief privacy officers and other senior
information management professionals.

To date the IAPP has certified over 1,000 professionals that work successfully in
the privacy field. These professionals represent a number of business sectors, government
agencies and world geographies. And they recognize the value and distinction that the
CIPP offers: industry research continues to show that more and more employers are
seeking the CIPP credential in their minimum requirements for hiring and promoting
candidates in their organizations.

I encourage you to take advantage of everything the IAPP has to offer—from industry-leading conferences and networking forums to valuable research reports and career development resources such as this reference book.

Make privacy certification the first step in your deeper engagement with our growing profession. The CIPP program is designed to help you achieve the professional goals that you seek as well as to elevate the privacy profession itself to new heights of growth and diversity.

On behalf of the IAPP, I thank you for participating in the CIPP program and for purchasing this reference book. Know that we consider you an important part of our privacy community and remain available to further support and promote your professional pursuits.

J. Trevor Hughes, CIPP
Executive Director
International Association of Privacy Professionals

March 2007

Chapter One

PRIVACY FUNDAMENTALS

Defining Privacy

In 1890, the U.S. Supreme Court justices Samuel Warren and Louis Brandeis published "*The Right to Privacy*" in the *Harvard Law Review*, setting forth the essential definition of privacy as "the right to be left alone."[1] Both fundamental and concise, the definition underscored the personal and social dimensions of the concept that would linger long after the publication of this landmark essay.

In the time since, numerous other individuals, organizations and world bodies have posited their own privacy definitions. Privacy has been defined, variously, as the desire of people to choose freely the circumstances and degree to which an individual will expose his attitude and behavior to others.[2] It has been connected to the human personality and used as a means to protect an individual's independence, dignity and integrity.[3] Privacy has been reduced to the elements of secrecy, anonymity and solitude, which themselves may be lost due to personal choice or state or third party action.[4]

More recently, privacy was defined by the United Kingdom's Calcutt Committee (1997) as "[t]he right of the individual to be protected against intrusion into his personal life or affairs, or those of his family, by direct physical means or by publication of information."[5] The Australian Privacy Charter states that "[a] free and democratic society requires respect for the autonomy of individuals, and limits on the power of both state and private organizations to intrude on that autonomy."[6]

Establishing an understanding of how privacy is defined and categorized—as well as how it has emerged as a social concern—are critical components to understanding data protection and privacy law as they have been established today in the United States and Europe as well as elsewhere around the world.

Classes of Privacy

While privacy can be defined in many different terms, it is equally important to understand how it is categorized. Four main areas of privacy are of particular interest with regard to data protection and privacy laws and practices:

1. *Information privacy* is concerned with establishing rules that govern the collection and handling of personal information. This can include credit information, medical data, and government records.[7]

2. *Bodily privacy* is focused exclusively on a person's physical being and any invasion thereof. Such an invasion can take the form of genetic testing, drug testing, or body cavity searches.[8]

3. *Territorial privacy* is concerned with placing limitations on the ability of one to intrude into another individual's environment. Environment is not limited to the home; it may be defined as the workplace or public space and environmental considerations can be extended to an international level. Invasion into an individual's territorial privacy typically comes in the form of video surveillance, ID checks, and use of similar technology and procedures.[8]

4. *Communications privacy* encompasses protection of the means of correspondence, including postal mail, telephone conversations, electronic email and other forms of communicative behavior and apparatus.[9]

While some of these categories may interrelate, this reference text will focus exclusively on the legal, technological, operational and practical components of information privacy.

The Social Origins of Privacy

The concept of privacy as a social concept is rooted in some of the oldest texts and cultures known to man.[10] Privacy is recognized in the Qur'an and in the sayings of Mohammed where there is discussion of the privacy of prayer as well as in the avoidance of spying or talking ill of someone behind their back.[11] Privacy is referenced numerous times in the Bible and in the laws of classical Greece. The concept of the freedom from being watched has historically been recognized by Jewish law.[12] Lastly, privacy protections were incorporated into the cultural fabric of ancient China.[13]

In addition to being intertwined with religion and culture, privacy has arisen within the context of human rights. In December 1948, the General Assembly of the United Nations adopted and proclaimed the Universal Declaration of Human Rights.[14] This declaration formally advanced the notion that "[n]o one shall be subjected to arbitrary interference with his privacy, family, home or correspondence[.]"[15] The statement was intended to encompass a wide range of conduct, as evidenced by Article 12 of the Declaration, which describes both the territorial and the communications notions of privacy.

Also in 1948, the Organization of American States (OAS) adopted the American Declaration of the Rights and Duties of Man.[16] This declaration pre-dated the Universal Declaration of Human Rights by six months and conveyed a similar sentiment: providing that "[e]very person has the right to the protection of the law against abusive attacks upon…his private and family life." [17]

In 1950, the Council of Europe set forth the European Convention for the Protection of Human Rights and Fundamental Freedoms.[18] The Convention acknowledged the goals of the aforementioned Universal Declaration of Human Rights and sought to secure the recognition and observance of the rights enunciated by the United Nations. The Convention provides that "[e]veryone has the right to respect for his private and family life, his home and his correspondence."[19] Article 8 of the treaty limits a public authority's interference with an individual's right to privacy, but allows for an exception with regard to inference that is in accord with the law and necessary to preserve a democratic society.

The legal protection of privacy rights has a similarly far-reaching history. It began in Europe in the mid-14th century with The Justices of the Peace Act (England, 1361). This act included provisions calling for the arrest of "peeping Toms" and eavesdroppers.[20]

In 1765, British Lord Camden struck down a warrant to enter and seize papers from a home, and, in so doing, wrote, "we can safely say there is no law in this country to justify the defendants in what they have done; if there was, it would destroy all the comforts of society, for papers are often the dearest property any man can have."[21] Parliamentarian William Pitt shared this view, writing that "[t]he poorest man may in his cottage bid defiance to all the force of the Crown. It may be frail: its roof may shake; the wind may blow through it; the storms may enter; the rain may enter—but the King of England cannot enter; all his forces dare not cross the threshold of the ruined tenement."[22]

In the ensuing centuries, other European countries advanced more particularized privacy protections. The Swedish Parliament enacted the Access to Public Records Act in 1776, requiring that information held by the government be used for legitimate purposes.[23] In 1858, France prohibited the publication of private facts with violators of the prohibition subject to strict fines.[24] The Norwegian Criminal Code prohibited publication of information that relates to an individual's personal or domestic affairs as early as 1889.[25]

Our contemporary concept of information privacy has its roots in the 1960s with the advent of information technology ("IT"): computer hardware and software systems that handle data processing and storage within businesses, government and educational institutions. The increased use of IT systems in the modern age for the purposes of managing and conveying data—including personal information—spurred an acute interest in privacy practices and the privacy rights of individuals. Demand for formal rules governing the collection and handling of personal information grew as powerful new computer systems and increased surveillance potential were developed.[26]

The first response to this concern can be traced to Europe where the German state of Hesse enacted the first known modern data protection law in 1970. This German law was motivated in part by the growing potential of IT systems as well as an attempt to prevent a reoccurrence of the personal information abuses that characterized the era of the Third Reich and post-WWII Germany. Such concerns were not confined to Germany however, and soon thereafter several European countries enacted national privacy laws of differing objectives and scope.

World Models of Data Protection

It is important to note that a wide variety of data protection models have evolved over time and exist around the world today; also, that different countries—through their social histories—have chosen to protect information by different means. Data protection varies from country to country both in terms of the legal scheme in place and the degree to which the data protection authorities enforce the law.

Some of the most common data protection models in use today include comprehensive and sectoral frameworks as well as the co-regulatory model, the self-regulatory model and the technology-based model.

Comprehensive laws (European Union). These laws govern the collection, use and dissemination of personal information in the public and private sectors.[27] Generally speaking, a country that has enacted comprehensive data protection laws hosts an official or agency responsible for overseeing enforcement.[28] This official—most commonly, a data protection authority ("DPA")—ensures compliance with the law and investigates alleged breaches of the law's provisions. In many countries, the official also bears the responsibility of educating the public on data protection matters and acts as an international liaison for data protection issues. Enforcement and funding are two critical issues in a comprehensive data protection scheme. Data protection officials are granted varying degrees of power from country to country. Further, countries choose to allocate varying levels of resources to the enforcement of data protection laws, leaving some countries inadequately funded and inadequately protected.

The movement towards comprehensive privacy and data protection laws can be attributed to a combination of three major factors: 1) to remedy past injustices; 2) to promote electronic commerce; and, 3) to ensure consistency with Pan-European laws.[29] A number of countries, particularly those previously subject to authoritarian regimes, are enacting comprehensive laws as a means to remedy past privacy violations. Countries, particularly in Asia, are in the process of developing laws so as to assure uneasy consumers and help promote and facilitate electronic commerce. Still more countries are adopting comprehensive laws to make certain that trade between E.U. and non-E.U. countries is unaffected by the requirements recently set forth by the E.U. Data Protection Directive (with the additional caveat that non-E.U. countries in Central and Eastern Europe are enacting laws in part to further their aspirations for joining the E.U.).

Sectoral laws (United States). This framework protects personal information by the enactment of laws that specifically address a particular industry sector.[30] For example, different laws delineate conduct and specify the requisite level of data protection for video rental records, consumer financial transactions, credit records, motor vehicle records, law enforcement, and medical records. Sectoral laws often are used as a complement to comprehensive laws in order to provide more specific protection for particular data.

The two major drawbacks to the sectoral model are technological relevancy and oversight.[31] Given that the sectoral approach requires new legislation to accompany the introduction of new technologies, legislation often lags behind the technology that needs to be regulated. Also, the sectoral model lacks a central agency (and a federal privacy mandate) to provide oversight of the myriad data protection laws, which can lead to overlapping regulations creating conflicting obligations and a plethora of compliance requirements.

The co-regulatory model (Canada, Australia). This data protection model is a variant of the comprehensive model (above). Under a co-regulatory approach, industry develops enforceable standards for privacy and data protection which are then enforced by the industry and overseen by a privacy agency such as an information and privacy commission.[32]

The self-regulatory model (United States, Japan, Singapore) requires companies to abide by codes of practice as set by a company or group of companies as well as industry bodies, and/or independent bodies as a means to protect data.[33] Two major issues with regard to codes of practice set by companies and industry bodies are adequacy and enforcement. In many countries, industry developed codes provide limited data protection and are coupled with weak mechanisms for enforcement. As a result, several coalitions and independent organizations have established codes of practice and seal programs.

The Online Privacy Alliance[34] (OPA), a coalition comprised of numerous online companies and trade associations and specifically established to encourage the self-regulation of online privacy, introduced Online Privacy Guidelines.[35] Under these guidelines, OPA members agree to post a privacy policy that informs users about how information about them is collected and used. Notably, the guidelines do not provide for enforcement and instead encourage members to establish enforcement mechanisms independently.[36]

Seal programs are another prominent form of self regulation. A seal program requires its participants to abide by codes of information practices and submit to some variation of monitoring to ensure compliance.[37] Companies that abide by the terms of the seal program are then allowed to display the program's privacy seal on their Web site.[38] Examples of such programs are TRUSTe, BBBOnline, and WebTrust.[39]

- **TRUSTe™**[40] was founded in 1997 by the CommerceNet Consortium and the Electronic Frontier Foundation (EFF). TRUSTe, a non-profit organization based in California, provides a license agreement that governs the licensee's collection and use of personally identifiable information. This agreement requires licensees to adhere to standards for notice, choice, access, and security, based primarily on the OPA guidelines. The program periodically reviews licensees' information practices as well as provides third party monitoring.

- **BBBOnline™**,[41] a subsidiary of the Council of Better Business Bureaus, started a seal program in 1999. In order for a company to post the BBBOnline seal on its Website, it must post a privacy policy conforming to the program's information practice principles, complete a Compliance Assessment Questionnaire, consent to participate in the specified dispute resolution system, and submit to monitoring.[42]

- **WebTrust™**[43] was created by the American Institute of Certified Public Accountants (AICPA) and the Canadian Institute of Chartered Accountants (CICA). It is a seal program that licenses qualifying certified public accountants.[44]

The technology based model for data protection utilizes technological security measures to protect individuals' personal data. While it is commonplace for companies to utilize technology to protect data, developments in commercially available hardware and software have enabled consumers to establish privacy protections for their own online activity. Consumers may now select from a variety of technological means to ensure, to varying degrees, the privacy and security of their communications.[45]

Several examples illustrate the fundamental element of the technology based model. Consumers may utilize digital cash to consummate an e-commerce transaction such as an online "shopping cart" function. Encryption is commonly used by both companies and individual consumers to ensure the privacy of communications between parties. Email senders can utilize anonymous remailers or proxy servers to try to preserve anonymity and privacy in email communication such as the "majordomo" email relaying system common in the 1990s.[46] Given the technology-based model's obvious dependence on technology and the array of new technology coming to market, the security and trustworthiness of technological systems remains a pertinent concern.

Fair Information Practices

While a data protection model provides an analytic framework to evaluate the flow of data, key aspects of the model must still be defined. These aspects include the coverage of the protection, the definition of the data to be protected and the scope and limitations of the use of the data.

Protection coverage. In a general sense, a data protection model must define what data are protected. The nature of data varies in its substance and its use, and such variation must be taken into consideration in determining whether a class of data merits protection and to what degree.

Personal information. Not only must a data protection model define what data are protected, but it must define what constitutes personal information.

Personal information can include name, age, gender, street address, email address, social security number (national identity number) and/or telephone number. This information can exist in many different forms (electronic or hard document as two examples) and may be managed or stored according to one or more general classifications. The key is to understand the source of personal information—whether from public records, publicly available information or non-public information.

1. ***Public records*** are information collected and maintained by a government entity and available to the general public. These government entities include the federal, state, and local governments. State and local public records laws vary from state to state and municipality to municipality as to their public availability.

   Many types of public records have important historical uses. For example, real estate records contain detailed information on parcels of property that reveal ownership, assessed value, amount paid for the parcel, taxes imposed on the parcel, and improvements. This information is public as a matter of law, so that each person that owns real estate can determine if the taxes assessed are fair relative to other parcels in the area.

2. ***Publicly available information*** is information that is generally available without restrictions. Some examples include names and addresses in telephone books and information from newspapers.

3. ***Non-public information*** is not generally available or easily accessed due to law or custom. Examples of this type of data include financial data, medical records, and adoption records. A company's customer or employee databases usually contain non-public information.

It is important to note that the same data elements may be public record, publicly available and non-public. For example, a name and address may be a matter of public record (on a real estate deed), publicly available in the telephone book, and included in non-public databases, such as in a healthcare patient file. To understand how to handle the name and address, you must understand the source that provided it.

Scope and limitations of use. Inherent to a data protection model are appropriate limitations and considerations of the scope of the rules the model sets forth. Particular types of data may be outside the scope of a given model if the rules do not sufficiently protect it. The scope of protection may vary for these different types of data:

- Secret, private, or sensitive data
  - Government filings
  - Consent requirements
  - National identifiers
  - Criminal records
  - Health data
  - Association or union memberships

- Consumer data

- Data collected online

- Aggregate or anonymous data

Notice is a description of an organization's information management practices. The typical notice will inform an individual what data are being collected; how that data are being used; whether the data are being disclosed or transferred to third-parties and, if so, to whom; how to exercise any choices that may exist with respect to use, disclosure and onward transfer; and, whether or not the individual can access or update the information.

Notices can serve two important purposes: consumer education and corporate accountability. They can provide individuals with the information they need to understand how a company will process information. They also provide regulators with a benchmark against which actual corporate practices are judged.

Access is the ability of an individual to view personal information held by an organization, and may be complemented by the ability to update and correct the information. Companies may not always offer access. For example, personal information may be very difficult or costly to retrieve, so access may not be appropriate. In general, if information is used for substantive decision-making, it becomes appropriate to offer access so that individuals can ensure that the information is correct and complete.

Choice is the ability to specify whether personal information will be collected and/or how it will be used or shared. Choice is generally appropriate when information is used for marketing communications. Choice is often not appropriate in other situations. For example, it would not make sense to offer choice about sharing a person's name and address with the shipping company that is delivering an order. Similarly, companies will not offer choice about the use of information for debt collection or legal compliance.

Where choice is appropriate, it should be offered in a meaningful manner, along with a notice that informs the individual about the processing and provides the option to opt out (or in) to the action.

Two central concepts of choice are "opt-in" and "opt-out."

- **Opt-in** means an individual makes an affirmative indication of choice (e.g., an individual checks a box stating that she wants to share her information with third parties).

- **Opt-out** means that an individual's failure to object to a use or disclosure implies that a choice has been made (e.g., unless an individual checks or unchecks a box, her information will be shared with third parties).

*It is important for privacy professionals to ensure that words used in choice statements are accurate. It is inappropriate to have a choice that says "I **opt in** to this use" if the box is pre-checked. Unless the individual checks the box personally, this is an **opt-out** offering.*

Regulating Privacy Activities

A critical component of data protection is regulating the activity involving personal information. Such information is subject to different actions that may include retrieval, processing, transfer, and sharing, among others.

Data processing can consist of a variety of activities. The European Data Protection Directive of 1995 ("E.U. Directive") defines the processing of personal data as "any operation or set of operations which is performed upon personal data, whether or not by automatic means, such as collection, recording, organisation, storage, adaptation or alteration, retrieval, consultation, use, disclosure by transmission, dissemination or otherwise making available, alignment or combination, blocking, erasure or destruction[.]"[47]

Under the E.U. Directive, data processing encompasses a wide array of individual, corporate, and government action. The breadth of data processing conduct can affect the overall impact of data protection regulation.

Data transfer and data sharing encompasses the movement of data between parties. Different data protection regulations place restrictions on a data holder's ability to transfer or share data. The E.U. Data Protection Directive permits personal data transfer to a third country only when the third country ensures an adequate level of protection.[48] In the United States, California's Online Privacy Protection Act imposes certain Web site notice requirements that must be met in order for a business or organization subject to the law to share data.[49]

Europe and the United States provide two excellent examples of how different data protection models have evolved. Historically, the United States has taken a sectoral approach to protecting personal data.[50] As explained earlier in this chapter, sectoral laws draw distinctions based on, among other things, industry, data sources, and the public and private sector.[51] In addition, individual states may enact privacy laws that address the actions of individuals and companies within state borders as well as persons outside the state whose activities bring them within state jurisdiction.[52]

Europe, by contrast, takes a comprehensive approach to data protection premised on the view of privacy as a fundamental human right. Under this approach, laws are designed to provide broad, comprehensive protection of an individual's privacy rights.

The variety of E.U. member nation privacy laws resulted in the blockage and delay of data transmissions. Companies were forced to assure government officials that trans-border data transfers did not place data subjects' privacy expectations at risk, a process that impeded the smooth transmission of data.[53] In some cases, multinational corporations integrated the data transmission approval process into their administrative procedures.[54] Ironically, due to the modest capabilities of IT systems in the 1980s and early 1990s (the predominant time period governed by these rules) government scrutiny fell primarily on internal corporate data transmissions between corporate facilities located in different nations.[55] Further, most of the transfers subject to scrutiny were conducted by physical, rather than electronic means; the technology of the time simply did not allow for the intra-corporate transfers of data that are now commonplace.

Privacy Principles

Underlying the views of privacy and the models for protecting data are certain fundamental privacy principles. These principles are foundational concepts that need to be considered in formulating any data protection regime.

Many of the frameworks described on the following pages have been influential in the development of information privacy laws around the world: the Fair Information Practices, OECD guidelines and APEC principles are chief among these. While not overtly redundant, these frameworks do share many common themes and definitions.

The Code of Fair Information Practices (also known as the "Code of Fair Information Principles") was first developed in the early 1970s by the U.S Department of Health, Education, and Welfare (known today as the Department of Health and Human Services) Advisory Committee on Automated Data Systems.[56] This code has become the backbone for more recent variations, most of which have the following core elements:[57]

1. *Openness.* The existence of record-keeping systems and databanks that contain personal data must be publicly known, along with a description of the main purpose and uses of the data.

2. *Individual Participation.* Individuals should have a right to view all information that is collected about them; they must also be able to correct or remove data that are not timely, accurate relevant, or complete.

3. *Collection Limitation.* There should be limits to the collection of personal data; data should be collected by lawful and fair means and should be collected, where appropriate, with the knowledge or consent of the subject.

4. *Data Quality.* Personal data should be relevant to the purposes for which they are collected and used; personal data should be accurate, complete, and timely.

5. *Finality.* There should be limits to the use and disclosure of personal data: data should be used only for purposes specified at the time of collection; data should not be otherwise disclosed without the consent of the data subject or other legal authority.

6. *Security.* Personal data should be protected by reasonable security safeguards against such risks as loss, unauthorized access, destruction, use, modification or disclosure.

7. *Accountability.* Record keepers should be accountable for complying with fair information practices.

In 1981, the Organization for Economic Cooperation and Development ("OECD"), a 23-nation body that includes the United States and Japan in addition to several European nations, published a set of privacy principles entitled "Guidelines Governing the Protection of Privacy and Transborder Data Flows of Personal Data."[58] Known more informally as the OECD Guidelines, these principles were subsequently endorsed by the U.S. Federal Trade Commission ("FTC") and have served as perhaps the most widely adopted of the frameworks for fair information practices.

The OECD Guidelines enunciated eight privacy principles, the importance of which has been further reinforced by the FTC.[59] These are:

1. *The Collection Limitation Principle.* There should be limits to the collection of personal data and any such data should be obtained by lawful and fair means and, where appropriate, with the knowledge or consent of the data subject.

2. *The Data Quality Principle.* Personal data should be relevant to the purposes for which they are to be used, and, to the extent necessary for those purposes, should be accurate, complete and kept up-to-date.

3. ***The Purpose Specification Principle.*** The purposes for which personal data are collected should be specified not later than at the time of data collection and the subsequent use limited to the fulfillment of those purposes or such others as are not incompatible with those purposes and as are specified on each occasion of change of purpose.

4. ***The Use Limitation Principle.*** Personal data should not be disclosed, made available or otherwise used for purposes other than those specified in accordance with Paragraph 8 except a) with the consent of the data subject; or b) by the authority of law.

5. ***The Security Safeguards Principle.*** Personal data should be protected by reasonable security safeguards against such risks as loss or unauthorized access, destruction, use, modification or disclosure of data.

6. ***The Openness Principle.*** There should be a general policy of openness about developments, practices and policies with respect to personal data. Means should be readily available of establishing the existence and nature of personal data, and the main purposes of their use, as well as the identity and usual residence of the data controller.

7. ***The Individual Participation Principle.*** An individual should have the right: a) to obtain from a data controller, or otherwise, confirmation of whether or not the data controller has data relating to him; b) to have data relating to him communicated to him, within a reasonable time, at a charge, if any, that is not excessive; in a reasonable manner; and in a form that is readily intelligible to him; c) to be given reasons if a request made under subparagraphs(a) and (b) is denied, and to be able to challenge such denial; and d) to challenge data relating to him and, if the challenge is successful to have the data erased, rectified, completed or amended.

8. ***The Accountability Principle.*** A data controller should be accountable for complying with measures which give effect to the principles stated above.

Also in 1981, the Council of Europe ("COE") passed "The Convention for the Protection of Individuals with Regard to the Automatic Processing of Personal Data" ("COE Convention").[60] These documents set forth the principles which form the basis for, or at a minimum constitute a component of, many European nations' data protection laws today.[61]

The COE Convention and OECD Guidelines enunciate specific rules addressing the handling of data and provide protection for personal information. These rules recognize personal information as data entitled to legal protection for the duration of its lifecycle: collection, processing, storage, use, transfer, and destruction.[62] Though these rules vary in degree, they require that personal information must be obtained fairly and lawfully; used only for the original specified purpose; kept accurate and up to date; made accessible to the subject; kept secure; and destroyed after its purpose is completed. [63]

Although the principles espoused by the COE Convention and OECD Guidelines provided a stepping stone toward uniform data protection throughout Europe, there were still significant differences between the privacy laws of the many individual European nations.[64] As a result of the disparate privacy laws between European Union ("E.U.") member nations, citizens of these nations were subject to a non-uniform level of privacy protection. Additionally, the non-uniform laws resulted in data transmission problems within the E.U. Many of the laws implementing the COE Convention set forth restrictions on the transborder flow of personal information whereby an individual or business that sought to export personal data required consent or approval from the originating country's authorities.[65] Upon export, public officials bore the responsibility of assuring that the information that was transported did not lose the protections that such information would be afforded within the originating country. These requirements placed substantial administrative burdens on companies and governments and in many cases prevented companies from enjoying the benefits of networking technology.

Enforcement Regimes

A critical element to a data protection model is the role of enforcement. Different data protection regimes implement enforcement in a different manner—whether in Europe, the United States.

Europe: the E.U. Directive and Data Protection Authorities ("DPA")

The E.U. Directive requires a data protection authority ("DPA") to supervise the information privacy principles embodied within the directive itself. Each E.U. member nation establishes its own DPA—in the form of an office or person—as a means to ensure compliance with the directive. These nations typically provide for either an elected or appointed data protection commissioner who holds this enforcement power.

Several different privacy roles are present in the variety of privacy and data protection regulations utilized across the world. The E.U. Data Directive defines a number of roles within the comprehensive data protection scheme so prevalent throughout the European Union: from data controller, processor and importer/exporter to data recipient.

- *Data Controller.* The natural or legal person, public authority, agency or any other body which alone or jointly with others determines the purposes and means of the processing of personal data; where the purposes and means of processing are determined by national or community laws or regulations, the controller or the specific criteria for his nomination may be designated by national or community law;[66]

- *Data Processor.* A natural or legal person, public authority, agency or any other body which processes personal data on behalf of the controller;[67]

- *Data Recipient.* A natural or legal person, public authority, agency or any other body to whom data are disclosed, whether a third party or not; however, authorities which may receive data in the framework of a particular inquiry shall not be regarded as recipients;[68]

- *Data Importer/Exporter.* Although not formally defined, importer and exporter are critical roles in the E.U.'s comprehensive data protection regulations. The Data Protection Directive requires importers and exporters to ensure the adequacy of data protection before data are shared.[69]

United States: Sectoral privacy laws and the Federal Trade Commission ("FTC")

The sectoral approach to data protection in the United States provides for different roles within different industries. Two roles of note with regard to the financial and credit industries, third parties and affiliates, are addressed by the Financial Services Modernization Act of 1999 ("Gramm-Leach-Bliley Act"[70] or, "GLBA") and the Fair Credit Reporting Act of 1970 ("FCRA").[71] These laws restrict the disclosure of personal information to third parties such as the exchange or transfer of financial, or credit information, respectively. For example, the GLBA prohibits financial institutions or their affiliates from disclosing non-public personal information to a nonaffiliated third party without providing notice to the consumer.[72]

The Health Insurance Portability an Accountability Act of 1996 ("HIPAA") provides a good example of sectoral privacy law in the medical field. As amended, the HIPAA[73] regulations provide for four covered entities: health plans, clearinghouses, particular healthcare providers, and prescription drug card sponsors.[74] The HIPAA regulations also apply to a business associate who performs a service or function involving personal health information on behalf of a covered entity.[75] This role may include lawyers, accountants, or consultants, but excludes the members of the covered entities' work force.

The U.S. Federal Trade Commission ("FTC") is the agency primarily charged with consumer protection in the United States. In this role, it aggressively enforces company-made privacy promises as well as obligations imposed on companies by privacy and security laws. In particular, the FTC brings actions against companies for failure to comply with promises made to individuals in privacy notices. The FTC also bring actions against companies for failure to meet obligations that are set forth under federal privacy laws, such as the Children's Online Privacy Protection Act ("COPPA"), the privacy and safeguards regulations promulgated under the GLBA and the Telemarketing Sales Rule ("TSR").[76]

The FTC can enforce both company-made privacy promises and privacy and security laws. The authority to enforce specific laws (and to promulgate rules under these laws) is provided in the laws themselves. For example, the Children's Online Privacy Protection Act ("COPPA") expressly gives the Commission the power to make rules and to enforce the Act and the rules.

The authority to enforce company-made privacy promises stems from the general authority that the Commission has under its consumer protection mission. Section 5 of the FTC Act (the U.S. law that created the Commission) enables the FTC to bring an action to address any unfair or deceptive trade practices that occur in the course of commercial activities. Understanding the meanings of (and differences between) "unfair" and "deceptive" trade practices is crucial for interpreting FTC actions. A deceptive trade practice is any commercial conduct that includes false or misleading claims, or claims that omit material facts. Consumer injury does not have to result; the mere fact that a company has engaged in a deceptive trade practice is actionable. Unfair trade practices are commercial conduct that (1) causes substantial injury, (2) without offsetting benefits, and (3) that consumers cannot reasonably avoid.

Accordingly, if a company makes a privacy or security promise, and then fails to live up to that promise, it has likely engaged in a deceptive trade practice. If a company puts consumers at risk, with no offsetting benefit, this may be an unfair trade practice. For example, even if a company does not promise to have reasonable security for its Website, if the company collects sensitive data (such as credit card numbers) without having reasonable security (and if consumers are not warned about the lack of security), the company has likely engaged in an unfair trade practice.

It is important to note that the FTC's authority is limited in some respects. For example, the FTC Act states that the FTC may not regulate or enforce against certain industries that are otherwise regulated, such as financial institutions subject to jurisdiction of the Office of Comptroller of the Currency, the Federal Reserve, et al., common carriers, etc.

U.S. federal agencies that regulate specific industries often work closely with the FTC on privacy regulations, however. For example, the FTC works with a group of federal financial institution regulators on GLBA rules, and it works with the Federal Communications Commission ("FCC") on telemarketing and email privacy rules.

Additionally, even where FTC authority does exist, companies are often subject to additional regulatory scrutiny. For example, many companies face both FTC and state attorney general actions for privacy or security breaches. Because the state attorneys general have independent authority, FTC actions do not preclude or supersede state action. In many cases, the consent decrees entered into with the state attorneys general for breaches exceed the FTC's requirements. Fines are also common at the state level.

The Enforcement Powers of the FTC
The FTC has broad powers to investigate companies and to bring enforcement actions. If the FTC suspects that a company has not lived up to privacy promises or complied with

applicable laws, it will typically launch an investigation of the company. Depending on the nature of the breach, the FTC may work with the company to resolve the matter informally. For more egregious breaches—or, where the FTC detects a pattern of non-compliance—the Commission may bring a formal enforcement action against the company. These actions generally result in the Commission and the company entering into a settlement agreement or consent decree. The FTC has authority to include many different types of provisions in consent decrees, consistent with its role as a consumer protection agency.

Common components of these FTC-mandated privacy and security programs in consent decrees include:

1. A prohibition on future misrepresentation of privacy or security program protections;

2. A requirement to establish and maintain a security program, including (i) training and proper oversight of employees and agents, (ii) identification of reasonably foreseeable risks, (iii) the design of reasonable and appropriate safeguards, and (iv) regular evaluation of the program;

3. An obligation to have the privacy or security program reviewed annually by an independent qualified third party;

4. A requirement to provide certain documents related to the representations made about the company's programs and compliance, upon request from the FTC;

5. An obligation to notify the FTC of any change which may affect the company's compliance; and,

6. Upon request from the FTC, filing a written report of compliance.

Conclusion

These privacy principles and regulatory structures establish an important foundation for information management practices around the world. Based on this foundation, privacy professionals can better understand how information privacy laws and practices evolve, take form and exert influence in the world marketplace today.

The next chapter will describe in much greater detail how the major U.S. and E.U. data protection laws work and will contrast these regulatory approaches to those of other world regions. Subsequent chapters will outline the technologies and operational practices that are universal to all jurisdictions on matters of information privacy.

Chapter Two

PRIVACY LAW AND COMPLIANCE

Introduction and Learning Objectives

Privacy Law and Compliance is the first of five chapters in this volume to address items that are tested on the Certified Information Privacy Professional ("CIPP") examination. This chapter provides a broad introduction to major U.S. and E.U. laws governing information privacy and information security as well as a selection of international privacy laws. It offers insights into the ways that privacy professionals develop programs in order to manage business-oriented legal compliance in these jurisdictions. Lastly, this chapter explores the risks associated with the failure to comply with major U.S. and E.U. privacy and security laws.

The CIPP will understand:

- The U.S. legal system, sources of privacy law and definitions of key legal terms;

- Key components of major U.S. information privacy and security laws;

- Basic theories of international data protection laws, specifically in the European Union; and,

- Theories of liability for privacy non-compliance.

The U.S. Legal System

The U.S. legal system is comprised of three co-equal branches of government designed to provide a separation of powers with a system of checks and balances amongst all branches. These three branches are found on both the federal and state (and often the local) levels. The Executive Branch's duties are to enforce and administer the law. The Legislative Branch is made up of elected representatives who write and pass laws. The Judicial Branch interprets the meaning of a law and how it is applied, and may examine such things as a law's constitutionality and the intent behind its creation.

Figure One: Three Branches of U.S. Government (source: IAPP)

Three Branches of U.S. Government			
	Executive Branch	**Legislative Branch**	**Judicial Branch**
Purpose	Enforces laws	Makes laws	Interprets laws
Who	President, VP, Cabinet, Federal agencies (such as FTC)	Congress (House & Senate)	Federal courts
Checks and Balances	President appoints Federal judges, President can veto laws passed by Congress	Congress confirms presidential appointees, can override vetoes	Determines whether the laws are constitutional

At the Federal level, the Executive Branch consists of the President, Vice-President, the President's Cabinet and other appointees, and the myriad of federal agencies. In addition to enforcing law, the President also has veto power over laws passed by Congress, and the power to appoint federal judges. The Legislative Branch is made up of Congress, which consists of the Senate and the House of Representatives. Aside from passing laws, Congress can confirm presidential appointees and override presidential vetoes. When enacting legislation, Congress may also delegate to federal agencies the power to promulgate additional regulations. For example, Congress has enacted several laws that give the U.S. Federal Trade Commission ("FTC") the authority to issue regulations to implement the laws.

Finally, the Judicial Branch encompasses the entire court system. The lowest courts in the federal system are the District Courts, which serve as federal trial courts. Cases decided by a District Court can be appealed to a federal Appeals Court, also referred to as a Circuit Court. The Federal Circuit Courts do not serve as trial courts but serves as the appeals court for federal cases. The Appeals Courts are divided into 12 regional circuits and each District Court is assigned to a circuit; appeals from a District Court are considered by the Appeals Court for that circuit.

At the top of the federal court system is the Supreme Court of the United States which hears appeals from the Circuit Courts and decides questions of federal constitutional law. In certain circumstances, the U.S. Supreme Court may also hear appeals from the highest state courts.

In addition to its appellate powers, the U.S. Supreme Court also has the ability to function as a trial court.

As mentioned above, when given the authority by Congress, federal agencies may also promulgate and enforce rules pursuant to law. In this sense, agencies may wield power that is characteristic of all three branches of government. This means that agencies may operate under statutes that give them legislative power to: issue rules and levy criminal and civil penalties; executive power to investigate and enforce violations of rules and statutes; and, to act in a judicial role over particular disputes.

> **Jurisdiction.** *The authority of a court to hear a particular case. Courts must have jurisdiction over both the parties to the dispute (**personal jurisdiction**) and type of dispute (**subject matter jurisdiction**).*

Several federal agencies engage in regulatory activities in the privacy sphere. The FTC issues regulations, conducts investigations and otherwise enforces a number of laws regarding marketing communications, financial privacy, children's privacy and consumer credit reporting. The FTC also investigates and enforces corporate privacy promises using its authority under the FTC Act, which prohibits unfair or deceptive practices.[77] Other federal agencies that are active in the privacy sphere include the federal banking regulatory agencies (such as the Office of the Comptroller of the Currency and the Federal Reserve Board), the Federal Communications Commission ("FCC") and the Department of Transportation ("DoT"), and the Department of Health and Human Services ("HHS").

In the United States, law-making power is shared between the national and state governments. In particular, the states have power to make law absent a federal law on the subject that prohibits state action. Under the Tenth Amendment to the Constitution, "[t]he powers not delegated to the United States by the Constitution, nor prohibited by it to the States, are reserved to the States respectively, or to the people."[78] In addition, state legislatures may also enact and enforce law that is stricter than federal law, unless the federal law explicitly preempts any state law on the subject.[80] Thus, where there is federal law, and absent any preemption, the federal law will always set a "floor," not a "ceiling" on a particular law unless such a law contains an explicit preemption provision.

> **Preemption.** *A superior government's ability to have its law(s) supersede those of an inferior government. For example, the U.S. federal government has said that no state government can regulate consumer credit reporting.*

At the state level, most privacy-related regulatory enforcement actions are taken by state attorneys general, pursuant to state laws.[81] Many states have successfully pursued such actions, including, among others, Washington[82] and Minnesota.[83]

Aside from the governmental ability to make and enforce laws and regulations, the U.S. legal system also relies on legal precedent based on court decisions, the doctrines implicit in those decisions and their customs and uses. Two key areas of the common law include contracts and torts.

Sources of Law and Their Interpretation

Constitutions

As discussed previously, various sources of law and enforcement exist in the United States. The supreme law in the United States is manifest in the U.S. Constitution which established the U.S. federal government when it was adopted in 1787. While the Constitution does not have an explicit clause or amendment guaranteeing privacy rights, various decisions by the U.S. Supreme Court have created a penumbra of rights (e.g., body of rights) around privacy.[85] State constitutions are also sources of law on the state level and may create stronger rights than are provided in the U.S. Constitution. For example, the California state constitution expressly recognizes a right to privacy.

Legislation

The primary function of the legislative branch of government is to enact laws. Both the federal Congress and the state legislatures have enacted a wide variety of privacy and security laws. These range from statutes that specifically focus on privacy (such as the Children's Online Privacy Protection Act) to laws that regulate the use of information for specific purposes (such as state laws that prohibit the consideration of certain types of information during the hiring process).

Regulations and Rules

Some laws direct regulatory agencies (such as the FTC or the FCC) to issue additional regulations. These place specific compliance expectations on the marketplace. For example, the U.S. Congress passed the CAN-SPAM Act in 2003, which requires the senders of commercial email messages to offer an "opt-out" to recipients of these messages. CAN-SPAM endows the FTC with the authority to issue regulations under the law itself that set forth exactly how the opt-out mechanism must be offered and managed.

Case Law

Generally speaking, "case law" refers to principles of law that have been established by judges in past decisions. When similar issues arise again, judges look to the past decisions as precedents and decide the new case in a manner that is consistent with past decisions. The following of past precedent is known as *stare decisis* (a Latin term meaning "to let the decision stand"). It should be noted that, as time passes, precedents often change in order to reflect society's changing values and laws.

Common Law

"Common law" refers to unwritten legal principles that have developed over time based on social customs and expectations. From a privacy perspective, this might mean that special privileges or relationships such as doctor-patient confidentiality may exist as a matter of common law even if there is not a statute that provides a legal right for the same concept.

Consent Decree

A consent decree is a judgment entered by consent of the parties whereby the defendant agrees to stop alleged illegal activity without admitting guilt or wrongdoing.[86] This legal document is approved by a judge and formalizes an agreement reached between a federal or state agency and an adverse party. The consent decree describes the actions the defendant will take and may be subject to a public comment period. Once approved, the consent decree has the effect of a court decision. In the privacy enforcement sphere, for example, the FTC in 2002 entered into a consent decree with Ohio Art over violations of the Children's Online Privacy Protection Act ("COPPA").[87] The Consent Decree required Ohio Art to pay $35,000 and to agree not to violate COPPA in the future.

Aside from agency rule and regulation promulgation, and enforcement actions, agencies also give guidance in the form of agency opinions. These opinions do not necessarily carry the weight of law, but do give specific guidance to interested parties trying to interpret agency rules and regulations.[88]

Figure Two: U.S. Regulatory Regime (Source IAPP)

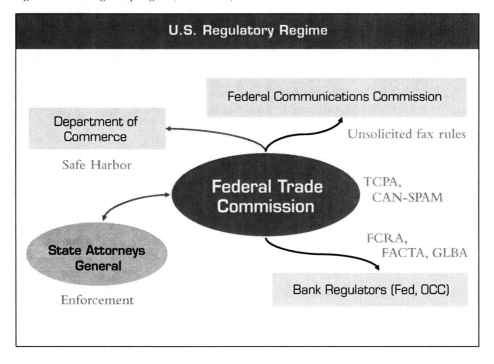

Contract Law

A contract is a legally binding agreement enforceable in a court of law. For example, a privacy-related contract might include abiding by the E.U. = U.S. Union's Safe Harbor framework,[89] which in turn might include making agreements on such issues as jurisdiction, data usage, and damages.

However, not every agreement is a legally binding contract. There are certain fundamental requirements for forming a binding contract[90] such as:

- *Offer.* An offer is the proposed language to enter into a bargain. An offer must be communicated to another person and remain open until it is accepted, rejected, retracted, or has expired. Some terms of an offer, like price, quantity, and description, must be specific and definite. Note: a counter-offer ends the original offer.

- *Acceptance* is the assent or agreement by the person to whom the offer was made that the offer is accepted. This acceptance must comply with the terms of the offer and must be communicated to the person who proposed the deal.

- *Consideration* is the bargained-for exchange. It is the legal benefit received by one person and the legal detriment imposed on the other person. Consideration usually takes the form of money, property, or services. Note: an agreement without consideration is not a contract.

   A privacy notice may be a contract if a consumer provides data to a company based on the company's promise to use the data in accordance with the terms of the notice.

Tort Law

Torts are civil wrongs recognized by law as the grounds for lawsuits. These wrongs result in an injury or harm which constitutes the basis for a claim by the injured party. The primary aim of tort law is to provide relief for damages incurred and deter others from committing the same wrongs.

There are three general tort categories:

1. *Intentional torts.* These are wrongs which the defendant knew or should have known would occur through their actions or inactions; for example, intentionally hitting a person;

2. *Negligent torts* occur when the defendant's actions were unreasonably unsafe; for example, causing a car accident by not obeying traffic rules; and,

3. *Strict liability torts.* These are wrongs that do not depend on the degree of carefulness by the defendant, but rather, are established when a particular action causes damage.[91] Product liability torts fall into this category since they concern potential liability for making and selling defective products.

Historically, the concept of a personal privacy tort has been a part of U.S. jurisprudence since the late 1890's.[92] However, in the modern privacy arena, the traditional concept of negligence is of particular importance to holders of personal information, particularly where privacy and security intersect, and adequate safeguards and procedures are crucial to data protection. An organization will be liable for damages if it breaches a legal duty to protect personal information and an individual is harmed by that breach.

> **Private Right of Action.** *Unless otherwise restricted by law, any individual that is harmed by a violation of the law can file a lawsuit against the violator.*

Enforcement of Law: Scope and Application

Two concepts are essential in considering the scope and application of the law. The first is the concept of the "person." A "person" is any entity with legal rights, whether it is an individual or a corporation. The second key concept is "jurisdiction." Jurisdiction defines the authority of the court to hear a particular case or dispute. A court must have jurisdiction over both the type of dispute (subject matter jurisdiction[93]) and the parties or persons (personal jurisdiction[94]).

The primary method for enforcing the law is through litigation. There are two types of litigation: criminal and civil. Criminal litigation occurs when the executive branch and its representative agencies bring an action against someone for violation of a criminal law. Civil litigation occurs when a person or party sues another party to redress a wrong. The person who sues (the plaintiff) often seeks a monetary judgment from the defendant, but may also seek an injunction, which is a court order telling the defendant not to do certain behaviors. The two main types of civil litigation include contract disputes and tort (personal injury) claims.

The U.S. legal system operates generally under the concept of preemption. Preemption is a conflict of laws doctrine that states that a superior government's law supersedes that of an inferior government on a particular topic. The preemption doctrine derives from the Supremacy Clause of the U.S. Constitution, which states that the "Constitution and the laws of the United States...shall be the supreme law of the land...anything in the constitutions or laws of any State to the contrary notwithstanding."[95] This means that any federal law, even a regulation of a federal agency, trumps any conflicting state law.

Self-regulatory regimes are a means by which industries have policed themselves and worked to stay in compliance with law, regulations, as well as industry best practices. In the privacy arena there are a number of organizations that offer certifications, reviews, and codes of conduct. Some of these include: TRUSTe,[96] the Direct Marketing Association,[97] and the BBBOnline.[98]

The Emergence of Privacy Laws

From a legal perspective, privacy law is a relatively recent phenomenon. In the United States, the concept of law surrounding a right to privacy was first articulated in 1890 by then Supreme Court Justices Louis Brandeis and Samuel Warren in a law review article aptly titled "The Right to Privacy."[99] Over the course of the next century, history and experiences in Europe and the U.S. would shape markedly different regulatory systems for managing and enforcing privacy laws.

The E.U. regulatory system: Privacy laws that protect privacy as a fundamental human right.

The European approach to privacy law was shaped largely by experiences from World War II, the Holocaust, and the policies of the former Soviet Bloc countries. Specifically, the past activities of secret policing bodies such as the Russian KGB and the East German Stasi led the European Union to treat and preserve privacy as a fundamental human right of all citizens and establish a socially-derived framework for privacy policy development and management. Generally speaking, in Europe today, no one can collect or use personal data unless they are permitted to do so by law. This philosophy is reflected in the European Convention on Human Rights[100] and, more recently, in the European Union's Directive on Data Protection (the E.U. Directive).[101]

The U.S. regulatory system: Privacy laws that prevent harmful uses of information.

The U.S. Constitution does not explicitly provide a right to privacy.[102] It was that absence and the rise of modern media that led Justices Brandeis and Warren to declare that privacy was the right to be free from intrusion, "the right to be left alone."[103] Seventy years later, the legal scholar William Prosser elaborated on these principles in a law review article[104] and then in the *Second Restatement of Torts*.[105] Over time, courts have taken the work of Brandeis and Warren and, using the U.S. Constitution, created a collection of privacy rights that give individuals rights over personal matters such as birth control,[106] abortion,[107] and sexual activities.[108] Generally speaking, in the U.S. government's use of data has been more restricted, while private use has been allowed unless shown to be harmful or covered by sector-specific laws.

Two major approaches to privacy prevail today in the United States. One is the fair information practices approach, the cornerstones of which are the concepts of notice and choice. This approach is process-oriented and is perhaps best exemplified by the Financial Modernization Act of 1999, known more broadly by reference to its three U.S. Senate authors as the **Gramm-Leach-Bliley Act (GLBA)**.[109]

The second approach is the "permissible purpose" approach which limits data usage to purposes permitted under laws, many of which are context-oriented. **The Fair Credit Reporting Act ("FCRA")**[110] is the best example of this approach. Lastly, newer privacy laws such as the **Health Insurance Portability and Accountability Act of 1999 ("HIPAA")**—and its namesake privacy rule—include both process elements and permissible uses, suggesting a convergence. For all these approaches, corporate accountability remains constant.

The Code of Fair Information Practices (also known as the "Code of Fair Information Principles") was first developed in the early 1970s by the U.S. Department of Health, Education, and Welfare Advisory Committee on Automated Data Systems. Today, this federal agency is known as the U.S. Department of Health and Human Services ("HHS"). The HEW/HHS Code has become the backbone for more recent variations, most of which have the following core elements:[112]

1. *Openness.* The existence of record-keeping systems and databanks that contain personal data must be publicly known, along with a description of the main purpose and uses of the data;

2. *Individual Participation.* Individuals should have a right to view all information that is collected about them; they must also be able to correct or remove data that are not timely, accurate relevant, or complete;

3. *Collection Limitation.* There should be limits to the collection of personal data; data should be collected by lawful and fair means and should be collected, where appropriate, with the knowledge or consent of the subject;

4. *Data Quality.* Personal data should be relevant to the purposes for which they are collected and used; personal data should be accurate, complete, and timely;

5. *Finality.* There should be limits to the use and disclosure of personal data: data should be used only for purposes specified at the time of collection; data should not be otherwise disclosed without the consent of the data subject or other legal authority;

6. *Security.* Personal data should be protected by reasonable security safeguards against such risks as loss, unauthorized access, destruction, use, modification or disclosure; and,

7. *Accountability.* Record keepers should be accountable for complying with fair information practices.

The major U.S. privacy laws are profiled in further detail in the next five sections of this chapter, which examine privacy laws and regulations within the U.S. private sector (concerning for-profit, commercial organizations) and the U.S. public sector (concerning government agencies). Key international privacy laws are also described.

U.S. Privacy Laws – Private Sector

The Fair Credit Reporting Act ("FCRA")

The Fair Credit Reporting Act ("FCRA") is one of the oldest U.S. federal privacy laws still in force today. It was enacted in 1970 to mandate accurate and relevant data collection, to give consumers the ability access and correct their information, and to limit the use of consumer reports to permissible purposes.[113]

The origins of FCRA can be traced to the rise of the use of credit in the United States. In the post-World War II era, merchants increasingly shared customer data in order to facilitate lending to households. By the 1960s consumer credit was critical, but increasingly, individuals were being harmed by inaccurate information that they could neither see nor correct. In response, Congress passed the Fair Credit Reporting Act ("FCRA"), the first federal law to regulate the use of personal information by private businesses.[114]

FCRA was amended in 1996 with provisions for non-consumer initiated transactions (also known as "pre-screening") and to establish standards for consumer assistance; it was also amended by the Fair and Accurate Credit Transactions Act of 2003 ("FACTA") with provisions related to identity theft.[115]

FCRA regulates all entities that compile "consumer reports" as well as persons who use consumer reports. The consumer report itself includes any information that pertains to:

• Credit worthiness,

• Credit standing,

• Credit capacity,

• Character,

• General reputation,

• Personal characteristics, or

• Mode of living,

• And that is used in whole or in part for the purpose of serving as a factor in establishing a consumer's eligibility for credit, insurance, employment, or other business purpose.[118]

Under FCRA, the following are required:

• Third-party data for substantive decision-making must be appropriately accurate, current, and complete;

• Consumers must receive notice when third-party data is used to make adverse decisions about them;

• Consumer reports may be used only for permissible purposes;

• Consumers must have access to their consumer reports and an opportunity to dispute or correct any errors;

• A covered entity must comply with all other requirements of users and furnishers of consumer data.

Violations of FCRA are enforced by the FTC and state attorneys general; individuals also have a private right of action. Non-compliance can include civil and criminal penalties. In addition to actual damages, violators are subject to statutory damages of at least $1,000 per violation, and at least $2,500 for willful violations.

FCRA defines a "consumer reporting agency" ("CRA") as any entity that routinely furnishes consumer reports to third parties for a fee. Among other things, the Act requires that CRAs:

• Provide consumers with access to the information contained in their consumer reports, along with the opportunity to dispute any inaccurate information;

• Must take reasonable steps to ensure the accuracy of information in the consumer report;

• Not report negative information that is outdated; in most cases this means account data more than seven years old or bankruptcies more than ten years old;

• Provide consumer reports only to entities that have a permissible purpose under the FCRA;

• Maintain records regarding entities that received consumer reports; and,

• Provide consumer assistance as required by FTC rules.

Notice requirements under FCRA

The FTC has published a notice that outlines the requirements for users of consumer reports.[117] Consumer reporting agencies are required to provide such notice to users.

These are the obligations of all users of consumer reports under FCRA:

1. *Users Must Have a Permissible Purpose.* Congress has limited the use of consumer reports to protect consumers' privacy. All users must have a "permissible purpose" under the FCRA to obtain a consumer report. Such purposes include:

   • As ordered by a court or a federal grand jury subpoena;

   • As instructed by the consumer in writing;

   • For the extension of credit as a result of an application from a consumer, or the review or collection of a consumer's account;

   • For employment purposes, including hiring and promotion decisions, where the consumer has given written permission;

   • For the underwriting of insurance as a result of an application from a consumer;

   • When there is a legitimate business need, in connection with a business transaction that is initiated by the consumer;

   • To review a consumer's account to determine whether the consumer continues to meet the terms of the account;

   • To determine a consumer's eligibility for a license or other benefit granted by a governmental instrumentality required by law to consider an applicant's financial responsibility or status;

   • For use by a potential investor or servicer, or current insurer, in a valuation or assessment of the credit or prepayment risks associated with an existing credit obligation; and,

   • For use by state and local officials in connection with the determination of child support payments, or modifications and enforcement thereof.

In addition, creditors and insurers may obtain certain consumer report information for the purpose of making "prescreened" unsolicited offers of credit or insurance. Section 604(c).

2. *Users Must Provide Certifications.* Section 604(f) The FCRA prohibits any person from obtaining a consumer report from a consumer reporting agency ("CRA") unless the person has certified to the CRA the permissible purpose(s) for which the report is being obtained and certifies that the report will not be used for any other purpose.

3. *Users Must Notify Consumers When Adverse Actions Are Taken.* The term "adverse action" is defined very broadly as including all business, credit, and employment actions affecting consumers that can be considered to have a negative impact, such as denying or canceling credit or insurance, or denying employment or promotion. No adverse action occurs in a credit transaction where the creditor makes a counteroffer that is accepted by the consumer.

FCRA also details a number of "adverse" actions that can be taken as result of obtaining or reviewing the information contained within a consumer credit report.

Adverse Actions Based on Information Obtained From a CRA. If a user takes any type of adverse action as defined by the FCRA that is based at least in part on information contained in a consumer report, The FCRA requires the user to notify the consumer. The notification may be done in writing, orally, or by electronic means. It must include the following:

- The name, address, and telephone number of the CRA (including a toll-free telephone number, if it is a nationwide CRA) that provided the report.

- A statement that the CRA did not make the adverse decision and is not able to explain why the decision was made.

- A statement setting forth the consumer's right to obtain a free disclosure of the consumer's file from the CRA if the consumer makes a request within 60 days.

- A statement setting forth the consumer's right to dispute directly with the CRA the accuracy or completeness of any information provided by the CRA.

Adverse Actions Based on Information Obtained From Third Parties Who Are Not Consumer Reporting Agencies. If a person denies (or increases the charge for) credit for personal, family, or household purposes based either wholly or partly upon information from a person other than a CRA, and the information is the type of consumer information covered by the FCRA, Section 615(b) (1) requires that the user clearly and accurately disclose to the consumer his or her right to be told the nature of the information that was relied upon if the consumer makes a written request within 60 days of notification. The user must provide the disclosure within a reasonable period of time following the consumer's written request.

Adverse Actions Based on Information Obtained From Affiliates. If a person takes an adverse action involving insurance, employment, or a credit transaction initiated by the consumer, based on information of the type covered by the FCRA, and this information was obtained from an entity affiliated with the user of the information by common ownership or control, Section 615(b) (2) requires the user to notify the consumer of the adverse action. The notice must inform the consumer that he or she may obtain a disclosure of the nature of the information relied upon by making a written request within 60 days of receiving the adverse action notice. If the consumer makes such a request, the user must disclose the nature of the information not later than 30 days after receiving the request. If consumer report information is shared among affiliates and then used for an adverse action, the user must make a similar adverse action disclosure.

Disclosures under FCRA

FCRA requires a disclosure by all persons that make or arrange loans secured by residential real property and that use credit scores. These persons must provide credit scores and other information about credit scores to applicants. Further, if a consumer report is used by an individual or organization in connection with an application for, or a grant, extension, or provision of, credit to a consumer on terms that are less favorable than the most favorable terms available to a substantial proportion of consumers from or through that person, the person must provide a risk-based pricing notice to the consumer in accordance with regulations jointly prescribed by the FTC and the Federal Reserve Board.

Consumer Reports and Employment

Other than within the trucking industry, FCRA mandates certain obligations of organizations that intend to use consumer report information in connection with the evaluation or hiring of a prospective new employee. The user of such information must:

- Make a clear and conspicuous written disclosure to the consumer before the report is obtained, in a document that consists solely of the disclosure, that a consumer report may be obtained.

- Obtain from the consumer prior written authorization to obtain a consumer report. Authorization to access reports during the term of employment may be obtained at the time of employment.

- Certify to the CRA that the above steps have been followed, that the information being obtained will not be used in violation of any federal or state equal opportunity law or regulation, and that, if any adverse action is to be taken based on the consumer report, a copy of the report and a summary of the consumer's rights will be provided to the consumer.

- Before taking an adverse action, provide a copy of the report to the consumer as well as the summary of the consumer's rights. (The user should receive this summary from the CRA.) An adverse action notice should be sent after the adverse action is taken.

An adverse action notice also is required in employment situations if credit information (other than transactions and experience data) obtained from an affiliate is used to deny employment.

Special rules apply for truck drivers where the only interaction between the consumer and the potential employer is by mail, telephone, or computer. In this case, the consumer may provide consent orally or electronically, and an adverse action may be made orally, in writing, or electronically. The consumer may obtain a copy of any report relied upon by the trucking company by contacting the company.

Employee Investigations

FCRA provides special procedures for investigations of suspected misconduct by an employee or for compliance with Federal, state or local laws and regulations or the rules of a self-regulatory organization, and compliance with written policies of the employer. These investigations are not treated as consumer reports so long as the employer or its agent complies with the procedures set forth in the Act, and a summary describing the nature and scope of the inquiry is made to the employee if an adverse action is taken based on the investigation.

Investigative Consumer Reports

Investigative consumer reports contain information about a consumer's character, general reputation, personal characteristics, and mode of living. This information is obtained through personal interviews by an entity or person that is a consumer reporting agency.

Consumers who are the subjects of such reports are given special rights under the FCRA. If a user intends to obtain an investigative consumer report, Section 606 of the Act requires the following:

- The user must disclose to the consumer that an investigative consumer report may be obtained. This must be done in a written disclosure that is mailed, or otherwise delivered, to the consumer at some time before or not later than three days after the date on which the report was first requested. The disclosure must include a statement informing the consumer of his or her right to request additional disclosures of the nature and scope of the investigation, and the summary of consumer rights required by the FCRA. (The summary of consumer rights will be provided by the CRA that conducts the investigation.)

- The user must certify to the CRA that the disclosures set forth above have been made and that the user will make the disclosure described below.

- Upon the written request of a consumer made within a reasonable period of time after the disclosures required above, the user must make a complete disclosure of the nature and scope of the investigation. This must be made in a written statement that is mailed, or otherwise delivered, to the consumer no later than five days after the date on which the request was received from the consumer or the report was first requested, whichever is later in time.

Medical Information under FCRA

FCRA limits the use of medical information obtained from CRAs (other than payment information that appears in a coded form that does not identify the medical provider). If the information is to be used for an insurance transaction, the consumer must give consent to the user of the report or the information must be coded. If the report is to be used for employment purposes—or in connection with a credit transaction (except as provided in regulations issued by the banking and credit union regulators)—the consumer must provide specific written consent and the medical information must be relevant. Any user who receives medical information shall not disclose the information to any other person (except where necessary to carry out the purpose for which the information was disclosed, or as permitted by statute, regulation, or order).

"Pre-screened" Lists

FCRA permits creditors and insurers to obtain limited consumer report information for use in connection with unsolicited offers of credit or insurance under certain circumstances. This practice is known as "pre-screening" and typically involves obtaining from a CRA a list of consumers who meet certain pre-established criteria. If any person intends to use pre-screened lists, that person must (1) before the offer is made, establish the criteria that will be relied upon to make the offer and to grant credit or insurance, and (2) maintain such criteria on file for a three-year period beginning on the date on which the offer is made to each consumer. In addition, any user must include with each written solicitation a clear and conspicuous statement that:

- Information contained in a consumer's CRA file was used in connection with the transaction;

- The consumer received the offer because he or she satisfied the criteria for credit worthiness or insurability used to screen for the offer;

- Credit or insurance may not be extended if, after the consumer responds, it is determined that the consumer does not meet the criteria used for screening or any applicable criteria bearing on credit worthiness or insurability, or the consumer does not furnish required collateral; and,

- The consumer may prohibit the use of information in his or her file in connection with future-prescreened offers of credit or insurance by contacting the notification system established by the CRA that provided the report. The statement must include the address and toll-free telephone number of the appropriate notification system.

In addition, once the Federal Trade Commission by rule has established the format, type size, and manner of the disclosure required, users must be in compliance with the rule. The FTC's complete set of regulations are available at www.ftc.gov/credit.

The Health Insurance Portability and Accountability Act ("HIPAA")

The Health Insurance Portability and Accountability Act of 1996 ("HIPAA") was enacted by Congress in order to improve the efficiency of delivery of healthcare services in the U.S. HIPAA required the Department of Health and Human Services ("HHS") to adopt national standards for electronic healthcare information transactions. Congress recognized, however, that the movement to electronic data exchange in the healthcare sector posed a possible threat to privacy. Accordingly, HIPAA mandated that HHS promulgate regulations to protect the privacy and security of electronically-transmitted healthcare information.

Entities that are directly covered under HIPAA include:

- Health care providers (e.g., a hospital)

- Health plans (a specific program offered by an insurer or other provider)

- Health care clearinghouses (third party organizations that host, handle or process medical information)[118]

Many other entities also maintain or transmit individually identifiable health information. Accordingly, HIPAA indirectly covers "business associates" and any other entity who uses or discloses personal health information ("PHI") whether or not such an entity falls under the definition of health care provider, health plan or health care clearinghouse.

> **Personal Health Information ("PHI").** *Any individually identifiable health information transmitted or maintained in any form or medium, which is held by a covered entity or its business associate, identifies the individual or offers a reasonable basis for identification, is created or received by a covered entity or an employer, and relates to a past, present, or future physical or mental condition, provision of health care or payment for health care to that individual.*

HIPAA is enforced by the U.S. Department of Health and Human Services, in addition to state attorneys generals. Enforcement actions can lead to both civil and criminal penalties, with fines of up to $250,000 and/or prison sentences of up to 10 years. It is important to note that HIPAA sets the floor for medical privacy and does not preempt stronger state statutes and legislation on health care privacy.

The HIPAA Privacy Rule

In August 2000, HHS promulgated a set of regulations on transaction sets known as the "Transactions Rule." This was followed in December 2000 by rules to protect the privacy of personal health information known as the "Privacy Rule."[119] The initial HIPAA Privacy Rule proved so complex and costly that HHS significantly amended it in 2002. In February 2003, HHS promulgated the final "Security Rule." All three of these Rules apply to entities that provide or pay for healthcare and that electronically transmit personal health data in connection with standard transactions.

The HIPAA Privacy Rule in force today applies to all "covered entities" under the Act. It recognizes the legitimate need for public health authorities and others responsible for ensuring public health and safety to have access to protected health information to carry out their public health mission. The Rule also recognizes that public health reports made by covered entities under the Act are an important means of identifying threats to the health and safety of the public at large, as well as individuals. The Rule permits covered entities to disclose protected health information without authorization for specified public health purposes."[120] HIPAA does require that a reasonable effort is made to disclose the minimum protected health information necessary to achieve the purpose of the report.[121]

The HIPAA Privacy Rule articulates a number of requirements around privacy notices, authorizations for use and disclosure of PHI (including limits to and accountings of such disclosure), the "de-identification" of information, security safeguards and the definition of "business associate." It also describes certain exceptions to the rule. These are all explained on the following pages.

Privacy Notices. Specific requirements for privacy notices are contained in the HIPAA Privacy Rule. There are also some defined exceptions to the notice requirements. For example, a privacy notice does not have to be provided when the healthcare provider has an "indirect treatment relationship" with the patient or in the case of medical emergencies. The Rule generally permits covered entities to use PHI for activities related to healthcare treatment, payment and operations (collectively, "TPO"). It requires covered entities to give individuals a detailed notice about the intended collection and use of their heath information.

Authorizations for Uses and Disclosures (Other than TPO). In general, a covered entity may use PHI for purposes other than treatment, payment or operations only with an individual's opt-in "authorization." An authorization must be an independent document that specifically identifies the information to be used or disclosed, the purposes of the use or disclosure, the person or entity to which a disclosure may be made, and other information. A covered entity may not require an individual to sign an authorization as a condition of receiving treatment or participating in a health plan.

Access and Accountings of Disclosures. Under the Rule, individuals have the right to access and copy their own PHI from a covered entity or a business associate. Additionally, individuals have a right to receive an accounting of the disclosures of their PHI that have been made. A reasonable charge may be assessed to cover the costs of providing access.

Individuals also have the right to amend PHI possessed by a covered entity. If the covered entity denies the request to amend the PHI, the individual may file a statement that must then be included in any future use or disclosure of the information.

"Minimum Necessary" Use or Disclosure. Covered entities must make reasonable efforts to limit the use and disclosure of PHI to the "minimum necessary" in order to accomplish the intended purpose. As discussed more fully below, covered entities may disclose PHI to a business associate (such as a billing company, third-party administrator, attorney, or consultant) only if the covered entity has a contract ensuring that the business associate will be bound by all of the obligations applicable to the covered entity, including the minimum necessary standards.

De-identification. The Privacy Rule does not apply to information that has been "de-identified," which is information that does not actually identify an individual and there is no reasonable basis to believe that the information could be used to identify an individual. The Privacy Rule contains a detailed list of data elements that must be removed from personal health information before it can be considered "de-identified."

Safeguards. The Privacy Rule requires that covered entities implement administrative, physical and technical safeguards to protect the confidentiality and integrity of PHI. Additional standards for protecting PHI were promulgated in February 2003, as the HIPAA Security Rule.

Business Associates. Under the Privacy Rule, a "business associate" is any person or organization, other than a member of a covered entity's workforce, that performs services and activities for, or on behalf of, a covered entity, if such services or activities involve the use or disclosure of PHI.[122] Business associates may provide the following types of services and activities: claims processing, data analysis, utilization review, and billing as well as legal, actuarial, accounting, consulting, data aggregation, management, administrative, accreditation, and/or financial services.

When a covered entity engages another entity to provide the activities and services described above, the Privacy Rule requires that covered entity to enter into a Business Associate Contract with that other entity. The Business Associate Contract must include provisions that pass the privacy and security standard down to the contracting entity. The Business Associate Contract must be in writing, although it may be signed electronically as long as such signatures are valid as "written signatures" under the applicable state's contract laws.

Exceptions. The Privacy Rule contains a number of exceptions under which PHI may be used without consent. These exceptions include information used for public health activities; to report victims of abuse, neglect, or domestic violence; in judicial and administrative proceedings; for certain law enforcement activities; for certain research purposes; and, for certain specialized governmental functions. A covered entity is required to release PHI to the individual it concerns (see accountings of disclosures above), and to the Secretary of HHS to investigate compliance with the privacy rules.

The HIPAA Security Rule

The HIPAA Security Rule was finalized in February 2003 along with the Privacy Rule. It establishes minimum security requirements for PHI that a covered entity receives, creates, maintains or transmits in electronic form.[123] The Security Rule is designed to require covered entities to implement "reasonable" security measures in a technology-neutral manner. The goal is for all covered entities to implement "policies and procedures to prevent, detect, contain, and correct security violations."

The Security Rule is comprised of "standards" and "implementation specifications," which encompass administrative, technical and physical safeguards. Some of the implementation specifications are required, while others are considered "addressable." This means that the covered entity must assess whether it is an appropriate safeguard for the entity to adopt. If not, the covered entity must document why it is not reasonable, and, if appropriate, adopt an alternative measure.

The Rule applies to "electronic protected health information," which is any PHI that is transmitted or maintained in "electronic media" (such as computer hard drives, magnetic tapes or disks, or digital memory cards, all of which are considered electronic storage media). Paper records, paper-to-paper fax transmissions, and voice communications (e.g., telephone) are not considered transmissions via electronic media.

The HIPAA Security Rule requires covered entities to:

1. Ensure the confidentiality, integrity, and availability of all electronic protected health information the covered entity creates, receives, maintains, or transmits;

2. Protect against any reasonably anticipated threats or hazards to the security or integrity of such information;

3. Protect against any reasonably anticipated uses or disclosures of such information that are not permitted or required under the Privacy Rule; and,

4. Ensure compliance with the Security Rule by its workforce.

As noted above, the Security Rule strives for a reasonable level of security. Accordingly, the Rule permits a covered entity to "use any security measures that allow the covered entity to reasonably and appropriately implement the standards and implementation specifications." As it develops its security program, each covered entity must consider the following factors:

1. The size, complexity, and capabilities of the covered entity;

2. The covered entity's technical infrastructure, hardware, and software security capabilities;

3. The costs of security measures; and,

4. The probability and criticalness of potential risks to electronic protected health information.

The HIPAA Security Rule also requires that:

1. Each covered entity must identify an individual who is responsible for the implementation and oversight of the Security Rule compliance program. (This person may be the same person that oversees the Privacy Rule compliance program, if the organization is simple enough for these duties to be consolidated.)

2. Each covered entity must conduct initial and ongoing risk assessments. In particular, the covered entity must "conduct an accurate and thorough assessment of the potential risks and vulnerabilities to the confidentiality, integrity, and availability of electronic protected health information held by

the covered entity." This assessment should identify potential risks and vulnerabilities, each of which must be addressed.

3. Each covered entity must implement a security awareness and training program for its workforce. Additionally, individual workers must be disciplined if they fail to comply with the policies and procedures.

4. Finally, covered entities must incorporate Security Rule requirements into the Business Associate Contracts required by the Privacy Rule.

HIPAA and Preemption Issues

It is important to note that the HIPAA Privacy and Security Rules are designed to establish *minimum* standards (e.g., to set the legal floor). States are free to develop more rigorous requirements as long as these requirements do not conflict with HIPAA. Thus, HIPAA itself lacks the power of preemption.

Each covered entity under the Act is therefore required to consider all state healthcare privacy and security laws, and to operate in accordance with these state laws even if they exceed the HIPAA standards. Accordingly, in discussions with covered entities, it is important to understand and consider the particular state requirements that may apply to that entity's information as well.

Gramm-Leach-Bliley Act (GLBA)

The Financial Services Modernization Act of 1999, known as the Gramm-Leach-Bliley Act ("GLBA"),[124] came about as a result of the standardization of the U.S. banking and insurance industries in the late 1990s. As financial institutions and insurance companies were allowed to merge, substantial concerns arose over the consolidation of consumer data and how this data were shared within and across these organizations and their subsidiaries in the finance and insurance sectors.

GLBA provided for sweeping changes in the financial services industry, allowing the creation of new financial services holding companies that could offer a full range of financial products. It also eliminated legal barriers to affiliations among banks, securities firms, insurance companies and other financial services companies.

Unfortunately, just prior to GLBA's passage, certain major financial institutions were found to have been selling detailed customer information (including account numbers and other highly sensitive data) to telemarketing firms, who then used the account numbers to charge customers for services they didn't want and which had no particular value. The largest case of this misuse of data, involving US Bancorp and the telemarketing firm MemberWorks, was brought by the Minnesota attorney general's office and resulted in a $3 million settlement by the bank for fraud, false advertising, deceptive trade practices, and violations of the Fair Credit Reporting Act and state consumer protection laws.

This US Bancorp/MemberWorks case focused both consumer and regulatory attention on the prevalence of banks' data sharing relationships with third-party marketers. A group of 25 attorneys general then brought actions against many of the country's leading and largest financial institutions in an attempt to regulate these practices. Congress responded to these events by including significant privacy and security protections for consumers in GLBA and mandating further rulemaking on privacy and security by the Federal Trade Commission, federal banking regulators and state insurance regulators.

Financial institutions were required to substantially comply with GLBA's requirements by July 2001.

GLBA applies to domestic financial institutions (e.g., any U.S. company that is "significantly engaged" in financial activities). Under GLBA, these companies are then considered "financial institutions" ("FI"). This definition encompasses companies such as insurance providers, securities firms, payment settlement services, check cashing services, credit counselors and mortgage lenders, among others.

GLBA addresses the handling of non-public financial information, although this includes a wide range of information that is not obviously financial in nature, such as a consumer's name and address. In addition it covers information:

- Provided by a consumer to an FI to obtain a financial product or service,

- Resulting from a transaction involving a financial product or service between an FI and a consumer; and,

- That the financial institution obtains in connection with providing a financial product or service to a consumer.

Non-Public Personal Information ("NPI"). Personally identifiable financial information (i) provided by a consumer to a financial institution, (ii) resulting from a transaction or service performed for the consumer, or (iii) otherwise obtained by the financial institution. Excluded from the definition are (i) publicly available information and (ii) any consumer list that is derived without using personally identifiable financial information.

GLBA requires a financial institution to safeguard consumers' personal data under privacy rules that are promulgated by the FTC and FI regulators. GLBA's basic requirements are to:

- Securely store personal financial information;

- Give notice of their policies regarding the sharing of personal financial information; and,

- Give consumers the alternative to opt-out of some sharing of personal financial information.

GLBA is enforced by the FTC and financial industry regulators, as well as state attorneys general. In addition, GLBA is not preempted by state law, thus each state may develop more stringent requirements.[125] The typical penalty for failure to comply with GLBA is an enforcement action; and, while there is no private right of action under GLBA, failure to comply with a notice is considered a deceptive trade practice by state and federal authorities, and some states have private rights of action for this type of violation.

GLBA's privacy protections generally apply to consumers, meaning individuals who obtain from a financial institution financial products or services to be used primarily for personal, family or household purposes. Many of the requirements relate to consumer customers—consumers with whom the organization has an ongoing relationship. Financial services companies that do not have consumer customers are not subject to many of GLBA's more onerous requirements, such as the notice requirements.

While it might appear that GLBA covers only financial information (based on the definition of nonpublic personal information), the federal agencies implementing GLBA determined that any information obtained by a financial institution in connection with providing a financial product or service is protected financial information, even if the information is not typically considered to be financial in nature. For example, the mere name of a financial institution's customer is non-public personal financial information because it indicates the existence of a relationship that is financial in nature between the institution and the consumer.

To comply with GLBA, financial institutions must:

1. Prepare and provide to consumer customers clear and conspicuous notice of the financial institution's information-sharing policies and practices—these notices must be given when a customer relationship is established and annually thereafter;

2. Clearly provide consumers the right to opt-out of having their non-public personal information shared with non-affiliated third parties (subject to a number of significant exceptions related largely to the processing of consumer transactions);

3. Refrain from disclosing to any non-affiliated third-party marketer, other than a consumer reporting agency, an account number or similar form of access code to a consumer's credit card, deposit or transaction account; and,

4. Comply with regulatory standards established by certain government authorities to protect the security and confidentiality of customer records and information, and protect against security threats and unauthorized access to or certain uses of such records or information.

Title V of Gramm-Leach-Bliley

While GLBA's privacy provisions are quite complex, Title V of the Act provides that financial institutions may share virtually any information with "affiliated" companies, but may share information with "non-affiliated" companies for marketing only after providing an opportunity for the consumer to "opt-out" of the disclosure. Thus, GLBA does not so much restrict information-sharing practices as require notice of such activities.

The provisions of Title V do not preempt or supersede state law if state law provides more stringent privacy protections. Section 505(a) requires that the Act and its regulations be enforced by various federal and state regulatory agencies having jurisdiction over the relevant financial institution. The Act gives federal enforcement authority to, among others, the Office of the Comptroller of the Currency, the Federal Reserve Board, the Federal Deposit Insurance Corporation and the Securities and Exchange Commission. The Federal Trade Commission has general enforcement authority for any financial institution that does not fall within the jurisdiction of any of the enumerated regulatory agencies.

While GLBA does not include a private right of action, financial institutions that are obligated to give notice could face liability under deceptive trade practices statutes if the notices are deceptive or inaccurate. Additionally, financial institutions that fail to comply may also be subject to penalties under the Financial Institution Reform, Recovery and Enforcement Act ("FIRREA"). FIRREA penalties range from up to $5,500 for violations of laws and regulations, to up to $27,500 if violations are unsafe, unsound or reckless, to up to $1.1 million for "knowing" violations.

GLBA and Privacy Notices

The FTC and financial regulators established a standard for privacy notices under which a financial institution must give initial and annual privacy notices to consumers on nine categories of information, and must process opt-outs within 30 days. The privacy notice itself must be a clear, conspicuous, and accurate statement of the company's privacy practices and include the following:

- What information the financial institution collects about its consumers and customers;

- With whom it shares the information;

- How it protects or safeguards the information; and,

- An explanation of how a consumer may opt-out of having his information shared. In addition, the financial institution must offer a reasonable way a consumer can do that.[126]

Provided that this standard is met, a financial institution may share any information it has with its affiliated companies.[127] In addition, other than for defined exceptions, a financial institution may also share consumer information with non-affiliated companies and other third parties, but only after disclosing information-sharing practices to customers and only after giving them the opportunity to opt-out.

It should be noted that financial institutions are prohibited from disclosing consumer account numbers to non-affiliated companies for purposes of telemarketing, direct mail marketing (including through email), even if the consumer has not opted out of sharing the information for marketing purposes. Also, a financial institution must ensure that service providers will not use provided consumer data for anything other than the intended purpose.

Situations may also arise in which the consumer has no opt-out right. For example, a consumer cannot opt out if:

- A financial institution shares information with outside companies that provide essential services like data processing or servicing accounts;

- The disclosure is legally required; and/or,

- A financial institution shares customer data with outside service providers that market the financial company's products or services.

The GLBA Safeguards Rule

Along with privacy standards and rules, GLBA requires financial institutions to have a security plan in place to protect the confidentiality and integrity of personal consumer information. The regulatory agencies established such standards in the form of a Final Rule (the "Safeguards Rule") that became effective on May 23, 2003.

The Gramm-Leach-Bliley Safeguards Rule[128] applies to both electronic and paper records. It requires financial institutions to develop and implement a comprehensive "information security program" (defined as a program that contains "administrative, technical and physical safeguards" to protect the security, confidentiality and integrity of customer information).[129] Such a program must be appropriate to the size, complexity, nature and scope of the activities of the institution. Thus, like the Privacy Rule, the Safeguards Rule distinguishes the concepts of security, confidentiality and integrity, but suggests that all three concepts are integral to a complete understanding of security.

The information security program required under the Rule must have certain elements, including a designated employee to coordinate it, audit systems to determine risks, and certain procedures to take with service providers to assure that the security of the information is maintained.

Under the GLBA Safeguards Rule, a financial institution must provide the following three levels of security:

1. *Administrative security,* which includes program definition, management of workforce risks, employee training, and vendor oversight;

2. *Technical security,* which covers computer systems, networks, applications, in addition to access controls and encryption; and,

3. *Physical security,* which includes facilities, environmental safeguards and disaster recovery.

Pursuant to the Safeguards Rule, the administrative, technical and physical safeguards to be implemented must be reasonably designed to (i) insure the security and confidentiality of customer information, (ii) protect against any anticipated threats or hazards to the security or integrity of the information, and (iii) protect against unauthorized access to or use of the information that could result in substantial harm or inconvenience to any customer.[130] Thus, the agencies that drafted the Rule appear to believe that security means protecting the confidentiality and integrity of information, and restricting access to it.

The Safeguards Rule does allow for flexibility in implementing a security program, stating that the program must contain safeguards that are "appropriate" to the entity's size and complexity, the nature and scope of the entity's activities, and the sensitivity of any customer information at issue.[131]

The Safeguards Rule requires that certain basic elements be included in a security program. Each institution must (1) designate an employee to coordinate the safeguards, (2) identify and assess the risks to customer information in each relevant area of the company's operation, and evaluate the effectiveness of the current safeguards for controlling those risks, (3) design and implement a safeguards program and regularly monitor and test it, (4) select appropriate service providers and enter into agreements with them to implement safeguards, and (5) evaluate and adjust the program in light of relevant circumstances, including changes in business arrangements or operations, or the results of testing and monitoring of safeguards.[132]

The Children's Online Privacy Protection Act of 2000 ("COPPA")

The Children's Online Privacy Protection Act of 2000 ("COPPA")[133] was passed in direct response to the FTC's 1998 *Privacy Online: A Report to Congress.*[134] This report raised concerns about the privacy of children using the Internet, and noted the rapid growth in the number of interactive services directed at children. The FTC report detailed how the children were actively engaging in discussion groups, online games, research surveys and contests. In the process, a large amount of personally identifiable information about children and their families was being collected by Web sites without the knowledge or permission of the children's parents or guardians.

COPPA applies to the operators of commercial Web sites and online services especially those directed to children under the age of 13. It also applies to general audience Web sites and online services that have actual knowledge that they are collecting personal information from children under the age of 13.

COPPA requires these Web site operators to do the following:

- Post a privacy policy on the homepage of the Web site and link to the privacy policy on every page where personal information is collected;

- Provide notice about the site's information collection practices to parents;

- Obtain verifiable parental consent before collecting personal information from children;

- Give parents a choice as to whether their child's personal information will be disclosed to third parties;

- Provide parents access and the opportunity to delete the child's personal information and opt-out of future collection or use of the information;

- Not condition a child's participation in a game, contest or other activity on the child's disclosing more personal information than is reasonably necessary to participate in that activity; and,

- Maintain the confidentiality, security and integrity of personal information collected from children.

COPPA enforcements are brought by the FTC and state attorneys general. FTC settlements have been as high as $400,000 dollars.[135] In addition to penalties from the FTC, there is the possibility of being sued for damages, to say nothing of the reputation risk involved in a COPPA violation.

Privacy Notices under COPPA

The COPPA privacy notice must be available via links on the Web site home page and any other page where personal information is disclosed. The link must be clearly labeled and placed in a prominent spot on each page that it appears. The privacy notice must include:

• contact information for the Web site operators collecting/maintaining information;

• the type of information collected;

• how the information will be used;

• if the information will be disclosed to third parties, and, if so, the general purpose of the third party, as well as a description of its business and acknowledgment of confidentiality;

• a disclaimer of an option to consent to collection but not disclosure;

• that no condition may be placed on the disclosure of information; and,

• the parent's final right to forfeit a child's disclosure of information, and the procedures to do so. Reasonable efforts must be taken to ensure that parents receive notice that information is being collected from their child, and that their consent is required for this collection.

As noted above, COPPA generally requires Web site operators to obtain verifiable parental consent before collecting personal information from a child. A variety of mechanisms have been developed to facilitate parental consent. According to the FTC's published guidance:[136]

> *If you are going to use the information only for **internal purposes**, that is, you will not be giving the information to third parties or making it publicly available through such activities as chat rooms or bulletin boards, then you can use what is being called the **email plus** method of obtaining consent. You may send an email to the parent containing the required notice, and request that the parent provide consent by responding in an email—as long as you take some additional, confirmatory step after receiving the parent's email. For example, after a reasonable time delay, you can send another email to the parent to confirm consent and let the parent know that he or she can revoke the consent if they wish. You may also request in your initial email that the parent include a phone number or mailing address in his or her reply so that you can follow up to confirm via telephone or postal mail.*

*If you are going to **disclose children's information to third parties or make it publicly available** through such activities as a chat room, message board, personal home page, pen pal service, or email service, then you must use the most reliable methods available to obtain parental consent. You can: provide a form for the parent to sign and mail or fax back to you; ask a parent to use a credit card in connection with a transaction (perhaps a fee just to cover the cost of processing the credit card); maintain a toll-free telephone number staffed by trained personnel for parents to call in their consent, or you can accept emails from parents where those emails contain a digital signature or other digital certificate that uses public key technology.*

There are several exceptions to the consent requirement which allow an operator to collect a child's name and email address: [137]

• If it is in addition to the parent's email address for purposes of providing the required notice and obtaining consent;

• To respond once to a specific request from a child, as long as the email address is deleted immediately after responding;

• To respond more than once to a specific request of a child (for example, one who is requesting a subscription to an online newsletter or requesting site updates), as long as, after the first communication with the child, the operator sends notice to the parent's email address to provide an opportunity for the parent to opt-out of the information collection and order the operator to delete the email address and stop contacting the child. With this multiple-contact exception, the parent needs only to contact the operator to discontinue the communication; affirmative consent is not required so that a non-response will be presumed to be parental consent. Of course, at any time, the parent may contact the operator and request that the information be deleted and the contact halted.

• To collect a child's name and email address where necessary to protect the safety of a child participating on the site or online service. The operator must give notice to the parent, use it only for such safety purpose, and not disclose it on the site or service.

• To collect a child's name and email address for the sole purpose of protecting the security or integrity of the site, take precautions against liability, respond to judicial process or for law enforcement on a matter related to public safety.

COPPA regulations have some additional requirements. For example, a child's participation in an online activity cannot be conditioned on the disclosure of detailed personal information. Additionally, upon request, parents must be provided with access to the specific information collected from their child; and the opportunity to terminate the use and collection of the information.

Web site operators are deemed to be in compliance with FTC-approved guidelines if:

- measures are implemented to ensure the protection of children;

- independent assessments of the operator's compliance are performed; and,

- incentives for compliance are provided. A number of third parties (such as TRUSTe, BBBOnline, and ESRB) offer COPPA certifications for this "Safe Harbor."

Children's online privacy is also addressed through marketplace initiatives among industry groups such as the Better Business Bureau's "Children's Advertising Review Unit" ("CARU"). The CARU *Guidelines for Children's Advertising* are a self-regulatory framework. If a company violates one or more of the guidelines, CARU will provide information on the violation directly to the FTC for enforcement.

The Drivers Privacy Protection Act ("DPPA")

The Drivers Privacy Protection Act ("DPPA") was originally enacted in 1994, and subsequently amended in 2000, for the purpose of protecting the privacy of personal information gathered by state departments or bureaus of motor vehicles (known more commonly as "DMVs" or "BMVs"). The DPPA was passed in the wake of a series of abuses of drivers' personal information held by DMVs, including the 1989 death of television actress' Rebecca Schaeffer, who was pursued and murdered by a stalker who had freely obtained the actresses' personal address from a publicly-available state database containing drivers' records. [139]

In essence, the DPPA prohibits the release or use by any state DMV/BMV of personal information about an individual obtained by the department in connection with a motor vehicle record. The "Shelby amendment" to the DPPA, introduced by U.S. Senator Richard Shelby, took effect June 1, 2000, and changed the DPPA to require states to get express permission (opt-in) from individuals before their personal information is sold or released to third-party marketers. This amendment survived a Constitutional challenge in the U.S. Supreme Court. [140]

Criminal fines are levied against anyone who knowingly violates the DPPA. In addition, violations by DMVs are subject to a civil penalty imposed by the state attorney general of not more than $5,000 a day for each day of substantial noncompliance. [141]

The DPPA establishes a "floor" of protections that each state was required to have in place in September 1997. Among these protections:

• DMV data can be provided by the state motor vehicle records offices for only certain permissible purposes or to certain permissible users. In particular, the DPPA sets forth 14 specific permissible purposes, including any use, if the user has written consent of the individual to whom the data pertains.

• Data resellers must certify to the states that the data will only be resold for the same types of permissible purposes. Resellers must maintain a rolling five-year audit trail showing who received data and what the purpose was for the data.

• State attorneys general are able to enforce the DPPA, using civil and criminal penalties. Additionally, individuals may bring civil actions against users who knowingly obtain, disclose or use DMV data about them, with statutory damages set at $2,500, plus punitive and other damages, as may be applicable or appropriate.

States had the option of enacting the federal DPPA's provisions or enacting other restrictions that were no less stringent than those set forth in the federal DPPA. States were free to establish restrictions that exceeded those established by the federal DPPA; the DPPA does not preempt other state restrictions on the use or disclosure of DMV data. Oklahoma and South Carolina challenged the constitutionality of the DPPA, but the Supreme Court ruled that the federal law was constitutional.[142]

Because each state has adopted its own version of the DPPA, there are many state-specific restrictions. For example, one permissible use under the federal DPPA is any use in connection with litigation and court proceedings. However, three states (Massachusetts, New Mexico and South Carolina) do not permit use of their data for this purpose. Additionally, other states have imposed different restrictions. For example, Texas, Oregon, Pennsylvania, West Virginia and Wyoming prohibit any distribution of their DMV data over the Internet.

U.S. Marketing Communications Laws

Within the body of law that governs the handling of personal information by organizations in the U.S. private sector are laws that regulate marketing communications to individual consumers. These laws relate to specific communications channels and methods such as telemarketing, electronic mail and fax marketing.

The major contrast between U.S. and other countries' approaches to marketing communications regards choice. In the E.U. (and internationally), laws generally require the consumer to opt-in to marketing programs,[143] whereas in the U.S., the laws generally provide for opt-out choice.

The U.S. Telemarketing Sales Rules ("TSR")

The U.S. Telemarketing Sales Rules ("TSR") apply to for-profit organizations, and cover charitable solicitations placed by for-profit telefunders. It requires that covered organizations:

- Call only between 8 a.m. and 9 p.m.

- Screen and scrub names against the national Do-Not-Call list ("DNC")

- Display caller ID information

- Identify themselves and what they are selling

- Disclose all material information and terms[144]

- Give special rules for prizes and promotions

- Respect requests to call back

- Retain records for at least 24 hours

- Gives special rules for automated dialers

The TSR does not apply to:

- Non-profits calling on their own behalf

- Calls to customers with an existing relationship within the last 18 months

- Calls to prospects within 90 days of an inquiry

- Inbound calls, provided that there is no "upsell"[145] of additional products or services

- Most business-to-business calls

The FTC issued the original Telemarketing Sales Rule in 1995 pursuant to the Telemarketing and Consumer Fraud and Abuse Prevention Act. The Rule has been amended several times since 1995 in order to address new types of practices. Most notably, the Commission amended the TSR in 2003 to implement the Do-Not-Call ("DNC") Registry regulations.

Under the Rule, telemarketing is defined as "a plan, program, or campaign…to induce the purchase of goods or services or a charitable contribution" involving more than one interstate telephone call.[146] With some exceptions,[147] all businesses or individuals that engage in "telemarketing" must comply with the TSR. As the FTC notes, compliance is required both of "telemarketers," entities that that initiate or receive telephone calls to or from consumers, or "sellers," the entities that provide or arrange to provide the goods and services being offered.

Limits on Calls to Consumers

The TSR limits when U.S. consumers may be called in three specific ways: calling time restrictions and entity-specific suppression lists as well as the National Do-Not-Call ("DNC") Registry.

1. *Calling time restrictions.* Outbound telemarketing calls may be madeonly between the hours of 8 a.m. and 9 p.m.

2. *Entity-specific suppression lists.* Any seller (or telemarketer calling on the seller's behalf) is prohibited from calling any consumer who has asked not to be called again. Sellers and telemarketers are required to maintain internal suppression lists to respect these do-not-call requests.

3. *The National Do-Not-Call Registry.* Any telemarketer must respect the requests of consumers to not receive any telephone-based solicitations from that telemarketers. This program has some exceptions and is defined in greater detail below.

The TSR does provide some latitude for companies that have distinct corporate divisions. In general, distinct corporate divisions are considered separate sellers under the Rule.

The FTC has offered a set of factors that should be used to determine whether do-not-call requests should be shared among divisions:

• whether there is substantial diversity between the operational structure of the divisions and,

• whether the goods or services sold by the divisions are substantially different from each other.

If a consumer tells one division of a company not to call again, a distinct corporate division of the same company may still make calls to that consumer. If the divisions are not distinct, however, the seller may not call the consumer even to offer different goods or services.

The U.S. National Do-Not-Call Registry

The U.S. National Do-Not-Call ("DNC") Registry[148] is perhaps the best known of the FTC's telemarketing sales rules and remains the most popular consumer program ever to be implemented by the FTC. The program provides a means for U.S. citizens to register residential and wireless phone numbers that they do not wish to be called for telemarketing purposes (with specific exceptions, below).

The FTC, the Federal Communications Commission ("FCC"), and state attorneys general enforce the DNC Registry which now contains the names of over 100 million participating U.S. citizens—and is still growing. Violations of the Rule can lead to civil penalties of up to $11,000 per violation. In addition, violators may be subject to nation-wide injunctions that prohibit certain conduct, and may be required to pay redress to injured consumers.

The FTC's National Do-Not-Call Registry provisions took effect in October 2003 and require sellers and telemarketers to access the Registry prior to making any phone-based solicitations. They are also required to update their call lists every 31 days with new Registry information.

The Registry is accessed via an automated Web site at *www.telemarketing.donotcall.gov*. Only sellers, telemarketers and their service providers may access the Registry. Each seller must establish a profile by providing identifying information about the organization. The seller then receives a unique "Subscription Account Number" ("SAN") upon payment of the appropriate fee.

Telemarketers accessing the Registry on behalf of seller-clients are required to identi-fy the seller-clients and provide the seller-client's unique SAN. (Telemarketers access the registry, at no cost, through the use of their seller-client's unique SANs—their access is limited to the area codes requested and paid for by the seller-client.)

The FTC's guidance specifically states that:

> *Even though they are not required by law to do so, telemarketers and service providers may gain access to the national registry on their own behalf, but they must pay a separate fee for that ability. But before placing calls on behalf of a seller-client, telemarketers are required to ensure that their seller-client has a valid SAN…In other words, each SAN belongs to a specific seller, and SANs are not transferable.*

Please note that it is a violation of the TSR to place any call to a consumer (absent an exception) unless the Registry is checked. In other words, even a call to a consumer whose phone number is not on the Registry is a violation of the TSR if the Registry was not checked prior to the call.

Exceptions to the DNC Rules—Existing Business Relationships

Sellers (and telemarketers calling on their behalf) may call a consumer with whom a seller has an established business relationship ("EBR"), provided the consumer has not asked to be on the seller's entity-specific do-not-call list. The TSR recognizes two distinct types of relationships: "customers" and "prospects."

An EBR exists with a customer if the consumer has purchased, rented or leases the seller's goods or services (or completed a financial transaction with the seller), within 18 months preceding a telemarketing call. The 18-month period runs from the date of the last payment, transaction, or shipment between the consumer and the seller.

An EBR exists with a prospect if the consumer has made an application or inquiry regarding the seller's goods and services. This EBR runs for three months from the date of the person's inquiry or application.

Telemarketing Sales Rule Case Study:
Executive Financial Home Loan Corporation

The Executive Financial Home Loan Corporation case is one example of how the FTC actively enforces the Telemarketing Sales Rule. This is the first of several FTC actions in the privacy and security arenas to be examined throughout this book.

Facts and Allegations
Executive Financial Home Loan is a California-based mortgage broker that both sells home loan services and engages in telemarketing of its services to consumers. For its telemarketing activities, Executive Financial Home Loan allegedly used phone numbers from "lead lists" it purchased from brokers, and relied upon the brokers' claims that the lists had been scrubbed against the DNC Registry. Despite the brokers' claims to the contrary, the lists contained numbers registered with the DNC Registry. In addition, although Executive Home Loan paid the brokers for the lead lists, it did not properly purchase access to the numbers on the registry.

The FTC complaint alleged that Executive Financial Home Loan violated the Telemarketing Sales Rule by:

1. Calling tens of thousands of consumers whose numbers were registered with the National Do-Not-Call Registry; and,

2. Failing to pay the annual fees required to gain access to the phone numbers on the DNC Registry.

Privacy and Security Promises
This case was primarily brought to enforce the TSR.

FTC Consent Agreement with Executive Financial Home Loan

1. TSR Compliance Program: Executive Financial Home Loan shall not (a) initiate any outbound telephone calls to a number on the Federal Do Not Call Registry unless it has obtained express agreement in writing or has an established business relationship, or (b) initiate any outbound telephone calls without paying the annual DNC Registry fee required.

2. Maintenance of Relevant Documents: For a period of five years, Executive Financial Home Loan shall maintain and provide, within seven days of request, any business records that demonstrate its compliance with this order.

3. Delivery of Order: Executive Financial Home Loan shall deliver a copy of the FTC order to all owners, principals, members, officers, directors, and managers and to all employees, agents and representatives having decision-making authority over the subject matter. In addition, it shall obtain a signed statement from each person acknowledging receipt of the order. Within 10 days of complying with the order, Executive Financial Home Loan shall file an affidavit containing the details of its compliance.

4. Reporting: Executive Financial Home Loan shall notify the FTC at least 30 days prior to any corporate change that may affect compliance with the order.

Duration of the FTC Order
Not specified

Fine Imposed
Executive Home Loan was assessed fines amounting to $1,138,551; however the company was required to pay only $50,000 due to its inability to satisfy the full judgment.

Please note that an EBR exists between sellers and customers—it does not generally extend to the seller's affiliates. The FTC guidance states that "[t]he test for whether a subsidiary or affiliate can claim an established business relationship with a sister company's customer is: would the customer expect to receive a call from such an entity, or would the customer feel such a call is inconsistent with having placed his or her number on the National Do-Not-Call Registry?" Per the guidance:

> Factors to be considered in this analysis include the nature and type of goods or services offered and the identity of the affiliate. Are the affiliate's goods or services similar to the seller's? Is the affiliate's name identical or similar to the seller's? The greater the similarity between the nature and type of goods sold by the seller and any subsidiary or affiliate and the greater the similarity in identity between the seller and any subsidiary and affiliate, the more likely it is that the call would fall within the established business relationship exemption.

Exceptions to the DNC Rules—Consent

The TSR also allows sellers and telemarketers to call consumers who consent to receive such calls. This consent must be in writing. It must state the number to which calls may be made, and it must also include the consumer's signature. (A valid electronic signature is acceptable.)

Please note that the seller's request for consent must be "clear and conspicuous." The request cannot be "hidden; printed in small, pale, or non-contrasting type; hidden on the back or bottom of the document; or buried in unrelated information where a person would not expect to find such a request." If online, the "please call me" button may not be pre-checked. The FTC's guidance also states:

In the FTC's enforcement experience, sweepstakes entry forms often have been used in a deceptive manner to obtain "authorization" from a consumer to incur a charge or some other detriment. Authorization or permission obtained through subterfuge is ineffective. The FTC scrutinizes any use of such sweepstakes entry forms as a way to get a consumer's permission to place telemarketing calls to her number.

The Do-Not-Call Safe Harbor

The TSR does have a "DNC Safe Harbor" that sellers and telemarketers can use to reduce the risk of liability. Per the guidance,

> [I]f a seller or telemarketer can establish that as part of its routine business practice, it meets the following requirements, it will not be subject to civil penalties or sanctions for erroneously calling a consumer who has asked not to be called, or for calling a number on the National Registry:

- The seller or telemarketer has established and implemented written procedures to honor consumers' requests that they not be called, [and]

- The seller or telemarketer has trained its personnel, and any entity assisting in its compliance, in these procedures, [and]

- The seller, telemarketer, or someone else acting on behalf of the seller ... has maintained and recorded an entity-specific Do-Not-Call list, [and]

- The seller or telemarketer uses, and maintains records documenting, a process to prevent calls to any telephone number on an entity-specific Do-Not-Call list or the National Do-Not-Call Registry. This, provided that the latter process involves using a version of the National Registry from the FTC no more than 31 days before the date any call is made, [and]

- The seller, telemarketer, or someone else acting on behalf of the seller... monitors and enforces compliance with the entity's written Do-Not-Call procedures, [then]

- The call is a result of error.

This DNC Safe Harbor provides an important protection for sellers and telemarketers because violations of the TSR can result in civil penalties of up to $11,000 per call.

Required Disclosures

The TSR requires telemarketers to make a prompt[149] disclosure to the consumer at the beginning of the call of:

• The identity of the seller,

• That the purpose of the call is to sell goods or services,

• The nature of those goods or services, and

• In the case of a prize promotion, that no purchase or payment is necessary to participate or win, and that a purchase or payment does not increase the chances of winning.

The FTC has issued guidance on how and when these four basic disclosures must be made. For example, disclosures must be truthful. A company cannot say it is making "a courtesy call" to the consumer, if the purpose of the call is telemarketing.

If a call has multiple purposes (such as the sale of different types of products or different overall purposes), these disclosures have to be given for all sales purposes. The following examples are from the FTC's "Complying with the TSR" guide:[150]

> *Say a seller calls a consumer to determine whether he or she is satisfied with a previous purchase and then plans to move into a sales presentation if the consumer is satisfied. Since the seller plans to make a sales presentation in at least some of the calls (the seller plans to end the call if the consumer is not satisfied), four disclosures must be made promptly during the initial portion of the call and before inquiring about customer satisfaction.*
>
> *However, a seller may make calls to welcome new customers and ask whether they are satisfied with goods or services they recently purchased. If the seller doesn't plan to sell anything to these customers during any of these calls, the four oral disclosures are not required. That's the case even if customers ask about the sellers' other goods or services, and the seller responds by describing the goods or services. Because the seller has no plans to sell goods or services during these calls, the disclosures are not required.*

Misrepresentations and Material Omissions

The TSR prohibits misrepresentations during the sales call. Telemarketers must provide accurate and complete information about the products and services being offered. They may also not omit any material facts about the products or services. There are six, broad categories of information that must always be disclosed:

1. Cost and quantity;

2. Material restrictions and conditions;

3. No-refund policy details (if applicable);

4. Prize and promotion details (such as odds of winning and value of the prize);

5. Credit card loss prevention program disclosures (for sellers offering this service); and,

6. Negative option feature details (if the seller uses a negative option).

The Rule also was amended to require specific disclosures when a telemarketer accepts payment by means other than a credit card or debit card, such as phone or utility billing. In this case, the seller must also obtain "express verifiable authorization." In amending the Rule, the Commission noted that many new payment methods lacked basic consumer protection provisions that exist in credit card transactions. Because the consumers may not have protections against, for example, unauthorized charges, or recourse in the event they are dissatisfied with the goods or services, the TSR now requires telemarketers to meet a higher standard for proving authorization when consumers use new payment methods.

Transmission of Caller ID Information

The TSR requires entities that make telemarketing calls to transmit accurate call identification information so that it can be presented to consumer with caller ID services. In particular, each telemarketer may transmit its own name and phone number or it may substitute the name of the seller on whose behalf the telemarketer is making the call. The telemarketer may also substitute the seller's customer-service telephone number for its number, provided that the seller's number must be answered during normal business hours.

Telemarketers are not liable if, for some reason, caller ID information does not reach a consumer, provided that the telemarketer has arranged with its carrier to transmit this information in every call. The FTC guidance states "telemarketers who can show that they took all available steps to ensure transmission of Caller ID information in every call will not be liable for isolated inadvertent instances when the Caller ID information fails to make it to the consumer's receiver. Nevertheless, a telemarketer's use of calling equipment that is not capable of transmitting Caller ID information is no excuse for failure to transmit the required information."

Prohibition on Call Abandonment

The TSR expressly prohibits telemarketers from abandoning an outbound telephone call, either with "hang ups" or "dead air." There is a Safe Harbor for the call abandonment provisions as well.

Under the TSR, an outbound telephone call is "abandoned" if a person answers it and the telemarketer does not connect the call to a live sales representative within two seconds of the person's completed greeting.

Abandoned calls often result from a telemarketer's use of predictive dialers to call consumers. Predictive dialers promote telemarketers' efficiency by simultaneously calling multiple consumers for every available sales representative. This maximizes the amount of time telemarketing sales representatives spend talking to consumers and minimizes representatives' downtime. But it also means that some calls are abandoned: consumers are either hung up on or kept waiting for long periods until a representative is available.

The use of pre-recorded message telemarketing, where a sales pitch begins with or is made entirely by a pre-recorded message, also violates the TSR because the telemarketer is not connecting the call to a live sales representative within two seconds of the person's completed greeting.[151]

Abandonment Safe Harbor

According to the FTC guidance, the abandoned call Safe Harbor provides that a telemarketer will not face enforcement action for violating the call abandonment prohibition if the telemarketer:

- Uses technology that ensures abandonment of no more than three percent of all calls answered by a live person, measured per day per calling campaign;

- Allows the telephone to ring for 15 seconds or four rings before disconnecting an unanswered call;

- Plays a recorded message stating the name and telephone number of the seller on whose behalf the call was placed whenever a live sales representative is unavailable within two seconds of a live person answering the call;

- Maintains records documenting adherence to the three requirements above.

To take advantage of the Safe Harbor, a telemarketer must first ensure that a live representative takes the call in at least 97 percent of the calls answered by consumers. Any calls answered by machine, calls that are not answered at all, and calls to nonworking numbers do not count in this calculation.

This three percent (3%) rule applies to each day and each calling campaign. The FTC does not allow a telemarketer to average abandonment rates, even if it is running simultaneous calling campaigns on behalf of different sellers. The Safe Harbor also requires the telemarketer to let the phone ring at least four times (or for 15 seconds). This requirement is designed to ensure that consumers have sufficient time to answer a call.

For the small number of calls that are abandoned, the TSR Safe Harbor requires the telemarketer to play a recorded greeting, consisting of the company's name and phone number and a statement that the call was for telemarketing purposes. This recorded message may not contain a sales pitch.[152] The phone number provided in the message must also be one to which the consumer can call to be placed on the company's own do-not-call list.

Finally, to be within the Safe Harbor, the telemarketer must keep records that demonstrate its compliance with the other Safe Harbor provisions. The records must demonstrate both that the per day, per campaign abandonment rate has not exceeded three percent (3%) and that the ring time and recorded message requirements have been met.

Prohibition on Unauthorized Billing

As you might expect, the TSR strictly prohibits telemarketers from billing consumers for any goods or services without the consumer's "express, informed consent." If the consumer provides the billing account information to the telemarketer during the call, then express, informed consent can be obtained in any non-deceptive manner.

If, on the other hand, the telemarketer has obtained the consumer's account information from some other source ("pre-acquired account information"), the TSR imposes a array of specific requirements on how express, informed consent must be obtained.

In particular, the TSR has special requirements for "free-to-pay conversion" offers (offers that begin with a free trial, but then convert to paid service at the end of the trial period). These rules are designed to combat the high-incidence of unauthorized charges made to consumer accounts where consumers did not understand that the service provider would charge the consumer at the end of the trial period. If pre-acquired account information is used in connection with a free-to-pay conversion offer, the telemarketer must:

- Obtain from the customer at least the last four digits of the account number to be charged, and

- Obtain the customer's express agreement to be charged for the goods or services and to be charged using the account number for which the customer has provided at least the last four digits, and

- Make and maintain an audio recording of the entire telemarketing transaction.

If pre-acquired account information is used in connection with any other type of transaction, the telemarketer must still (at minimum) identify the account to be charged with enough specificity for the consumer to understand which account will be charged, and obtain the consumer's express agreement to be charged using that account number.

Record-Keeping Requirements

The TSR requires sellers and telemarketers to keep certain records that relate to their telemarketing activities. In general, the following records must be maintained for two years from the date that the record is produced:

• Advertising and promotional materials,

• Information about prize recipients,

• Sales records,

• Employee records, and

• All verifiable authorizations or records of express informed consent or express agreement.

These records may be maintained in whatever manner, format or medium that the companies use in the normal course of business. For example, the records may be maintained in electronic or paper formats.

Additionally, the TSR requires only one copy of the records to be maintained. In particular, sellers and telemarketers can decide which party should maintain which records as part of the services contract. As the FTC's guidance states:

> Sellers and telemarketers do not have to keep duplicative records if they have a written agreement allocating responsibility for complying with the recordkeeping requirements. Without a written agreement between the parties, or if the written agreement is unclear as to who must maintain the required records, telemarketers must keep employee records, while sellers must keep the advertising and promotional materials, information on prize recipients, sales records, and verifiable authorizations.
>
> In the event of dissolution or termination of the business of a seller or telemarketer, the principal of the business must maintain all records of the business. In the event of a sale, assignment, or other change in ownership of the seller or telemarketer's business, the successor business must maintain the records.

For each type of record listed above, the TSR includes lists of the information that must be retained. For example, sales records must include: (a) the name and last known address of each customer; (b) the goods or services purchased; (c) the date the goods or services were shipped or provided; and (d) the amount the customer paid for the goods or services.

Similarly, for all current and former employees directly involved in telephone sales, records must include: (a) the name (and any fictitious name used); (b) the last known home address and telephone number; and (c) the job title(s) of each employee. Additionally, if fictitious names are used by employees, the TSR also requires that each fictitious name be traceable to a specific employee.

Other Provisions

The TSR also includes specific regulations designed to address:

• Credit card laundering;

• Telemarketing sales of credit repair programs, loss recovery services and advance-loans; and,

• "Telefunding" activities (for-profit companies that call on behalf of charitable organizations).

The TSR also includes enforcement provisions. As noted earlier, the TSR can be enforced by the FTC, the state attorneys general or private individuals.[153] The FTC aggressively enforces the TSR. As noted above, violations of the TSR are punishable by civil penalties of up to $11,000 per call.

State Telemarketing Laws

It is important to note that the Telemarketing Sales Rule does not preempt state telemarketing laws.[154] Today, 42 U.S. states have their own telemarketing laws, where registration and often the posting of a bond are mandatory, and penalties may include private rights of action and statutory damages. Process rules may also differ from the TSR (such as different calling times), and many states also maintain their own DNC lists. A few states (Indiana, Florida, Arizona and Wisconsin for example) limit or do not recognize the EBR exception for their own DNC lists.[155]

Telemarketers must therefore be vigilant to ensure that their activities comply with the TSR as well as any applicable state law requirements.

Controlling the Assault of Non-Solicited Pornography and Marketing Act of 2003

Controlling the Assault of Non-Solicited Pornography and Marketing Act of 2003 (CAN- SPAM)[156] applies to anyone who advertises products or services by electronic mail directed to or originating from the U.S. The law covers the transmission of commercial email messages whose primary purpose is advertising or promoting a product or service.

The CAN-SPAM Act:

• Prohibits false or misleading headers;

• Prohibits deceptive subject lines;

• Requires commercial emails to contain a functioning, clearly and conspicuously displayed return email address that allows the recipient to opt out of future emails from that sender;

• Prohibits sending commercial email (following a grace period of 10 business days) to an individual who has asked not to receive future email;

• Requires all commercial email to include (i) clear and conspicuous identification that the message is an advertisement or solicitation (unless the recipient has provided prior affirmative consent to receive the email), (ii) clear and conspicuous notice of the opportunity to opt out, and (iii) a valid physical postal address of the sender;

• Prohibits "aggravated violations" relating to commercial emails such as (i) address harvesting and dictionary attacks, (ii) the automated creation of multiple email accounts, and (iii) the re-transmission of commercial email through unauthorized accounts; and,

• Requires all commercial email containing sexually-oriented material to include a warning label (unless the recipient has provided prior affirmative consent to receive the email).

CAN-SPAM is enforced primarily by the FTC and carries penalties of fines of up to $11,000 per violation. In addition, deceptive commercial email also is subject to laws banning false or misleading advertising. The FTC has the authority to issue to regulations implementing the CAN-SPAM Act and, as of this writing, is in the processing of developing these rules.

Commercial email messages are distinguished in the Act from "transactional or relationship messages," which are messages whose primary purpose is to (i) facilitate or confirm an agreed-upon commercial transaction, (ii) provide warranty or safety information about a product purchased or used by the recipient, (iii) provide certain information regarding an ongoing commercial relationship, (iv) provide information related to employment or a related benefit plan, or (v) deliver goods or services to which the recipient is entitled under the terms of an agreed-upon transaction. Because it may be difficult to discern based on the Act's provisions when a specific email is a "commercial" email, Congress instructed the FTC to issue regulations within one year on how to determine the primary purpose of an email message.

CAN-SPAM contains a number of requirements generally applicable to the sender of a commercial email message. A "sender" is anyone who initiates an email message and whose product or service is advertised or promoted by the message. More than one person may be deemed to have initiated a message. The FTC is currently developing regulations that would provide additional guidance on the definition of "sender."

CAN-SPAM grants the FTC and other federal regulators enforcement authority. In addition, the Act provides for enforcement by state attorneys general and other state officials. Internet service providers that have been adversely affected by a violation also may sue violators for injunctive relief and monetary damages. Unlike a number of state spam laws that are now superseded, the Act does not provide for a private right of action.

The Act provides for injunctive relief and damages up to $250 per violation, with a maximum award of $2 million. The Act further provides that a court may increase a damage award up to three times the amount otherwise available in cases of willful or aggravated violations. Certain egregious conduct is punishable by up to five years imprisonment.

CAN-SPAM does preempt most state laws that restrict email communications, although state spam laws are not superseded by CAN-SPAM to the extent such laws prohibit false or deceptive activity.

Wireless Message Rules Under CAN-SPAM

In addition to the email rules discussed above, the Federal Communications Commission ("FCC") has also issued rules implementing the CAN-SPAM Act with regard to *mobile service commercial messages* ("MSCMs").

The CAN-SPAM Act defines an MSCM as "a commercial electronic mail message that is transmitted directly to a wireless device that is utilized by a subscriber of a commercial mobile service..." The message must have (or utilize) a unique electronic address that includes "a reference to an Internet domain." The FCC also notes in its commentary that the rule is designed to apply only to mail addresses designed by carriers for mobile services messaging (e.g., messages to mobile devices).

The FCC rule defers to the FTC rules and interpretation regarding the definitions of "commercial" and "transactional" (with respect to the mail messages) as well as the mechanisms for determining the "primary purpose" of messages. Accordingly, the FCC rule must always be analyzed in the context of the FTC regulatory framework for the CAN-SPAM Act.

Express Prior Authorization

The CAN-SPAM Act prohibits senders from sending any MSCMs without the subscriber's "express prior authorization." Express prior authorization must be obtained for each MSCM, regardless of sender or industry. The FCC requirements can be summarized as follows:

- "Express prior authorization" must be "express," meaning that the consumer has taken an affirmative action to give the authorization. Authorization may not be obtained in the form of a negative option. If the authorization is obtained via a Web site, the consumer must take an affirmative action, such as checking a box or hitting a button.

- The authorization must also be given prior to the sending of any MSCMs. There is no provision to grandfather any existing authorizations that senders may have obtained. Because of the disclosure requirements in these authorizations, the FCC notes that senders who claim they have obtained authorization prior to the effective date of these rules will not be in compliance unless they can demonstrate that these existing authorizations have met each and every one of the requirements set forth in the rule.

- Consumers must not bear any cost with respect to the authorization or revocation processes.

- Each authorization must include certain required disclosures. These require disclosures consist of statements that:

  1. The subscriber is agreeing to receive MSCMs sent to his/her wireless device from a particular (identified) sender,

  2. The subscriber may be charged by his/her wireless provider in connection with the receipt of such messages, and

  3. The subscriber may revoke the authorization at any time.

These disclosures must be clearly legible and in sufficiently large type (or volume, if given via audio). They must be presented in a manner that is readily apparent to the consumer. These disclosures must be separate from any other authorizations contained in another document. Additionally, if any portion of the authorization/disclosure is translated into another language then all of the portions must also be translated into that language.

- As noted above, the authorization must clearly identify the entity that is being authorized to send the MSCMs. The authorizations are personal as to the sender. The FCC rule prohibits any sender from sending MSCMs on behalf of other third parties, including affiliates and marketing partners. Each entity must obtain separate express prior authorizations for the messages it sends.

- Authorization may be obtained in any format, oral or written, including electronic. Although a writing is not required, the FCC requires that each sender of MSCMs must document the authorization and be able to demonstration that a valid authorization (meeting all the other requirements) existed prior to sending the commercial message. The commentary notes that the burden of proof rests with the sender.

- With regard to revocations, senders must enable consumers to revoke authorizations using the same means that the consumers used to grant authorizations. (For example, if a consumer authorizes MSCMs electronically, the company must permit the consumer to revoke the authorization electronically.) Additionally, the MSCMs themselves must include functioning return electronic mail addresses or another Internet-based mechanism that is clearly and conspicuously displayed for the purpose of receiving opt-out requests.

Note: Consumers must not be required to view or hear any further commercial content during the opt-out process (other than institutional identification).

- The FCC rule maintains the CAN-SPAM Act mandated 10-business-day grace period after which messages cannot be sent following a revocation of an authorization.

The Wireless Domain Registry

In order for senders of commercial messages to determine whether those messages might be MSCMs (rather than regular commercial email), the FCC has created a registry of wireless domain names. This list is available on the FCC Web site at www.fcc.gov/cgb/policy/DomainNameDownload.html (or, follow the link to Consumer Bureau). It is updated on a periodic basis, as new domains are added.

Senders are responsible for obtaining this list and ensuring that the appropriate authorizations exist before sending commercial messages to addresses within the domains. In other words, the requirements listed above will apply to messages sent to any address whose domain name is included on the wireless domain name list.

Note that messages are not MSCMs if they are sent to domains that are not on the registry, even if those messages are sent or forwarded to wireless devices (such as "smart phones" or personal digital assistants). The FCC rule relies on the carriers to identify the appropriate domain names. The commentary provides some discussion of the FCC position that messages do not become MSCMs merely by virtue of consumer forwarding to wireless devices.

With regard to the domain name list, all commercial mobile radio service providers are required under the rule to identify all electronic mail domain names that are dedicated for use by subscribers for wireless devices. The providers are also responsible for updating information on the domain name list to the FCC within 30 days before issuing any new or modified domain names.

The Telephone Consumer Protection Act of 1991 ("TCPA")

The Telephone Consumer Protection Act of 1991 ("TCPA")[157] is enforced by the U.S. Federal Communications Commission ("FCC") and prohibits unsolicited commercial fax transmissions. The Act requires specific written authorization for any commercial faxing and gives no exception for existing business relationships. Penalties include a private right of action, and statutory damages of up to $500 per fax.[158]

The TCPA requires senders to have opt-in consent for fax communications. However, many businesses rely on faxes to communicate with existing customers. Senders historically understood these faxes to be permissible because the consent to the communication was implicit in the business relationship that existed with the recipient.

In July 2003, the FCC revised the TCPA regulations and required fax senders to document that they had consent to send faxes by obtaining signed, written authorizations from all prospective recipients. The authorizations had to include the fax numbers to which faxes could be sent. The FCC required these authorizations to be obtained for all faxes, even for faxes sent to recipients with whom the senders had existing business relationships. Due to concerns about the costs and difficulty of obtaining authorizations from customers, the FCC stayed implementation of these regulations to allow companies to continue to send faxes to existing customers while obtaining the necessary consents.

The Junk Fax Prevention Act of 2005 ("JFPA")

The Junk Fax Prevention Act of 2005 ("JFPA") was enacted to enable organizations to continue to send faxes to recipients with whom they have an existing business relationship, provided that the sender offers the recipient an opportunity to opt-out of receiving future commercial faxes.

The JFPA overrides the FCC's regulations and permits businesses to obtain consent to send faxes in writing or by other means. It specifically provides that consent can be inferred from an existing business relationship ("EBR"), and it permits sending faxes to recipients based on an EBR, as long as the sender offers an opt-out in accordance with the Act.

Established Business Relationships

For purposes of the JFPA, "existing business relationship" has the same definition as it does in the FCC's Do-Not-Call Rule. Specifically, an existing business relationship exists if the fax recipient has entered into a purchase or services transaction with the sender within the past 18 months or if the recipient has made an inquiry or application with the sender during the past three months. The JFPA permits faxes to both consumers and businesses, if the EBR exists.

The JFPA authorizes the FCC to examine these time periods in the future, and to make rules to revise the time periods that establish the EBR. In particular, three months after the effective date of the JFPA, the FCC can revise the EBR time periods after considering various factors, including complaints received about faxes and the costs associated with demonstrating that an EBR exists.

The JFPA also imposes requirements on how fax numbers can be obtained. After the effective date, senders wishing to rely on the EBR may collect fax numbers from new customers only through (1) the voluntary communication of the fax number from the customer within the context of the business relationship, or (2) from a directory or Internet site where recipients have voluntarily agreed to make fax numbers available for public distribution. EBR customer fax numbers possessed prior to the effective date are not subject to this requirement.

State Fax Regulations

Unfortunately, neither the TCPA nor the JFPA preempt more restrictive state regulations. Understanding the federal requirements is only the beginning of the analysis. Companies that wish to use fax communications must consider the state regulatory context as well.

California enacted a true opt-in fax law shortly after the JFPA was enacted, to regulate all "unsolicited fax advertisements." The California law is problematic because it applies to all faxes sent to or from California. This law took effect on January 1, 2006 although the law is being challenged in court. A federal judge has stayed the interstate provisions until the constitutionality of the law can be determined.

Additionally, several other states had enacted TCPA-mirror statutes prior to the JFPA, and these state laws retain the old opt-in rules (without an EBR exception). States that do not recognize an EBR include Arizona, Connecticut, Florida, Michigan, Minnesota, Montana, Nebraska, Oregon, Pennsylvania, Tennessee, Utah and Virginia.

Other states do recognize an EBR exception, but define specific opt-out process requirements that senders must respect. States with specific opt-out requirements include Colorado, Georgia, Kansas, Kentucky, Maine, Massachusetts, New Jersey, New Mexico, New York, North Carolina, North Dakota, Oklahoma, Rhode Island, South Carolina, Texas, Washington, West Virginia, and Wisconsin. These rules specify opt-out methods that must be offered (such as toll-free numbers) and the time period in which opt-outs must be processed.

Finally, several states have general process requirements for faxes, including specific times when faxes may not be sent and page lengths for faxes.

U.S. State Security Breach Notification Laws

The state of California enacted the first security breach notification law in the United States with SB 1386 in 2003.[159] This law provides that California government agencies and commercial entities that do business in California must disclose the breach of any computer system that contains the unencrypted personal information of California residents.

"Personal information" is defined under SB 1386 as an individual's name in combination with any one or more of: (i) Social Security number, (ii) California identification card number, (iii) driver's license number, or (iv) financial account number or credit or debit card number in combination with any required security code, access code or password that would permit access to an individual's financial account.

SB 1386 requires organizations to disclose any breach of the security of the system to any resident of California whose unencrypted personal information was or is reasonably believed to have been acquired by an unauthorized person. A "breach of the security of the system" means unauthorized acquisition of computerized data that compromises the security, confidentiality, or integrity of personal information maintained by the person.

The disclosure must be made "in as expedient manner as possible." The disclosure may be delayed if law enforcement requests a delay to meet its investigative requirements.

SB 1386 provides an exception for the good faith acquisition of personal information by an employee or agent of the business, provided that the personal information is not used or subject to further unauthorized disclosure.

Since 2003, approximately 23 U.S. states have enacted similar security breach notification laws. With the exception of Indiana's law, which applies only to state agencies, the new laws generally require that any person or organization that maintains personal information about state residents must notify relevant individuals following a security breach. Most of these bills define a security breach as the unauthorized acquisition of computerized data that compromises the security, confidentiality or integrity of personal information. Montana's law allows entities more autonomy in deciding whether to notify individuals by defining a breach to have occurred when security is materially compromised and the acquisition "causes or is reasonably believed to cause loss or injury to a Montana resident."

Generally, the new state laws define "personal information" as an individual's first initial or name and last name, in addition to one or more of the following data elements when the name or data element is *unencrypted*:

• Social Security number;

• Driver's license or state ID number; or,

• Account number, credit or debit card numbers in combination with the required password or access code.

Some states have varied this definition, however. For example, in addition to these data elements, Arkansas' breach notification law includes medical information in its definition of "personal information" and North Dakota's law includes mother's maiden name, employer-assigned ID numbers and electronic signatures.

Lastly, the federal financial regulators issued joint security breach notification guidelines interpreting section 501(b) of the Gramm-Leach-Bliley Act. The guidelines advise financial institutions to develop and implement a response program for security breaches involving customer information. The guidelines describe (i) the standard for providing customers with notice, (ii) the recommended components of a response program, and (iii) the recommended content of a customer notice.

U.S. Unfair and Deceptive Trade Practices ("UDTP")

The FTC has administered a wide variety of consumer protection laws, including the Telemarketing Sales Rule,[160] and these trade regulations carry the full force of law. State attorneys general have additional enforcement power over activities deemed unfair and deceptive and do so through specific state statutes.[161]

Unfair trade practices are defined as commercial conduct that intentionally causes substantial injury, without offsetting benefits, and that consumers cannot reasonably avoid.

Deceptive trade practices are defined as commercial conduct that includes false or misleading claims, or claims that omit material facts. However, there is no intent requirement.

Section 5 of the U.S. Federal Trade Commission Act (the Act that created the Commission itself) declares "unfair or deceptive acts or practices in or affecting commerce" to be illegal.[162] Section 5 confers on the FTC the plenary power to prevent such acts and practices.[163]

Organizations must be very careful in constructing privacy notices and other consumer-facing statements. In exercising its Section 5 authority, the FTC has taken the position that misrepresenting why information is being collected from consumers or how the information will be used constitutes a deceptive practice.[164]

As the FTC notes on its Web site:[165]

A key part of the Commission's privacy program is making sure companies keep the promises they make to consumers about privacy and, in particular, the precautions they take to secure consumers' personal information. To respond to consumers' concerns about privacy, many Web sites post privacy policies that describe how consumers' personal information is collected, used, shared, and secured. Indeed, almost all the top 100 commercial sites now post privacy policies. Using its authority under Section 5 of the FTC Act, which prohibits unfair or deceptive practices, the

Commission has brought a number of cases to enforce the promises in privacy statements, including promises about the security of consumers' personal information. The Commission has also used its unfairness authority to challenge information practices that cause substantial consumer injury.

Unfair and Deceptive Trade Practices Case Study:
Gateway Learning

The Gateway Learning case is perhaps the most widely known example of an enforcement action taken by the FTC against an organization for conducting what the commission considered to be an "unfair" trade practice under its general theory of unfairness.

Facts and Allegations

Gateway Learning Inc., markets educational aids for children such as the popular "Hooked on Phonics" audio reading program. The company's primary customers include parents and teachers. The company had a posted privacy statement on its Web site that said it would not share personal information with third parties without the consumer's consent, but the statement also included a notice that the statement could be changed at any time.

In April 2003, Gateway Learning began renting personal information provided by consumers that the company had captured through online mechanisms on its Web site. Such information included first and last name, address, phone number, and purchase history. Gateway Learning did not seek or receive any consent from the consumers. Further, the company released personal information—such as the age range and gender of consumers' children—to third parties for the purposes of direct mail and telemarketing solicitations on behalf of Gateway Learning.

On June 20, 2003, Gateway Learning posted a revised privacy statement on its Web site notifying consumers that their personal information would be shared and providing them with a post office address at which consumers could opt-out of such use. Gateway Learning posted a second revised privacy policy on July 17, 2003, but took no additional steps to notify consumers of the information change in the policy.

Around July 1, 2003, Gateway Learning suspended rental of any customer data collected on its Web site.

The FTC alleged that:
• Despite initial promises to the contrary, Gateway Learning did rent personal information collected from consumers to third parties without receiving consumers' explicit consent and did provide personal information about children under the age of 13 without providing notice to consumers of material changes to its information practices.

• Gateway Learning retroactively applied its materially changed and revised privacy policy to information collected under the original privacy statement.

• Substantial injury to consumers occurred.

The FTC also characterized the retroactive application of a materially-changed privacy policy to previously collected information as "unfair" and the failure to provide notice to consumers of material changes to the privacy policy as promised as "misleading."

Privacy and Security Promises

Gateway Learning made the following representations regarding the security and privacy of personal information collected on the Web site:

• **Original Privacy Policy:** "We do not sell, rent or loan any personally identifiable information regarding our consumers with any third party unless we receive a customer's explicit consent…" [then, later in the policy] "…If at some future time there is a material change to our information usage practices that affects your personally identifiable information, we will notify you of the relevant changes on this Site or by email. You will then be able to opt-out of this information usage by sending an email….You should also check this privacy policy for changes."

• **Revised Privacy Policy (June, 2003):** "From time to time, we may provide your name, address and phone number (not your email address) to reputable companies whose products or services you may find of interest. If you do not want us to share this information with these companies, please write to us at …or email us at … ."

• **Revised Privacy Policy (July, 2003) added the following:** "The Site is not targeted to children, and we do not knowingly collected personally-identifiable information from children under the age of 13 on this site. We do not sell products for purchase by children; we sell children's products for purchase by adults. This site is entirely aimed at adults."

FTC Consent Agreement with Gateway Learning

1. **Bar on Misrepresentation:** Gateway Learning shall not misrepresent (a) that they will not sell, rent, or loan to third parties such personal information; (b) that they will not provide to any third party personal information about children under the age of 13; (c) the manner Gateway Learning notifies customers of changes to its privacy policy; or (d) the manner Gateway Learning will collect, use, or disclose personal information.

2. **Ban on Disclosure of Personal Information to 3rd Parties:**

   a. Gateway Learning shall not disclose to any third party any personal information collected on the Web site prior to the date Gateway posted its revised privacy policy permitting third-party sharing (June 20, 2003), without first obtaining the express, affirmative (opt-in) consent of the consumers to whom such personal information relates.

b. Gateway Learning shall not apply material privacy policy changes to information collected from or about consumers before the date of the posting unless Gateway obtained the express, affirmative (opt-in) consent of the consumers to whom such personal information relates.

3. **Maintenance of Relevant Documents:** For a period of five years, Gateway Learning must make available to the FTC all documents demonstrating compliance with the order, including:

   a. A copy of each different privacy statement or communication with the date, full text, URL address, and graphics;

   b. A copy of documents seeking to obtain opt-in consent of consumers and any documents demonstrating such consent provided by consumers; and,

   c. All invoices, communications, and records relating to the disclosure of personally identifiable information to third parties.

4. **Delivery of Order:** Gateway Learning must deliver a copy of this order to all current and future principals, officers, directors, managers and all employees with managerial responsibility over the subject matter of the order.

5. **Reporting:** Gateway Learning shall notify the FTC at least 30 days prior to any corporate change which may affect its compliance with the order. Within 60 days after service of the order and thereafter as requested, Gateway Leaeninf shall file a report with the FTC setting forth Gateway Learning's compliance with the order.

Duration of the FTC Order and Penalties for Violations
Except as otherwise indicated in the final order, the final order terminates in 20 years. Each violation of the final order may result in a civil penalty of $11,000.

Fine Imposed
$4,608 (which reflected all profits received for renting personal information).

U.S. Laws that Compel Disclosure of Personal Information

In addition to laws that provide data protection, a number of U.S. statutes and regulations require disclosure of personal information—rather than restrict it. In general, these laws mandate that personal information must be provided to third parties (either government agencies or private persons) when necessary in order to combat crime, serve justice, ensure product safety or accomplish another essential purpose.

These laws are often referred to as "anti-privacy" since they contradict the notion of data protection in the interest of serving specific banking or national security concerns.

The U.S. Bank Secrecy Act of 1970 ("BSA")[166] authorizes the U.S. Secretary of the Treasury to issue regulations that impose extensive record keeping and reporting requirements on financial institutions.[167] Specifically, financial institutions must keep records and file reports on certain financial transactions, including those in excess of $10,000 that move into, out of, and within the United States. The Act was significantly expanded by the USA PATRIOT Act (addressed below), both in terms of scope and industries covered.

The BSA, by its terms, applies to "financial institutions", which are defined to include banks, securities brokers and dealers, money services businesses, telegraph companies, casinos, card clubs, and other entities subject to supervision by any state or federal bank supervisory authority. The BSA contains regulations relating to currency transactions, transportation of monetary instruments, and the purchase of currency-like instruments. For example, the BSA generally requires that currency transactions over $10,000 are to be reported to the IRS per the regulations, using a Currency Transaction Report ("CTR"), Form 4789.

Similarly, the BSA regulations also cover purchases of bank checks, drafts, cashier's checks, money orders, or traveler's checks for $3,000 or more in currency. The rules require that the entity collect and report information including the name and address and social security number of the purchaser, the date of purchase, type of instrument, serial numbers of instruments, and dollar amounts of the instruments.

The BSA regulates certain wire transfers, including funds transfers and transmittals of funds by financial institutions. Certain funds transfers are exempted from the regulation, however, including funds transfers governed by the Electronic Funds Transfer Act and fund transfers made through an automated clearing house, ATM, or point of sale systems.

Records Retention Requirements

Financial institutions are required to maintain records of all extensions of credit in excess of $10,000, but does not include credit secured by real property. Records must include the borrower's name and address, credit amount, purpose of credit and the date of credit. Such records must be maintained for five years. As to deposit account records, a financial institution must keep the depositor's taxpayer identification number, signature cards, checks in excess of $100 that are drawn or issued and payable by the bank, and, as to certificates of deposit, such financial institution must obtain the customer name and address, a description of the CD, and the date of the transaction. For wire transfers or direct deposits, a financial institution must maintain all deposit slips or credit tickets for transactions in excess of $100.[168] Additionally, the BSA includes detailed rules regarding information that banks must retain in connection with payment orders.

Suspicious Activity Reports

A Suspicious Activity Report ("SAR") must be filed with the Department of Treasury's Financial Crimes Enforcement Network ("FinCEN") in the following circumstances: (i) when a financial institution suspects that an insider is committing (or aiding the commission of) a crime, regardless of dollar amount; (ii) when the entity detects a possible crime involving $5,000 or more and has a substantial basis for identifying a suspect; (iii) when the entity detects a possible crime involving $25,000 or more (even if it has no substantial basis for identifying a suspect); and (iv) when the entity suspects currency transactions aggregating $5,000 or more that involve potential money laundering or a violation of the act.[169]

BSA Enforcement

Liability for violations of the BSA and its regulations include the following: civil penalties, including fines up to the greater of $25,000 or the amount of the transaction (up to a $100,000 maximum), as well as penalties for negligence ($500 per violation); additional penalties up to $5,500 per day for violations of law and regulations; penalties of up to $27,500 per day if violations or unsafe or unsound practices are engaged in recklessly or are part of a pattern of misconduct that causes more than a minimal loss to the bank or any pecuniary gains to the parties involved; and penalties up to $1,100,000 per day against persons who knowingly commit a violation and knowingly or recklessly cause a substantial loss to the bank for a substantial benefit to the party; and criminal penalties up to a $100,000 fine and/or one year imprisonment and up to a $10,000 and/or five year imprisonment.[170]

The Uniting and Strengthening America by Providing Appropriate Tools Required to Intercept and Obstruct Terrorism Act of 2001 ("USA PATRIOT")

The BSA was modified 10 years after its enactment by *The Uniting and Strengthening America by Providing Appropriate Tools Required to Intercept and Obstruct Terrorism Act of 2001* ("USA PATRIOT").[171] This federal law grants permission to financial institutions, upon providing notice to the U.S. Department of the Treasury, to share information with one another in order to identify and report to the federal government activities that may involve money laundering or terrorist activity.[172]

USA PATRIOT was drafted by the U.S. Congress in the wake of the September 11, 2001 terrorist acts on the United States. An omnibus law, it contains separate titles that are designed to meet specific national security objectives such as enhancing domestic security against terrorism (Title I); providing for additional surveillance authority (Title II); increased border protection and immigration requirements (Title IV); removing obstacles to law enforcement investigations of terrorism (Title V); creating the September 11 Relief Fund (Title VI); increasing information-sharing and intelligence for critical infrastructure protection and counter-terrorism (Titles VII and IX); and establishing additional criminal laws against terrorism (Title VIII).

The International Money Laundering Abatement and Anti-Terrorist Financing Act of 2001

The International Money Laundering Abatement and Anti-Terrorist Financing Act of 2001 expanded the reach of the Bank Secrecy Act and made other significant changes to U.S. anti-money laundering laws. The Act also gave the Secretary of the Treasury the ability to promulgate broad rules to implement modified "Know Your Customer" requirements and to otherwise deter money laundering.

For covered financial services companies, the major USA PATRIOT Act compliance issues can be grouped into the following categories:

- Information-sharing regulations, and participation in the cooperative efforts to deter money laundering, as required by Section 314 of the Act;

- Know Your Customer rules, including the identification of beneficial owners of accounts—procedures required by Section 326 of the Act;

- Development and implementation of formal money-laundering programs as required by Section 352 of the Act; and,

- The Bank Secrecy Act expansions, including new reporting and record keeping requirements for different industries (such as broker-dealers) and currency transactions.

The U.S. Communications Assistance to Law Enforcement Act of 1994 ("CALEA")

The U.S. Communications Assistance to Law Enforcement Act of 1994 (CALEA)[173] (sometimes referred to as the "Digital Telephony Bill") lays out the duties of a telecommunications carrier to cooperate in the interception of communications for law enforcement and other needs relating to the security and safety of the public. It preserves, but does not expand, law enforcement wiretapping capabilities by requiring telephone companies to design their systems to ensure a certain basic level of government access. At present, CALEA does not apply to voice-over-Internet communications ("VOIP").

The Federal Communication Commission ("FCC") has implemented CALEA through various rule-making processes.[174]

Other Regulatory Disclosure Requirements

Various federal and state agencies require companies to report certain information for government affairs, law enforcement, public health, public safety and other purposes. For example, at the federal level, the following agencies have reporting requirements that may encompass personal information:

- The U.S. Food and Drug Administration ("FDA") requires health professionals and drug manufacturers to report serious adverse events, product problems or medication errors suspected to be associated with the use of an FDA-regulated drug, biologic, device or dietary supplement under the Food, Drug and Cosmetic Act.[175]

- The U.S. Department of Labor's Occupational Health and Safety Administration ("OSHA") requires compilation and reporting of information about certain workplace injuries and illnesses.[176]

- The U.S. Department of Health and Human Services, through its Centers for Disease Control, collects information on various public health matters, including outbreaks of contagious diseases.[177]

Privacy laws generally provide exceptions for all necessary or useful disclosures to law enforcement and public health/safety offices. For example, the HIPAA Privacy Rule specifically "recognizes the legitimate need for public health authorities and others responsible for ensuring public health and safety to have access to protected health information to carry out their public health mission. The Rule also recognizes that public health reports made by covered entities are an important means of identifying threats to the health and safety of the public at large, as well as individuals. Accordingly, the Rule permits covered entities to disclose protected health information without authorization for specified public health purposes."[178]

Subpoenas and Court Orders

Privacy laws also recognize that personal information must occasionally be disclosed to third parties in the interest of justice. Accordingly, privacy laws generally provide that companies with personal information may disclose that information when required to do so by a valid court order or subpoena.

> *Subpoena. A written court order issued in an administrative, civil or criminal action that requires the person named in the subpoena to appear in court in order to testify under oath on a particular matter which is the subject of an investigation, proceeding, or lawsuit. A subpoena may also require the production of a paper, document, or other object relevant to an investigation, proceeding, or lawsuit that discloses personal information.*

Subpoenas are commonly issued where a person's information is subject to the litigation at hand. For example, if an individual sues another person to recover damages caused by an automobile accident, the person being sued will likely issue a subpoena to the medical provider who treated the injuries. Having the medical records is vital to understanding what damages may be appropriately claimed during the litigation.

On occasion, a party to a lawsuit may want to see records about a person that is not party to the lawsuit. For example, in a workplace safety lawsuit, the worker filing the complaint may want to see medical records of other employees who suffered similar injuries on the job. These records may help the employee demonstrate that the workplace was truly unsafe.

Entities that believe a subpoena is requesting data inappropriately can ask the court to narrow or "quash" the subpoena. Entities can also ask the court to have the recipient of the data agree to confidentiality or use restrictions. In many cases, courts are sensitive to the privacy interests of individuals whose information is subject to the request, especially if they are not party to the litigation. In the example above, the court might decide that justice requires the worker to see other employees' medical records, but might take steps to protect those employees by anonymizing the records or requiring the receiving party to execute a non-disclosure agreement.

U.S. Privacy Laws—Public Sector

U.S. public sector privacy laws regulate the activities of U.S. government agencies and departments with regard to how public records are procured, managed and maintained as well as how personal information is exchanged between and among agencies and third parties (such as government contractors). These laws also mandate certain requirements around public access to records including personal information.

Major public sector privacy laws in force today across the U.S. include the *Privacy Act of 1974, the Freedom of Information Act ("FOIA")*, the *E-Government Act, the Data Quality Act of 2002* and the *Government in the Sunshine Act.* For the purposes of this section—and this text generally—only the first two of these laws will be examined.

More complete information on U.S. government privacy laws, policies and practices is available through a separate IAPP credentialing program, the Certified Information Privacy Professional/Government (CIPP/G).

The Privacy Act of 1974

The Privacy Act of 1974 is a U.S. federal government privacy law passed in response to the Executive Branch's less-than-scrupulous data-gathering practices in the late 1960s and 1970s. The Act regulates the federal government's use of computerized databases of information about U.S. citizens and permanent, legal residents. It also establishes certain "fair information practices" that each agency must follow when collecting, using or disclosing personal information, including rights of citizen action and redress for violations.

The Privacy Act assures individuals on whom information is collected that:

- There are not federal government personal recordkeeping systems whose existence are secret;

- Federal personal information files are limited to those that are clearly relevant and necessary;

- Citizens will have an opportunity to see what information about them is kept and to challenge its accuracy;

- Personal information collected for one purpose may not be used for another purpose without their consent; and that,

- If disclosures are made, they will find out to whom they were made, for what purpose and on what date.

The U.S. Office of Management and Budget ("OMB") is in charge of developing guidelines for use by the agencies in the implementation of the Act. Enforcement comes through a private right of action, with both civil and criminal penalties for agencies and government employees that violate the act.

The Privacy Act generally requires government agencies to provide notice about all "systems of records" that they establish. Personal information contained in the systems of records must be relevant and necessary for the government agency's stated purposes, and the information cannot be used for any other purpose. Individuals are entitled to have access to the information about them stored in the system of records. Individuals may also sue the government for violations of the Privacy Act.

As noted above, the Privacy Act generally applies to federal government agencies (and their contractors and agents). One provision applies more broadly: section 7 of the Privacy Act imposes requirements on all federal, state and local government agencies that collect or use Social Security numbers. Government agencies generally cannot require individuals to provide a Social Security number unless the number is needed to comply with a federal statutory requirement. When a government agency asks for a Social Security number from an individual, it must also tell the individual whether the disclosure is mandatory or voluntary, what laws give the agency the authority to request the Social Security number, and how the number will be used. Please note that this provision only applies to government agencies—it does not regulate or restrict the collection of Social Security numbers by private entities for their own behalf.

The Privacy Act does have several critical exceptions. For example, law enforcement agencies and activities can be exempted from the Act's requirements.

The Freedom of Information Act ("FOIA")

The Freedom of Information Act ("FOIA")[179] was enacted in 1966 to ensure citizen access to Federal government agency records. FOIA covers all government records, not just those that contain personal information.

FOIA provides access to all federal agency records, subject to nine specific exemptions. Agencies do not have to disclose any records (or portions thereof) that contain materials:

1. Classified as national defense and foreign relations information;

2. Internal agency personnel rules and practices;

3. Prohibited from disclosure by another law;

4. Trade secrets and other confidential business information;

5. Certain inter-agency or intra-agency communications;

6. Personnel, medical, and other files involving personal privacy;

7. Compiled for law enforcement purposes;

8. Matters relating to the supervision of financial institutions; and,

9. Geological information on oil wells.[180]

FOIA only applies to federal Executive Branch documents—it does not apply to Legislative (Congressional) or Judicial records. It also does not apply to state or local records, but nearly all state governments have their own FOIA-type statutes.[181] Most FOIA statutes provide specific exceptions for personal information, so that sensitive data (such as Social Security numbers) are not disclosed inadvertently during the open government processes.

Other Public Sector Privacy Laws

States have adopted various laws that regulate government processing of personal information. For example, the California Security Breach Notification law discussed earlier applies to California government agencies as well as private companies. Other state laws (discussed previously) restrict the collection and use of certain data elements (such as motor vehicle data or Social Security numbers) by public and private sector entities.

International Data Protection Laws

Canada

Despite its proximity to the United States, Canada is closer in philosophy and approach to the European model of data protection. As discussed in Chapter One, Canada's system is *co-regulatory* such that information privacy matters are managed by the industries concerned as well as overseen by the Canadian federal, provincial and territorial data protection commissioners (known officially as the "Information Privacy Commissioners" and in some cases as "Ombudsmen"). These Canadian government officials hold broad oversight powers but lesser degrees of enforcement ability—if any at all.

The Personal Information Protection and Electronic Documents Act of 1998 ("PIPEDA")

The Personal Information Protection and Electronic Documents Act of 1998 ("PIPEDA")[182] is Canada's comprehensive national privacy legislation and applies to personal information that is collected, used, or disclosed by the federal government, the retail sector, publishing companies, the service industry, manufacturers and other provincially regulated organizations. The Act became fully applicable to all industry segments on January 1, 2004 and has two goals: (1) to instill trust in electronic commerce and private sector transactions for Canadian citizens, and (2) to establish a level playing field where the same marketplace rules apply to all businesses.

PIPEDA applies to "every organization" with respect to "personal information" that the organization collects, uses or discloses in the "course of commercial actives":

- *"Personal information"* is defined as information about an identifiable individual, but does not include business contact information.[183]

- *"Commercial activity"* is defined as any transaction, act or conduct, or any regular course of conduct that is of a commercial character, including the selling, bartering or leasing of donor, membership or other fundraising lists.

The principles behind PIPEDA are similar to the Code of Fair Information Practices that was previously discussed. The Act requires organizations to adhere to 10 standards regarding the information that they collect. These 10 standards were previously developed and adopted in 1996 by the Canadian Standards Association ("CSA") as a voluntary industry code called the *Model Code for the Protection of Personal Information*.[184]

The CSA Model Code principles are:

1. *Accountability.* An organization is responsible for personal information under its control and shall designate an individual or individuals who are accountable for the organization's compliance with the following principles.

2. *Identifying Purposes.* The purposes for which personal information is collected shall be identified by the organization at or before the time the information is collected.

3. *Consent.* The knowledge and consent of the individual are required for the collection, use or disclosure of personal information, except when inappropriate. Organizations must also obtain new consent whenever the use for which the information was collected has changed.

4. *Limiting Collection.* The collection of personal information shall be limited to that which is necessary for the purposes identified by the organization. Information shall be collected by fair and lawful means.

5. *Limiting Use, Disclosure, and Retention.* Personal information shall not be used or disclosed for purposes other than those for which it was collected, except with the consent of the individual or as required by the law. Personal information shall be retained only as long as necessary for fulfillment of those purposes.

6. *Accuracy.* Personal information shall be as accurate, complete, and up-to-date as is necessary for the purposes for which it is to be used.

7. *Safeguards.* Personal information shall be protected by security safeguards appropriate to the sensitivity of the information.

8. *Openness.* An organization shall make readily available to individuals specific information about its policies and practices relating to the management of personal information.

9. *Individual Access.* Upon request, an individual shall be informed of the existence, use and disclosure of his or her personal information and shall be given access to that information. An individual shall be able to challenge the accuracy and completeness of the information and have it amended as appropriate.

10. *Challenging Compliance.* An individual shall be able to address a challenge concerning compliance with the above principles to the designated individual or individuals for the organization's compliance.

Under PIPEDA, an organization is prohibited from using personal information without the person's consent except in particular situations, such as for law enforcement investigations and emergency situations. Similarly, an organization is prohibited from disclosing personal information without consent, except in particular situations, such as for debt collection, or when doing so is required for compliance with a law or court order, or for law enforcement or national security purposes.

Oversight of PIPEDA is done on the national level by the Office of the Information Privacy Commissioner of Canada located in Ottawa, Ontario.[185] The Commissioner has broad powers to enforce the Act. For example, the Commissioner can audit any organization collecting personal information on Canadian citizens, and has the power to investigate, compel the production of evidence, make findings and recommendations, and to take such cases to the courts for judicial action. Individuals may also hold organizations liable for violations of the Act, seeking injunctive relief and/or monetary damages.

PIPEDA also provides for the enactment of provincial privacy legislation, and each province has an active, independent data protection authority. If a provincial law is deemed "substantially similar" to PIPEDA, it generally supersedes PIPEDA with respect to the regulation of intra-provincial and provincial government activities. At present, the provinces of Alberta, British Columbia and Quebec have such substantially similar laws. This model is designed to enable the enactment of locally-appropriate laws that are harmonized with and substantially similar to the federal law.

Exceptions to PIPEDA are allowed for some groups, such as law enforcement agencies and journalists, which have a lawful or investigative need to collect, use and disclose personal information without having to obtain the consent of the concerned individuals. PIPEDA does not apply to the personal information of employees of organizations regulated by one or more of Canada's provinces or territories such as Ontario, Quebec, Alberta, Yukon or Nunavut.

Each Canadian province and territory has an oversight officer to monitor and enforce provincial and territorial privacy law.[186]

Extensive information on Canadian privacy laws, policies and practices is available to interested students through a separate IAPP credentialing program, the Certified Information Privacy Professional/Canada (CIPP/C).

Europe

As previously discussed, European law is based on the protection of privacy as a fundamental human right. The general rule is to not allow any collection or use of personal data unless permitted under law.

The E.U. Data Protection Directive
The data protection framework now in force across the European Union includes the

E.U. Data Protection Directive (95/46/EC) and other directives, such as the *Electronic Communications Directive and the E-Privacy Directive (2002/58/EC).*[187] In addition, there are specific E.U. member nation laws that apply to data protection, employment, and general civil activities. Finally, guidance is given by the *Article 29 Working Party,*[188] a special group formed under the E.U. charter for the expressed purpose of overseeing specific issues such as workplace privacy and employee data handling. All of these laws are enforced by the national data protection commissioners of E.U. member states as well as the data protection authority of the European Commission itself.

In 1995, the European Union passed *the Directive 95/46/EC of the European Parliament and of the Council on the protection of individuals with regard to the processing of personal data and on the free movement of such data* (known more commonly as *The E.U. Data Protection Directive* or "The Directive"). This is the E.U.'s comprehensive, over-arching law to protect the fundamental rights and freedoms of E.U. citizens, in partic-ular their right to privacy with respect to the processing of personal data.

Section I, Article 6[189] of The Directive codifies the fair information practices first developed in the U.S. in the 1970's, and states that E.U. member states shall provide that personal data must be:

• Processed fairly and lawfully;

• Collected for specified, explicit and legitimate purposes and not further processed in a way incompatible with those purposes. Further processing of data for historical, statistical or scientific purposes shall not be considered as incompatible provided that member states provide appropriate safeguards;

• Adequate, relevant and not excessive in relation to the purposes for which they are collected and/or further processed;

• Accurate and, where necessary, kept up to date; every reasonable step must be taken to ensure that data which are inaccurate or incomplete, having regard to the pur-poses for which they were collected or for which they are further processed, are erased or rectified;

• Kept in a form which permits identification of data subjects for no longer than is necessary for the purposes for which the data were collected or for which they are further processed. Member states shall lay down appropriate safeguards for personal data stored for longer periods for historical, statistical or scientific use.

A cornerstone principle of The Directive is that it prohibits the transfer of personal data to non-E.U. jurisdictions unless an "adequate level of protection" is guaranteed or another exception applies. One of the main challenges presented in attempting compliance with with The Directive is the broad definitions found in the language of the Act:

• *Personal Data* are any and all data that relates to an identifiable individual;

• *Special Categories of Data* are all data revealing race, ethnic origin, political opinions, religion or beliefs, trade union membership, sexual orientation or sex life, or criminal offenses—as well as biometric, health or disability data, and national ID numbers; and,

• *Processing* means any and all operations on personal data (including collection, storage, handling, use, disclosure and deletion)—regardless of form or format (manual or automatic processing).

E.U. member states (and their internal political divisions) have their own implementation schedule[190] which should be consulted when doing business with that particular country.

Similar to the dynamic between U.S. federal legislation and U.S. state law, The Directive sets the floor for E.U. member states and allows them to enact more stringent national data protection laws should they chose to. The Directive is designed to be a model for privacy legislation among the E.U. member states.[191] In particular, The Directive was designed to ensure the free movement of personal data across member states by providing a foundation for harmonized national legislation. As the preamble to The Directive notes: "in order to remove the obstacles to flows of personal data, the level of protection of the rights and freedoms of individuals with regard to the processing of such data must be equivalent in all Member States."

Each E.U. member state is obligated to enact national law to provide for appropriate data protection within that state. The Directive has also served as a model for other countries in the European Economic Area, such as European Free Trade Agreement members Switzerland, Norway, Iceland and Liechtenstein, as well as other countries, such as Argentina.

Of note, however, is that The Directive has not in practice created harmonized national privacy legislation. The Directive established a floor for privacy protection, and national laws often exceed the Directive's base requirements. The Directive has also been supplemented by other directives and guidance regarding privacy in certain specific contexts.[192] Accordingly, to fully understand E.U. law, it is necessary to consider the actual provisions of each applicable Directive, as well as the national laws enacted by each member state and the applicable published guidance, an exercise that is well outside of the scope of this text.

The E.U. Directive imposes strict requirements on any person that collects or processes data pertaining to individuals in any capacity. It is based on a set of data protection principles, which include the legitimate basis, purpose limitation; data quality, proportionality, and transparency principles; data security and confidentiality; data subjects' rights of access, rectification, deletion, and objection; restrictions on onwards transfers; additional protection where special categories of data and direct marketing are involved; and a prohibition on automated individual decisions.

As noted, The Directive's scope is very broad. It applies to all sectors of industry and to all types of personal data. The Directive's key provisions impose serious restrictions on personal data processing, grant individual rights to "data subjects," and set forth specific procedural obligations, including notification to national authorities. It should be noted, however, that many of The Directive's provisions are vague and effectively leave much discretion to national data protection authorities ("DPAs").

Definitions and Scope

The Directive regulates the "processing" of "personal data." The term "personal data" is broadly defined as data that relates to an identified or identifiable individual, including (for example) business contact information and information about an individual acting in a business or professional capacity. Personal data obtained from public sources are also covered.

The term "processing" is defined to cover all operations involving personal data, including collection, storage, handling, use, and deletion. Both manual and automated processing activities are covered. To accommodate other important interests, The Directive provides for partial exemptions for certain activities, such as journalism and research, but only if such exemptions are necessary to reconcile the right to privacy with the rules governing the freedom of expression and if the member states provide "appropriate safeguards," such as an obligation to render personal data anonymous.

General Processing Prohibition and Exceptions

Personal data may be processed only in certain specific situations described in The Directive. For example, processing is permitted if the "unambiguous consent" (as discussed below) of the individual has been obtained.

Processing is also permitted if it is necessary for the performance of a contract to which the data subject is party. This scenario is particularly important in business-to-consumer transactions, although the exception is applied quite narrowly. For example, a contractual clause agreed with a third party, which provides for processing of data other than those needed to service the customer, would not be covered.

Processing is also permitted when "necessary for the purposes of the legitimate interests" of the company or a third party or parties to whom data are disclosed, except where the business interests are overridden by the interests for fundamental rights and freedoms of the consumer. In this vaguely defined category of cases, processing is justified if there is an acceptable balance between the company's business interests and the consumer's interests. Unlike the situations described above, this ground requires that a balancing test be applied in each specific case.

Legitimate Purposes and Fair Processing

Qualifying under one of these categories is a necessary—but not sufficient—condition for lawful processing of personal data. In addition, personal data may be collected only for "specified, explicit and legitimate" purposes, and then may be processed only for purposes that are compatible with the original purposes, unless individual consent has been obtained.

Additionally, personal data must be processed "fairly." This concept of fairness is not further defined in The Directive. The fairness requirement is generally interpreted to require that data subjects be adequately informed about the processing. Fairness may also require other measures, depending, for example, on the nature of the data involved and the nature of the proposed processing.

Notice

The Directive requires that individuals whose data are collected and processed be adequately informed. For example, when data are collected directly from the data subject, the data controller should inform the individual about (1) the controller's identity, (2) the intended purposes of the collection and use of their data, and (3) "in so far as necessary to guarantee fair processing", the categories of recipients of the data, and the right of access and to rectify incorrect data.

Choice

Individual choice (or control) is a key element of the E.U. model. Under The Directive different situations call for prior opt-in consent for processing, while in other situations individuals must be given an opportunity to object (opt-out) to processing. In each case, the opportunity to exercise consent may not be made dependent on the payment of a fee or other burdensome conditions.

Opt-in consent is generally required for (1) the processing of sensitive data, (2) uses that are incompatible with the purpose of which the data subject has been informed, (3) depending on national law, direct marketing, and (4) disclosure of personal data to third parties. Opt-out consent is required, in general, depending on national law, for direct marketing and (in the context of transfers to outside the E.U.), with respect to onward transfers (i.e., transfer by a data importer to another third party).

Access and Rectification

Data controllers must respect the data subject's right of access. Data subjects have a right to access, at reasonable intervals and without excessive delay or expense, all information relating to them that is on file with the data controller, subject to limited exceptions such as the privacy of other persons. The data subject also has the right to have the controller rectify, erase, or block data which is inaccurate or incomplete and the processing of which does not comply with The Directive. In addition, unless it is impossible or it involves a disproportionate effort, the data subject has the right to have the controller notify third parties (to whom data have been disclosed) of the rectification, erasure or blocking of such data.

Data Quality

Data must be accurate and, where necessary, kept up to date. The data must be "adequate, relevant and not excessive" in relation to the purposes for which they are collected and processed. They must be destroyed when no longer needed. Member States must provide adequate safeguards for personal data that are stored for longer periods for historical, statistical, or scientific use.

Confidentiality and Security

The Directive requires also that confidentiality and security of processing be guaranteed. The controller must implement "appropriate technical and organizational measures" to protect personal data against accidental or unlawful destruction; accidental loss, alteration; unauthorized disclosure or access, especially where the processing involves the transmission of data over a network; and against all other unlawful forms of processing. In implementing such measures, the technology available as well as the costs of implementing the measures should be considered. The measures must ensure a level of security appropriate to the risks represented by the processing and the nature of data to be protected (e.g., sensitive data may require strong encryption).

The Directive prohibits any processor or any person acting on behalf of the controller or processor and who has access to personal data, from processing such data except pursuant to instructions of the controller (unless it is required by law). This prohibition is aimed at ensuring that the processor, controller or their representative process data in a confidential manner.

Data Transfers Outside of the European Union

As discussed in depth below, transfers of personal data from the E.U. to a transferee outside of the E.U. are subject to a specific export regime. In principle, subject to exceptions, such transfers are prohibited, unless the country at issue offers an "adequate level" of privacy protection or another established mechanism for ensuring privacy protection exists.

Prior Notification

The controller or his representative must notify the applicable DPAs before carrying out any fully or partly automated processing. At a minimum, at least the following information must be provided to such authorities; (1) the name and address of the controller or his representative, if any; (2) the purpose(s) of the processing; (3) the description of the category or categories of data subjects and the data or the categories of data relating to them; (4) the recipients or categories of recipients to whom such data may be disclosed; (5) any proposed transfer of data to third countries; and (6) general description of the measures taken to ensure the security of the processing (to allow a preliminary assessment of the measures taken).

In addition, a public register of processing operations is supposed to be established by each member state, and member states must provide a procedure pursuant to which changes to the aforementioned information is to be provided to the data protection authorities. Member states, however, may provide for the simplification of, or exemption from, notification for certain categories of data processing and under certain conditions.

Enforcement

The Directive is aimed also at giving individuals adequate means to enforce their rights. Data protection legislation provides for complaint and mediation procedures involving the national DPAs. In addition, it provides for civil and criminal enforcement of the data controller's obligations. In connection with data transfers, DPAs consider it essential that the data importer's obligations and the data subject's rights can be adequately enforced in the data importer's jurisdiction.

International Transfers of Personal Data

As noted above, the purpose of The Directive is precisely to enhance the free flow of data among the E.U. member states, while providing for a high level of data protection. The Directive is designed to ensure the free movement of data within Europe, and European data protection laws do not impose data transfer restrictions on data flows within the E.U. However, The Directive strictly regulates transfers of personal data to non-E.U. countries. In particular, personal data may not be transferred to jurisdictions outside of the E.U. unless the jurisdictions offer an "adequate level of protection" for the data or another basis for the transfer exists.[193]

With regard to adequacy, the European Commission has declared the following countries to offer adequate legal protection, so that data transfers can occur in these instances without further approvals or processes:[194] Argentina, Canada (based on PIPEDA, discussed above), Switzerland, Guernsey, and the Isle of Man.

Transfer Mechanisms

Absent a finding of adequacy, transfers of personal information may occur only pursuant to The Directive's other exceptions or formally-approved transfer mechanisms. Currently there are five main exceptions to the general prohibition on transfers of personal data. In particular, transfers are permissible if:

1. The unambiguous consent of each of the individuals involved has been obtained;

2. The transfer is strictly "necessary for the performance of a contract" with the individual or for the performance of a contract in the interest of the individual;

3. The transfer is to a U.S. recipient that has joined the "Safe Harbor" program;

4. The national authorities of the E.U. member state from which the data are transferred have granted specific authorization; or,

5. The transferor (in Europe) and transferee (outside of the E.U.) have entered into a contract providing for an "adequate level" of data protection. Such a contract may take the form of a general Model Contract as approved by the Commission, or a specific contract agreed between the transferor and transferee and approved by the applicable national authority.

Each of these transfer mechanisms can be considered in greater detail:

Consent. To utilize this exception, unambiguous consent must be obtained from each individual whose data are to be transferred. The Directive defines the data subject's consent as "any freely-given, specific and informed indication of his wishes by which the data subject signifies his agreement to the processing of personal data about him." "Freely-given" generally means that consent is given without undue external pressure. In two situations the freedom to consent may be deemed diminished.

First, consent may be deemed not freely given if there is a hierarchical relationship between the controller and data subject or if the data subject is otherwise dependent on the controller. This may be the case, for instance, in an employment context, where an employee may feel that his refusal will be held against him. If the data subject is significantly dependent on the controller, additional guarantees may be required for consent to be regarded as freely-given

Second, consent may be tainted if refusal to consent is penalized directly. For instance, refusing to deal with an individual unless consent is given, in some situations, may render consent coerced. If a refusal to consent results in significant disadvantages for the individual (e.g., he will not be entitled to procure certain types of services or other benefits), consent may be deemed not freely-given. In other words, for consent to be freely-given, the data subject must not face any serious adverse consequences.

Performance of a Contract. The exception for transfers that are "necessary for the performance of a contract" may permit data to be exported if a contract with the data subject (or with a third party in the interest of the data subject) so requires. For example, personal data of a credit card holder may automatically be transferred to an issuing bank outside of the E.U. during the credit card authorization process at the point of credit card use. However, an entity's ability to rely on this exception is limited by the necessity test: performance of the contract must be all but impossible but for the transfer.

Additionally, while use of this exception does not necessarily require an explicit agreement with the data subject regarding to the transfer, it is likely not useable if the data subject cannot actually anticipate that the data will be transferred.

Safe Harbor Framework. Under The E.U. Directive, the E.U. member states are prohibited from transferring data to the U.S. because, in their estimation, the U.S. does not meet the definition of "adequate" in a data protection context. To navigate around this impediment, the U.S. Department of Commerce, in consultation with the European Commission, developed a "Safe Harbor" framework.

The principles of the Safe Harbor Framework[195] involve a number of rights that U.S.-based signatories agree to grant to European data subjects, including, specifically:

• The right to be adequately informed about the purposes of data collection;

• The right to opt-out if personal data are intended to be disclosed to a third party or are intended to be used for a purpose that is incompatible with original collection purposes; and,

• The right to access, amend or delete inaccurate information, subject to certain restrictions where employee data are involved.

With regard to enforcement, the *Safe Harbor* Principles require that corporations subject themselves to the authority and jurisdiction of a U.S. enforcement authority. Currently two U.S. regulatory agencies, the Federal Trade Commission ("FTC") and the Department of Transportation ("DOT") have agreed to enforce Safe Harbor violations.[196] The FTC agreed that not following a self-certified standard is an unfair and deceptive trade practice, and thus subject to enforcement. Companies that implement a Safe Harbor privacy program then annually certify their compliance with the Department of Commerce.

The following seven Safe Harbor requirements are, in large part, based upon the earlier, commonly established, fair information practices:[197]

Notice. Organizations must notify individuals about the purposes for which they collect and use information about them. They must provide information about how individuals can contact the organization with any inquiries or complaints, the types of third parties to which they disclose the information and the choices and means the organization offers for limiting its use and disclosure.

Choice. Organizations must give individuals the opportunity to choose (opt out) whether their personal information will be disclosed to a third party or used for a purpose incompatible with the purpose for which it was originally collected or subsequently authorized by the individual. For sensitive information, affirmative or explicit (opt in) choice must be given if the information is to be disclosed to a third party or used for a purpose other than its original purpose or the purpose authorized subsequently by the individual.

Onward Transfer (Transfers to Third Parties). To disclose information to a third party, organizations must apply the notice and choice principles. Where an organization wishes to transfer information to a third party that is acting as an agent, it may do so if it makes sure that the third party subscribes to the Safe Harbor principles or is subject to The Directive or another adequacy finding. As an alternative, the organization can enter into a written agreement with such third party requiring that the third party provide at least the same level of privacy protection as is required by the relevant principles.

Access. Individuals must have access to personal information about them that an organization holds and be able to correct, amend, or delete that information where it is inaccurate, except where the burden or expense of providing access would be disproportionate to the risks to the individual's privacy in the case in question, or where the rights of persons other than the individual would be violated.

Security. Organizations must take reasonable precautions to protect personal information from loss, misuse and unauthorized access, disclosure, alteration and destruction. Personal information must be relevant for the purposes for which it is to be used. An organization should take reasonable steps to ensure that data are reliable for their intended use, accurate, complete, and current.

Enforcement. In order to ensure compliance with the Safe Harbor principles, there must be (a) readily available and affordable independent recourse mechanisms so that each individual's complaints and disputes can be investigated and resolved and damages awarded where the applicable law or private sector initiatives so provide; (b) procedures for verifying that the commitments companies make to adhere to the Safe Harbor principles have been implemented; and (c) obligations to remedy problems arising out of a failure to comply with the principles. Sanctions must be sufficiently rigorous to ensure compliance by the organization. Organizations that fail to provide annual self certification letters will no longer appear in the list of participants and Safe Harbor benefits will no longer be assured.

Significantly, participation in the Safe Harbor program is not available to financial institutions and others that are not regulated by the U.S. FTC or Department of Transportation.

Alternatives to Safe Harbor. Companies seeking to provide adequate protection for E.U. purposes, but not wanting to go through Safe Harbor certification, may also execute "model contracts"[198] which mandate certain safeguards and standard clauses. These clauses have been approved by the E.U. Commission and stipulate that:

- Data exporters and importers provide notice, access, and other data protection provisions as provided by local law;

- Both exporter and importer are liable to the data subject for illegal data flows; and,

- The Data Protection Authority (in most member states) is notified about the contract.

The model form may be modified so long as the basic provisions providing adequate protection remain intact.

Consent is yet another alternative to Safe Harbor. Data transfers can generally be authorized by consent. Such consent must be freely-given and unambiguous, but standards vary in each E.U. member state. Individuals must also be able to withhold or revoke consent with no adverse consequences. E.U. authorities do not always recognize consent for human resources data because of the subordinate nature of the employment relationship.

Authorization. The national DPAs of the member states from which the transfers occur may also authorize transfers. Before granting any such authorization, the authorities must assess the adequacy of the data protection regime that will be applied in a specific case, taking into account all the circumstances surrounding a data transfer.

In terms of substantive protection, however, the authorities will likely require at least the same level of protection that the Safe Harbor Principles or model contract provide. Also, obtaining authorizations may be very onerous, especially if data from more than a few countries are involved, because the approval process is very resource-intensive for both the DPAs and companies seeking approval.

If a company decides to use non-model data transfer contracts, these contracts will have to be approved by the applicable DPAs in the same manner as an authorization.

Transfer Contracts. The European Commission permits adequate protections to be assured by contract.[199] Prior to June 2001, organizations wishing to use contracts had to have each contract approved by the application data protection authority. This approval process presented a real barrier to the use of contracts, resulting in the Commission's movement to develop "model" contracts whose use could be relied on without specific approval.[200] Currently three form model contracts have been authorized; the original June 2001 model controller-to-controller form, a controller-to-processor form (approved in 2002) and a model contract developed by the International Chamber of Commerce (ICC) and approved in January 2005.

As noted above, if data transfers are made pursuant to the model contract clauses, no authorization from the member state national authorities is required (or where member states nonetheless require authorization, they must give it automatically), regardless of the location of the data recipient. Parties using the model contracts specify in appendices the specific purposes of the data transfer, the specific categories of data that are transferred (including sensitive data), the recipients of the data (onward transfer), and the data storage limit.

With respect to the substantive rules governing the data processing abroad, the parties have some options. For example, they may choose to comply with a set of mandatory data protection principles, which are annexed to the contract. The parties must warrant that the exported data are processed in accordance with the mandatory data protection principles,[201] which generally mirror those of The Directive.

With regard to onward transfer, the model clauses provide that further transfers of personal data from the data importer to another controller established in a non-adequate third country may take place only if (a) data subjects have given their unambiguous consent to the onward transfer if sensitive data are involved (or have been given the opportunity to object in other cases),[202] and (b) the data exporter and the data importer agree to the adherence of set of standard contractual clauses (thereby having the same obligations as the original data importer).

The enforcement of the contract regime is built on two pillars: (1) the contract includes a third party beneficiary clause enabling data subjects to enforce the principles against both the exporter and importer; and (2) joint and several liability of the data exporter and importer for damages resulting from any violation of the contractual provisions. According to the Commission, data subjects must be entitled to take action and receive compensation from either contracting party for any damage resulting from any act incompatible with the annexed principles. Additionally, the contracts are always governed by the national laws where the data exporter resides. In the event of a dispute, the data subject has the right to choose between third party mediation or referring the dispute to the courts in the data exporter's country.[203]

The DPAs have no right to audit the data importer's processing operations outside their jurisdiction. However, all data exporters and importers must agree to cooperate with inquiries and investigations by any competent supervisory authority. They must also comply with any decisions of the authorities. In addition, the data importer must agree to submit its data processing for audit by the data exporter. DPAs do have the authority to suspend data flows that are occurring pursuant to a contract. They may suspend the data flows if (1) the law to which the data importer is subject requires it to deviate from the contract other than as required for national security; (2) a competent authority has established that the data importer has not respected the contractual clauses; or (3) there is a substantial likelihood that the contract terms are not being followed, and the continuing transfer would create an imminent risk of grave harm to the data subjects.

Special Rules for Sensitive Data

Under The Directive, "special categories of data" (or "sensitive data") are personal data relating to:

a. The racial or ethnic origin of the data subject;

b. His or her political opinions;

c. His or her religious beliefs;

d. Trade union membership;

e. Sex life or sexual orientation;

f. Physical or mental health or conditions; and,

g. Criminal records (or allegations of crimes) or any proceedings related to offenses committed (or alleged) including the outcome or sentencing in court of such proceedings

To the extent that sensitive data elements are processed, additional requirements apply. In general, companies may process sensitive data only if required to do so by law or with the express consent of the data subject. Transfers of sensitive data are also restricted. The model contracts and Safe Harbor Principles provide limited utility for the transfer of sensitive data.

In order to transfer sensitive data, a company must determine if the transfer of the data is strictly necessary for a recognized legal purpose. Next, the company must generally obtain the explicit consent of the data subject for the disclosure of sensitive personal data to other entities. (All of the considerations relating to consent discussed above apply in this context a well.) Alternatively, (if, for example, consent cannot be obtained), sensitive data may be transferred pursuant to another exception, such as with the explicit authorization by the applicable DPAs.

The E-Privacy Directive

Over the past several years, the European Commission has issued various directives to address different types of technology and business practices (such as the adoption of distance contracts). Many of these directives address privacy implications of the technology or practice. For example, in 1997, the Telecommunications Directive[204] was promulgated to address the use of telephonic marketing (phone and fax) by means of automated calling systems and predicative dialers. This directive prohibited the use of these technologies unless express (opt-in) consent of the individuals had been obtained.[205]

In 2002, given concerns about the rise of unsolicited commercial email, the European Commission revised, renamed and re-enacted the Telecommunications Directive as the E-Privacy Directive[206] so that it could better address all issues related to electronic communications.

Known formally as the *Privacy and Electronic Communications Directive* (2002/58/EC),[207] the E-Privacy Directive was adopted with the purpose of regulating the privacy and data protection issues inherent in online marketing practices. Some of the key provisions of this directive include:

• Individuals must give prior consent in the form of an opt-in prior to receiving email. However, if there is an existing customer relationship, companies may email (or text) such customers provided that they are marketing their own similar products and the customer is easily able to opt out of receiving such communications in the future.

• "Cookie" files and similar online identification mechanisms are required to be more transparent, and anyone using them should provide information about them to subscribers or users and offer an opportunity to refuse them.

• Stronger rights for individual subscribers to decide whether or not they want to be listed in subscriber directories. Subscribers must be given clear information about the directories and must be informed of any reverse search.

• Value-added services (e.g., location-based advertising to mobile phones) are permitted, so long as subscribers have given their consent and are informed of the data processing implications.

The E-Privacy Directive extends controls on unsolicited direct marketing to all forms of electronic communications including unsolicited commercial email (UCE) and SMS (i.e., text messages) to mobile telephones. The E-Privacy Directive requires prior (opt-in) consent for electronic marketing communications, although it has a limited exception for communications within an established customer relationship. This exception permits companies to email or SMS to market products and services to customers who have purchased similar products or services from the company under the same brand name. In this case, the company must offer an opt-out, so that individuals can discontinue receiving the communications if they choose.

The E-Privacy Directive also imposes controls over the use of cookie files on Web sites. In particular, it requires transparency of the use of cookies. Companies must clearly display the terms under which they use cookies on their Web sites. Additionally the E-Privacy Directive gave Member States the authority to introduce provisions on the retention of traffic and location data for law enforcement purposes.

The European Economic Area ("EEA") and Switzerland

The European Economic Area ("EEA") is comprised of the 25 E.U. Member States plus the three members of the European Free Trade Association ("EFTA"), which are Iceland, Liechtenstein, and Norway. These three nations chose not to become members of the E.U., but do wish to participate in Europe's internal marketplace.

The objective of the EEA is to promote a continuous and balanced strengthening of trade and economic relations between the contracting parties with the view toward creating a homogenous European Economic Area.[208] The European Data Protection Directive extends to all member states of the EEA.

Switzerland opted not to join the EAA, but has passed its own omnibus privacy legislation. *The Swiss Federal Act on Data Protection*[209] is compatible with the Council of Europe's "*Convention for the Protection of Individuals with Regard to Automatic Processing of Personal Data*" with the standards set forth by The Directive.

The Asia Pacific Region

The Asia-Pacific Economic Cooperation ("APEC") is a multi-national organization with 21 Pacific-coast members in Asia and the Americas. Unlike the E.U., the APEC organization operates under non-binding agreements (e.g. as a cooperative). It was established in 1989 to enhance economic growth for the region.

In February 2003, the APEC Privacy Subgroup was established under the auspices of the Electronic Commerce Steering Group ("ECSG") in order to develop a framework for privacy practices. This framework was designed to provide support to APEC-member economy legislation that would both protect individual interests and ensure the continued economic development of all APEC member economies.

The APEC Privacy Framework was approved by the APEC ministers in November 2004.[211] It contains nine information privacy principles which closely mirror the Fair Information Principles, and the OECD Privacy Principles described earlier in this text.

The APEC Privacy Principles are:

1. ***Preventing Harm***. Recognizing the interests of the individual to legitimate expectations of privacy, personal information protection should be designed to prevent the misuse of such information. Further, acknowledging the risk that harm may result from such misuse of personal information, specific obligations should take account of such risk and remedial measures should be proportionate to the likelihood and severity of the harm threatened by the collection, use and transfer of personal information.

2. ***Notice***. Personal information controllers should provide clear and easily accessible statements about their practices and policies with respect to personal information that should include:

   a. the fact that personal information is being collected;

   b. the purposes for which personal information is collected;

   c. the types of persons or organizations to whom personal information might be disclosed;

   d. the identity and location of the personal information controller, including information on how to contact it about its practices and handling of personal information; and,

   e. the choices and means the personal information controller offers individuals for limiting the use and disclosure of, and for accessing and correcting, their personal information.

   All reasonably practicable steps shall be taken to ensure that such information is provided either before or at the time of collection of personal information. Otherwise, such information should be provided as soon after as is practicable.
   It may not be appropriate for personal information controllers to provide notice regarding the collection and use of publicly available information.

3. ***Collection Limitation.*** The collection of personal information should be limited to information that is relevant to the purposes of collection and any such information should be obtained by lawful and fair means, and, where appropriate, with notice to, or consent of, the individual concerned.

4. ***Uses of Personal Information***. Personal information collected should be used only to fulfil the purposes of collection and other compatible purposes except:

a. with the consent of the individual whose personal information is collected;

b. when necessary to provide a service or product requested by the individual; or,

c. by the authority of law and other legal instruments, proclamations and pronouncements of legal effect.

5. **Choice.** Where appropriate, individuals should be provided with clear, prominent, easily understandable, accessible and affordable mechanisms to exercise choice in relation to the collection, use and disclosure of their personal information. It may not be appropriate for personal information controllers to provide these mechanisms when collecting publicly available information.

6. **Integrity of Personal Information.** Personal information should be accurate, complete and kept up-to-date to the extent necessary for the purposes of use.

7. **Security Safeguards.** Personal information controllers should protect personal information that they hold with appropriate safeguards against risks, such as loss or unauthorized access to personal information, or unauthorized destruction, use, modification or disclosure of, information or other misuses. Such safeguards should be proportional to the likelihood and severity of the harm threatened the sensitivity of the information and the context in which it is held, and should be subject to periodic review and reassessment.

8. **Access and Correction.** Individuals should be able to:

a. obtain from the personal information controller confirmation of whether or not the personal information controller holds personal information about them;

b. have communicated to them, after having provided sufficient proof of their identity, personal information about them;
    i.   within a reasonable time;
    ii. at a charge, if any, that is not excessive;
    iii. in a reasonable manner;
    iv. in a form that is generally understandable; and,

c. challenge the accuracy of information relating to them and, if possible and as appropriate, have the information rectified, completed, amended or deleted. Such access and opportunity for correction should be provided except where:
    i.   the burden or expense of doing so would be unreasonable or disproportionate to the risks to the individual's privacy;

    ii. the information should not be disclosed due to legal, security or commercial proprietary reasons; or,

    iii. the information privacy of persons other than the individual would be violated.

If a request under (i) or (ii) or a challenge under (iii) is denied, the individual should be provided with reasons why and be able to challenge such denial

9. *Accountability.* A personal information controller should be accountable for complying with measures that give effect to the principles stated above. When personal information is to be transferred to another person or organization, whether domestically or internationally, the personal information controller should exercise due diligence and take reasonable steps to ensure that the recipient person or organization will protect the information consistently with these principles.

Japan

Japan's data protection law, the *Law Concerning the Protection of Personal Information*, was enacted in 2003 and became effective for private sector entities on April 1, 2005. The Law represents one part of a complex, comprehensive privacy regulatory regime, as it is implemented through guidelines promulgated by the various ministries charged with the enforcement of the Law within their respective industry sectors.[212]

Japan's Law contains several key definitions:

• *Personal Information* means information that relates to living individuals and which can be used to identify specific individuals by name, date of birth, or other description (including that which can be easily compared with other information and thereby used to identify specific individuals).

• *Personal Information Databases, etc.* refers to the collection of information including personal information, as follows: (i) Information which is structurally constituted so as to be able to easily retrieve specific personal information by use of a computer; (ii) manual or paper-based records that are structurally constituted so as to be able to easily retrieve specific personal information.

• *Businesses Handling Personal Information* refers to a person who uses personal information databases, etc., for business operations. Certain exceptions exist, including "persons designated by government ordinance as being little or no threat to the rights or welfare of individuals from the standpoint of the quantity of Personal Information handled and the method of use."[213]

- *Personal Data* refers to personal information which makes up a personal information database.

- *Held Personal Data* generally refers to personal data over which a business handling personal information has the authority to disclose, to make corrections, additions, or deletions of content, to cease use, to eliminate, or to cease providing to third parties.

- *Principal* as used with respect to personal information refers to the specific individual identified by personal information. (i.e., the data subject). Additionally, the definition of "third parties" is also critical for understanding the data transfer provisions of the Japanese Law. All separate legal entities are third parties, even if they are related to (or affiliated with) an organization. The definition of third parties does not, however, apply to "delegates" or true data processors that handle data only pursuant to the instructions of the original organization.

Japan's Law sets forth a general approach for privacy protection, called the "Basic Policy," which outlines the following duties of businesses handling personal information, including:

- Specification of and limitation on the "Purpose of Use"
- Appropriate (fair) acquisition of personal information
- Notification of the purpose of use (at collection)
- Securing accuracy of data content
- Security control measures
- Supervision of employees and delegates (data processors)
- Restrictions on providing information to third parties
- Public announcement of items relating to held personal data
- Disclosure (access), correction, cease use, etc.
- Explanation of reasons (for refusal to correct, cease use, etc.)
- Procedures for responding to request for disclosure
- Processing of grievances by businesses handling personal information
- Collection of reports and advice (ministerial notification and guidance)
- Admonishments and orders (Enforcement)

Rules for International Transfer of Personal Data
The Japan Law does not provide any specific regulation of international transfers. Instead, it imposes strong consent-based requirements on all transfers of personal information to third parties, regardless of the location of the recipient. Additionally, as noted above, the restrictions on transfer apply to all third parties (other than delegates), including affiliated entities.[214]

In particular the Law provides that businesses handling personal information shall not provide personal data to any third party without first acquiring the explicit consent of the principal.[215] The Law does provide for certain transfers outside of this rule, including transfers to delegates as needed to achieve the purpose of use, transfers in connection with business succession operations (such as mergers), and transfers in connection with joint use arrangements, if certain conditions are met.

Additionally, while the general rule requires explicit consent for transfers, the Law does provide a mechanism for companies to share personal information using an opt-out regime. A company may transfer personal data if the company has provided notice to the principal stating: (1) that the transfer of personal data to third parties is included in the purpose of use; (2) the categories of personal data that will be provided; (3) the means and methods of transferring the personal data; and (4) the principal can, upon request, have the business cease transfer of the personal data to the third parties.

It is important to note that the ministerial regulations may provide additional limitations on the data transfers. For example, the Financial Services Administration ("FSA") has prohibited the use of the opt-out consent regime for certain transfers of credit information.[216] Additionally, the various guidelines also address issues of corporate accountability for transfers. The transfer rules clearly imply that businesses are accountable for actions of delegates regardless of where those entities reside. Similarly, with respect to human resources data, Guidelines from the Ministry of Economy, Trade and Industry and the Ministry of Health, Labor and Welfare provide that companies remain accountable for the processing of personal information by third parties even if the principal has explicitly consented to the transfer.

Australia

Australia's Federal Privacy Act contains eleven information privacy principles ("IPPs")[217] which apply to Commonwealth and "ACT" (Australian Capital Territory) government agencies. On December 21, 2001, amendments to the Australian Privacy Act extended the country's existing National Privacy Principles into the private sector. This Privacy Amendment (Private Sector) Act 2000[218] now regulates how businesses collect, use and store information personal information across the country.

Australia's Act has 10 National Privacy Principles ("NPPs")[219] which apply to parts of the private sector and all health service providers as well as private sector data processing activities. These principles dictate that:

1. Collection must be fair and lawful;
2. Use and disclosure of data must occur only with consent;
3. Reasonable data quality and accuracy must be maintained;
4. Reasonable security must be maintained;
5. Openness (publication of organization's privacy policies) must be fulfilled;
6. A means for access and correction must be provided;

7. Use of government-issued identifiers must be limited;

8. Reasonably anonymity options must be offered;

9. Transborder data flows should be limited; and,

10. Special protection must be implemented for sensitive data.

Part IIIA of The Act regulates credit providers and credit reporting agencies. Under the Act, the Australian National Privacy Commissioner has some regulatory functions under other enactments, including the Telecommunications Act 1997, National Health Act 1953, Data Matching Program Act 1990 and the Crimes Act 1914.

Instead of defining specific procedures and standards within the national law, Australia has encouraged industry organizations to develop sets of self-regulatory codes that reflect the national privacy principles. The Australian National Privacy Commissioner assists with code development, approves the codes, and provides an independent enforcement mechanism for resolving complaints.

Additionally, instead of strict standards, the Australian law generally ties the obligations of an organization to what is "reasonable" for the organization under the circumstances. Data subjects do not have absolute rights under the Australian law. This hybrid regulatory/self-regulatory approach and the focus on "reasonableness" reflects the Australian government's attempt to provide adequate privacy protection within a business-facilitating framework.

Latin America

The Latin American region includes 30 individual countries. Privacy rights are provided by constitutional guarantees or amendments to the existing constitutional laws of these countries.

The process began first in Brazil in 1990 with a formal amendment to the Brazilian Constitution in order to permit the right of citizen access to personal information. This continued throughout the 1990s with similar provisions in the constitutions of Columbia, Paraguay, Venezuela, Ecuador and Uruguay.

Common themes among Latin American data protection laws include:

- A constitutional mandate to ensure privacy;
- A traditional privacy clause;
- A definition of sensitive personal information;
- The right for citizens to rectify information;
- An express consent requirement; and,
- A provision for "habeas data."

Data protection laws in Latin America are generally based on rights of *habeas data*. These are constitutional guarantees that the citizenry may "have the data" archived about them by governmental and commercial repositories. This translates into individual rights to compel organizations to provide access to data and, generally, includes rights to mandate correction of inaccurate data and to limit distribution (or mandate destruction) of the data.

Habeas data rights cover both consumer and employee data files. They do not generally include specific restrictions on the international transfer of personal information. Instead, organizations subject to these rules would likely be required to provide access and respect the other *habeas data* rights with regard to data maintained anywhere.

The *habeas data* doctrine varies from country to country, but generally, is designed to protect the image, privacy, honor, information, self-determination and freedom of information of a person. These concepts are imperative because they establish the legal framework that governs privacy law in the region.

In many Latin American countries, *habeas data* rights are being supplemented with statutory rights in traditional data protection legislation such as the laws in force across the European Union and defined earlier in this chapter.

Argentina's historical approach to privacy and data protection in many ways mirrors the European experience and remains one of the leading examples of Latin American privacy laws. In 1994, as a reaction to government abuses including the forced detainment of political foes (the "desaparecidos" or "disappeared"),[220] Argentina amended its Constitution to include a right of *habeas data*, making the protection of personal data a fundamental right.[221]

Argentina next passed the *Law for the Protection of Personal Data ("LPPD")* in 2000.[222] This law conformed to the Argentinean Constitution, and is based on the E.U. Data Protection Directive. It contains provisions relating to general data protection principles, the rights of data subjects, the obligations of data controllers and data users, the supervisory authority, sanctions, and rules of procedure in seeking *habeas data* as a judicial remedy. The law also prohibits the international transfer of personal information to nations without "adequate protection." The E.U. considers Argentina as providing an adequate level of protection for data transfer. Argentina's privacy laws are enforced by a government agency, the National Directorate for the Protection of Personal Data.

Also in 2000, Chile enacted the *Law for the Protection of Private Life.* This law mandates, among other requirements, that sensitive personal data cannot be stored in a database even *with* the consent of the data subject. Paraguay also has comprehensive privacy laws in force.

Other Latin American countries—such as Columbia, Brazil and Mexico, (below)—do not currently have omnibus data protection laws in force (e.g., a privacy law that broadly applies to the entire country)—despite the constitutional provisions that have been in force for many years. These countries do have specific data protection draft laws currently under consideration. The proposed laws tend to follow the E.U. model, reflecting the desire to ensure that data transfers from Europe are not disrupted.

Lastly, some Latin American countries have incorporated habeas data-type rights in other varieties of laws, such as e-commerce laws or consumer protection laws.[223] For example, the *Mexican Federal Consumer Protection Law*[224] now includes provisions that give consumers rights to restrict data transfers and use of their data for targeted marketing.[225] This law is enforced by the Mexican Consumer Protection Agency (the Procuraduría Federal del Consumidor or "PROFECO"), an agency with powers similar to that of U.S. Federal Trade Commission.

Compliance with Privacy Laws

In order to understand any law, statute or regulation, it is important to ask six key questions:

1. Who is covered by this law?
2. What types of information (or what applications of information) are covered?
3. What exactly is required or prohibited?
4. Who enforces the law?
5. What happens if I don't comply?
6. Why does this law exist?

The first two questions give you the scope of the law. If you are outside the scope of the law, it may still be useful for you to understand the law. For example, the law may suggest good practices that you want to emulate. It may provide an indication of legal trends. It may also provide a proven way to achieve a particular result, such as protecting individuals in a given situation.

Assuming you are within the scope of the law, question three tells you what you need to know to comply with the law. Questions four and five help you assess the risks associated with non-compliance or less than perfect compliance. In most cases, companies do whatever it takes to be materially compliant with all applicable laws. However, there may be a situation where the costs of compliance outweigh the risks of non-compliance for a particular period of time. For example, if a system that is not appropriately compliant with a new law is going to be replaced in a few months, a company may decide that the risks of non-compliance outweigh the costs of trying to accelerate the system transition.

The final question helps you understand the motivation behind the law. Most companies try to comply with both the letter and the spirit of the law, and knowing why the law was written helps you understand the spirit of the legislation. Knowing why a law was written can also help you improve other processes, to achieve desired results. It may also help you anticipate regulatory trends.

Consider, for example, California's security breach notification law (SB 1386): [236]

- *Who is covered?*

This law regulates entities that do business in California that own or license computerized data including personal information. It applies to persons—natural persons, legal persons and government agencies.

If you do business only in Montana or New York, you are not subject o this law. Even if you do business in California, you are not subject tot this law if you don't have computerized data.

- *What is covered?*

This law regulates computerized personal information of California residents. "Personal information" is an individual's name in combination with any one or more of (i) Social Security number, (ii) California identification card number, (iii) driver's license number, or (iv) financial account number or credit or debit card number in combination with any required security code, access code or password that would permit access to an individual's financial account, when either the name or the data elements are not encrypted.

If your databases contain only names and addresses, you are not subject to this law. If your database contains only encrypted information, you are not subject to this law.

- *What is required or prohibited?*

This law requires you to disclose any breach of the security of the system to any resident of California whose unencrypted personal information was or is reasonably believed to have been acquired by an unauthorized person. A "breach of the security of the system" means unauthorized acquisition of computerized data that compromises the security, confidentiality, or integrity of personal information maintained by the person. The disclosure must be made "in as expedient manner as possible."

There is an exception for the good faith acquisition of personal information by an employee or agent of the business, provided that the personal information is not used or subject to further unauthorized disclosure.

You may also delay providing notice, if law enforcement requests such a delay.

- *Who enforces?*

The California attorney general, and there is a private right of action.

- *What happens if I don't comply?*

The California attorney general or any citizen can file a civil lawsuit against you, seeking damages and forcing you to comply.

- *Why does this law exist?*

SB 1386 was enacted because there is a fear that security breaches of computerized databases cause ID theft—and individuals should be notified about the breach so that they can take steps to protect themselves.

If you have a security breach that puts people at real risk of identity theft, you should consider notifying them even if you are not within the scope of this law.

Compliance Basics

The ability to collect and use personal information is essential to any information-driven economy. Organizations rely on information collected from prospective and existing customers, suppliers, and government agencies to further many legitimate commercial purposes—and the ability to supplement and enhance the data with both experiential and third-party information is essential. These data sets are the infrastructure of our personalized, customer relationship management-driven systems, and the information is used to promote business, target and improve products and services, collect debts, screen customers and employees, and prevent fraud and other crimes. These data sets are also shared with a multitude of data processors, outsourced service providers, affiliates, business partners and government agencies. However, given the proliferation of technologies which permit the storage and manipulation of vast quantities of personal data, and the ever-growing threat of identity theft, individuals, privacy advocates, and policy makers are concerned about the potential for misuse of information.

Many information-dependent companies struggle to understand and quantify the harms related to the actual or perceived loss of privacy or security by customers. Privacy and security are often not even defined in a way that anticipates consumer concerns and objections. Security is objective, limiting access of information to authorized users and processes. Privacy is subjective, the use of information in ways that are appropriate, given the context.

Because privacy is subjective, even the sensitivity of the personal data collected is oftentimes not definitive. Intellectually, it is reasonable to assert that it is a greater privacy violation to reveal confidential or embarrassing information about an individual than it is to reveal publicly-known facts about the individual. However, many individuals believe that they have a privacy interest in public record information about themselves as well as in their names and addresses. In addition, the use of any data for targeted marketing purposes without adequate disclosure is almost always perceived as a privacy violation by individuals. Further, a security breach, such as inappropriate disclosure of information or an identity theft incident, is also perceived by consumers as a privacy issue. The bottom line: privacy violations are whatever individuals think they are.

Managing the Four Privacy and Security Risks

There are four risks that every organization must manage around information use, and the most effective organizations manage all of these risks in a holistic manner. These risks are:

1. *Legal Compliance.* The organization must comply with all applicable laws—state, federal and international—regarding its use of information. These include traditional privacy and data protection laws as well as new security standards, all of the laws regulating advertising, government reporting, and all other laws that touch information. The company must also comply with its contractual commitments.

2. *Reputation.* The organization must protect its reputation as a trusted institution with respected brands. The company must also protect all of its relationships with its non-consumer stakeholders, including its employees, independent agents, brokers or dealers, investors, vendors, regulators and business partners. The company must understand the nuances of consumer, media and government relations.

3. *Investment.* The organization must receive the proper return on the investments that are made in communications and information technology, including CRM systems and other data management technology. If the company invests in businesses, products or corporate initiatives that are information-dependent, the company must understand the return on investment needs for these endeavors as well. The company must understand the real revenue implications of its corporate information assets.

4. *Reticence.* The organization must use information as robustly as its competitors; it must use information to retain, add and up-sell customers by delivering the right offer at the right time to the right individuals. Appropriate corporate growth, leveraging the company's informational assets, is essential to success.

Balancing these four risks requires trade-offs to be made. One can minimize legal compliance and reputation risks by using information only in the most conservative ways, but this strategy creates too much reticence risk. If a company is meek, it leaves too much money on the proverbial table because of opportunities that are not taken. It does not provide investors or employees with appropriate growth, and it is not successful in the long term.

The same tradeoffs exist on the security side. A company can require multiple authentication steps to help ensure that it knows its customers. If these added steps increase the transaction times, however, the customer may reject the transaction in favor of a more efficient vendor. Similarly, consumers may be comfortable being asked to show a photo ID to complete a credit transaction, but they may balk at a request for biometric identity confirmation, such as fingerprint. They may believe that the added security is too invasive of their privacy.

The task of finding the right balance for an organization is typically given to a Chief Privacy Officer or other privacy manager. Effective privacy officers rely on a combination of good instincts and sound processes to achieve the right risk balance. For example, a Chief Privacy Officer will rely on processes to ensure that proposed data uses are consistent with legal requirements and expectations. They weigh investment plans against the probability of future changed expectations. They then build consensus around the results of the processes, offering solutions that meet corporate goals in a manner consistent with the corporate culture.

A Sensible Approach to Fair Information Practices

The secret for information industry and information-dependent companies is to develop balanced information management programs. This program serves as a framework that enables companies to achieve a variety of information policy goals ranging from development of privacy and security policies to compliance with U.S. or international data protection laws. It also provides a foundation for achieving other company goals, such as guiding marketing programs and enabling the company to anticipate business threats, the requirements of new laws, and consumer and policy-maker concerns.

Many companies have developed a number of privacy and security policies, but the polices are typically created in an *ad hoc* or as needed manner—for example, most companies have a "privacy policy" on their Web sites or a formal program to comply with the HIPAA requirements for the employee health plan. This *ad hoc* approach solves short term problems, but does not provide the company with the holistic benefits that a formal information management program can offer.

A better approach is for each organization to develop a list of specific information policy objectives, then create a holistic, enterprise-wide set of business/policy standards and tools that enable the company to realize the defined objectives. This holistic approach allows the company to generate value for the company from personal information while maintaining as much flexibility within the organization for use and distribution of data as is needed for the company to achieve both short and long term business goals. This approach also allows the company to make more informed decisions about the potential risks and returns on its investments in infrastructure technologies that facilitate communication, information management and customer relationship management. Most importantly, this approach allows the company to articulate its information policy values and link these values to the ultimate corporate goal of building trust with company stakeholders.

By imposing a formal process approach on procedure development, companies can preserve business flexibility and maximize the success of the information management program. Companies can also anticipate future changes both in the regulatory environment and in their business needs. Additionally, by considering all of the issues related to the data collected and used by the company, the company is well-positioned to leverage its program to build consumer and business partner trust. Many companies are discovering that they can gain real top and bottom-line revenue advantages by being good corporate citizens who are privacy-sensitive and who can intelligently address any questions about their information management practices.

Key Components of an Information Management Program

Both risk management and good corporate citizenship require that organizations develop policies for the appropriate collection and use of personal information. Depending on the organization's business, these polices may include such things as maintaining opt out lists for direct marketing, developing appropriate security for customer financial or medical records, executing proper contracts to authorize international data flows, or publishing an online privacy notice if data are collected over the Internet.

Corporate privacy leaders must assist their organizations in thinking about privacy policy development in a formal, objective way, meeting policy goals as well as preserving business flexibility. Privacy executives must also understand and anticipate future changes both in the regulatory environment and in their companies' business needs. To achieve these objectives, companies should consider four distinct tasks.

Figure Three: Steps for Information Management (source: IAPP)

Information Management — Four Basic Steps

1

Discover
- Issue identification & self-assessment
- Determination of best practices

2

Build
- Procedure development & verification
- Full implementation

3

Communicate
- Documentation
- Education

4

Evolve
- Affirmation and monitoring
- Adaptation

Phase 1: Discover

Before you can begin to draft a privacy policy, you must first consider the company's informational goals and corporate culture. What laws regulate the company's collection or use of information? Does the company want to be able to use information as aggressively as possible? Does the company want to limit its use of information to try to achieve a competitive advantage as a privacy-sensitive leader? Does the company's executive management or shareholders have privacy issues that should be considered? How do the company's information policy objectives mesh with those of its competitors, customers and business partners? The answers to these questions, can begin to help an organization define its core information policy goals. These goals serve as the foundation upon which the company's polices are built.

In addition to the myriad of state, federal and international laws that regulate the collection, use and/or disclosure of personal information, many industry groups have promulgated self-regulatory guidelines, some of which are mandatory for members of the specific industry group. For example, the Direct Marketing Association ("DMA") requires its members to comply with the provisions of the DMA's "Privacy Promise." Other "mandatory" codes of fair information practices have been adopted by the Software and Information Industry Association, the Online Privacy Alliance, and the online seal providers TRUSTe™ and BBBOnline™.

In the world of e-commerce, the Federal Trade Commission has been actively and aggressively pursuing companies that post privacy policies and then do not comply with their posted policy. The FTC initiates these actions under Section 5 of the Federal Trade Commission Act, which prohibits unfair and deceptive trade practices. Similarly, several of the state attorneys general have initiated enforcement activities against companies that breach promises made to consumers in privacy policies. Accordingly, it is essential that, to the extent you advise your company on privacy policies, you make it clear to your management team that failure to comply with your posted privacy policies is a deceptive trade practice actionable by the FTC and other state and federal authorities.

In order to provide useful advice to your organization regarding privacy, it is essential that you understand all of the company's actual practices with regard to personal data as well as what its goals are with respect to the use of the personal data that it has collected. The success of this exercise hinges on asking the right people the right questions. The successful privacy professional forges honest and open relationships with individuals in all departments and at all levels. For example, the privacy professional should have regular dialogue with the individuals responsible for legal compliance, customer service, marketing, IT, and sales to determine if the company's current practices (and future goals) are clearly understood. The leader should also communicate regularly with the individuals who implement the policies and procedures to help ensure that the policies are properly adopted and that the policies address all of the questions that company personnel face.

Phase 2: Build

Once you understand your company's current practices and goals, you can help your company find the best way to address consumer expectations while meeting its business goals. By undertaking a formal balancing exercise, a company can realize its information policy objectives while maintaining flexibility within its organization for use and distribution of data as is needed for the company to achieve both short and long term business goals.

Additionally, by considering all of the issues related to the data collected and used by the company, the company will be well-positioned to leverage its program to build consumer and business partner trust.

Phase 3: Communicate

Once your company has developed and implemented an information management program, it is essential that you communicate the elements of the program to internal and external audiences. Internal audiences must be trained on the procedures and processes that are established, and individuals must be accountable for complying with the company's program. More importantly, the company's information policy values need to be shared with all company decision-makers and consumer-facing employees, so that they are able to use these values to shape the messages given to the company's customers and other stakeholders.

Consumer education is also critical. The primary goal of a written privacy statement is to educate consumers honestly about the actual practices of the company. The policy must accurately reflect the company's practices, and it must not mislead consumers, even by omission. A secondary goal of the privacy statement is to provide a basis for accountability of the organization with respect to its practices. We recommend that companies adopt a layered privacy notice approach—placing a template-based, standardized form privacy notice on top of a longer, more detailed statement of privacy and security practices.

With regard to all privacy statements, there is a good deal of consensus as to what types of organizational practices a privacy policy must address. At minimum, a privacy statement must include a clear notice as to what data are being collected by the organization and notice as to the intended uses and recipients of the data. Additionally, companies should inform consumers about what choices (if any) the individual has with respect to the intended uses of the data. If the data are to be used for direct marketing purposes or are otherwise shared with non-affiliated companies, companies are generally expected to offer individuals the ability to opt out of having the data used in these ways. Finally, the notice should include contact information for the company.

Phase 4: Evolve

Finally, in order to help ensure continued compliance with the company's policies and procedures (and to help anticipate when revisions to the policies are needed), each company should initiate an ongoing education-affirmation cycle. To do this, the company would define and implement a schedule of periodic reviews of the policies, complete with employee training, and legislative monitoring (and advocacy, if appropriate). The goals of the education-affirmation cycle are to verify compliance with your company's published procedures and to position the company to proactively respond with education to any problematic legislative proposals and/or media events.

Conclusion

Privacy professionals must assist their organizations in thinking about privacy and security policy development in a formal, objective way that respects the relevant laws in the jurisdictions in which they operate. Successful privacy professionals must also understand and anticipate future changes both in the regulatory environment and in their organization's business needs. In order to do this, privacy professionals must be conversant in all of the business, legal, economic, social and political factors that may be relevant to the organization's situation—including how these many factors continue to evolve around the world.

By imposing a formal process approach on procedure development, organizations can maximize the success of the information management program because the structure of the program will permit the organizations to anticipate future changes both in the regulatory environment and in their business needs. Additionally, an organization can use a well-designed information policy program to develop consumer and business partner trust, and to make better investment decisions about technology infrastructure, resulting in top and bottom-line revenue advantages for the organization.

Chapter Three

WORKPLACE PRIVACY

Introduction and Learning Objectives

Privacy issues in the workplace arise before employment, during employment, and after the employment relationship ends. Each country (and, increasingly, each state, province or nation within a region) addresses these issues differently.

The laws of the United States provide comparatively fewer protections for employees than European nations', which have comprehensive data protection laws and Works Council consultation rules in place today. However, a few U.S. laws are, in some senses, stricter than their European counterparts—such as U.S. state laws requiring disclosure of security breach incidents.

Given the multiple schemes of privacy law in force today around the world, employee privacy remains a complicated issue for global employers. Even a U.S.-based employer must be cognizant of the legal obligations inherent in transferring or sharing employee data with third parties that are located outside of the U.S.

"Workplace Privacy" focuses on information management within the U.S. workplace—from employee hiring and management to termination or departure. The chapter also addresses the privacy implications of employee evaluation, testing and monitoring as well as the handling and processing of employee personal information in jurisdictions within and outside of the U.S. It examines the relevant workplace privacy laws, policies and practices in use today within the U.S. and around the world.

The CIPP will understand:

- The privacy concerns around human resources management including information outsourcing, employee records management and document retention and destruction;

- The regulatory and enforcement powers of the U.S. Federal Trade Commission ("FTC"), U.S. Equal Employment Opportunity Commission ("EEOC"), and U.S. state labor relations boards as well as the European Union Works Councils;

- The legal framework around employee screening, hiring, evaluation, and testing; and,

- International guidelines for employee privacy from Canada and Europe to Latin America and the Asia Pacific region.

U.S. Employment Privacy Basics

In general, the United States' legal system gives more rights to employers than employees, and imposes some obligations on employers regarding the workplace environment that motivates employers to more aggressively monitor, investigate and control their employees. In the U.S., security concerns still largely outweigh employees' rights. Continuous and multi-dimensional employee monitoring is allowed under the U.S. scheme. Frequently, aggressive background checks by employers are required by law.

Under U.S. privacy laws, employee expectations of privacy are limited, particularly for electronic systems where the employer provides notice to the employees that they have no reasonable expectation of privacy.

Even though almost every labor law in the United States mandates some data collection or management practice, employees do get some limited protection from federal and state laws. These laws require and prohibit specific information handling practices at all stages of the employment relationship. Often, the state laws afford stronger employee privacy protection than federal laws.

U.S Laws Protecting Employee Privacy

Federal Laws

The United States has several federal laws that prohibit discrimination, and therefore afford employees some privacy protection by limiting inquiries. These laws include:

- *The Civil Rights Act of 1964*—Bars discrimination due to race, color, religion, sex, and national origin;[227]

- *The Pregnancy Discrimination Act*—Bars discrimination due to pregnancy, childbirth, and related medical conditions;[228]

- *The Americans with Disabilities Act*—Bars discrimination against qualified individuals with disabilities;[229]

- *The Age Discrimination Act*—Bars discrimination against individuals over 40 years of age; and,

- *The Equal Pay Act of 1963*[230]—Bars gender-based wage discrimination.[231]

The United States also has several federal laws that regulate employee benefits management. Although these laws often mandate collection of employee medical information, they do offer limited privacy protection and impose some restrictions on the use of and security of the data. These laws include:

- *The Health Insurance Portability and Accountability Act of 1996 ("HIPAA")* — Privacy and security rules that regulate "protected health information" for self-funded health plans;[232]

- *The Consolidated Omnibus Budget Reconciliation Act ("COBRA")*—Requires qualified health plans to provide continuous coverage after termination to certain beneficiaries;[233]

- *The Employee Retirement Income Security Act ("ERISA")*—Ensures that employee benefits programs are created fairly and administered properly; and,

- *The Family and Medical Leave Act ("FMLA")*[234]—Entitles certain employees to leave in the event of birth or illness of self or a family member.[235]

Other federal laws that have privacy implications are those that regulate data collection and record-keeping. These laws include:

- *The Fair Credit Reporting Act ("FCRA")*—Regulates the use of "consumer reports" obtained from "consumer reporting agencies" in reference checking and background checks of employees;[236]

- *The Fair Labor Standards Act ("FLSA")*—Establishes minimum wage and sets standards for fair pay;[237]

- *The Occupational Safety and Health Act ("OSHA")*—Regulates workplace safety;[238]

- *The Whistleblower Protection Act*—Protects federal employees and applicants for employment who claim to have been subjected to personnel actions because of whistleblowing activities;[239]

- *The National Labor Relations Act ("NLRA")*—Sets standards for collective bargaining;[240]

- *The Immigration and Reform Control Act ("IRCA")*—Requires employment eligibility verification;[241]

- *The Privacy Act of 1974*—Affects federal employers only; requires privacy notices and limited collection of data;[242] and,

• *The 4th Amendment of the United States Constitution*—Affects federal employers only; limits the government's ability to conduct searches and seizures.[243]

State Laws

U.S. state laws also provide some privacy protections to employees. Many state constitutions have a right to privacy that applies to state government employees. Some states, including California, have extended this protection to employees of private employers.[244]

Specific state statutes give protection to employees, such as prohibition of marital status discrimination,[245] limits on employers' abilities to give drug and polygraph tests, and specific prohibitions on inquiries regarding prospective employees, such as inquiring into whether a worker has ever filed a claim for worker's compensation benefits.[246]

State laws also give protection to employees through common law torts. Employers can be sued for the tort of "invasion of privacy" which includes four distinct injuries:

1. "intrusion upon seclusion,"
2. "appropriation of likeness,"
3. "public disclosure of private facts," and,
4. "false light publicity."

Regulatory Bodies that Protect Employee Privacy

U.S. employees are also protected by several government organizations that include the U.S. Department of Labor, the U.S. Equal Employment Opportunity Commission ("EEOC"), the U.S. Federal Trade Commission ("FTC"), state departments of labor, and the U.S. National Labor Relations Board ("NLRB").

The Department of Labor oversees "the welfare of the job seekers, wage earners, and retirees of the United States by improving their working conditions, advancing their opportunities for profitable employment, protecting their retirement and health care benefits, helping employers find workers, strengthening free collective bargaining, and tracking changes in employment, prices, and other national economic measurements."[247] To achieve this mission, the Department administers a variety of federal laws including, but not limited to, the Fair Labor Standards Act ("FLSA"), the Occupational Safety and Health Act ("OSHA"), and the Employee Retirement Income Security Act ("ERISA").

The Equal Employment Opportunity Commission ("EEOC") works to prevent discrimination in the workplace. The EEOC oversees many laws including Title VII of the Civil Rights Act, the Age Discrimination in Employment Act of 1967 ("ADEA"), and Titles I and V of the Americans with Disabilities Act of 1990 ("ADA").

The Federal Trade Commission ("FTC") regulates the free market. To do this, the FTC administers several federal laws including the Fair Credit Reporting Act, which limits employers' ability to receive an employee's or applicant's credit report, driving records, criminal records and other "consumer reports" obtained from a "consumer reporting agency."[248]

U.S. State Department of Labor oversees state labor laws. These laws include state minimum wage laws and state minor labor laws. This Department also administers state unemployment insurance programs and employee rehabilitation programs. Some subdivisions also conduct safety inspections of worker conditions.

The National Labor Relations Board administers the National Labor Relations Act. The Board conducts elections to determine if employees want union representation and investigates and remedies unfair labor practices by employers and unions.

Workplace Privacy Case Study:
Eli Lilly

The Eli Lilly case serves to illustrate the legal exposure an organization will face as the result of an employee's mishandling of personal information. The FTC held the company liable both under the grounds of unfair and deceptive trade practices as well as for failing to uphold its own stated organizational security standards. Importantly, the FTC maintained that it was the company's obligation to offer effective privacy training to all employees so that responsible information management practices could be effectively maintained.

Facts and Allegations
Eli Lilly and Company, a large U.S.-based pharmaceutical company, offered consumers an online reminder service called the "Medi-messenger." This service sent automated, personalized messages to registered consumers via electronic email that reminded them to take or refill their depression medications as individually prescribed.

Using a new software program, an Eli Lilly employee inadvertently sent an email notice to all subscribers of the Medi-messenger service. This notice contained (for all to see) the email addresses of all 669 individuals who were registered to the service at that time.

The FTC complaint alleged that Eli Lilly failed to implement or maintain reasonable and appropriate measures to protect consumer information including a failure to properly train employees, provide oversight, and implement appropriate checks and controls.

Privacy and Security Promises

Eli Lilly had made the following representations regarding its privacy and security measures:

1. "Our Websites have security measures in place, including the use of industry standard secure socket layer encryption, to protect the confidentiality of Your Information"

2. "Eli Lilly and Company respect the privacy of visitors to its Websites and we feel it is important to maintain our guests privacy as they take advantage of this resource. As a result, we have developed this privacy code."

3. "Any and all uses would comply with applicable laws."

FTC Consent Agreement with Eli Lilly

1. Bar on Misrepresentation: Eli Lilly shall not misrepresent the extent to which it maintains and protects the privacy or confidentiality of the collected personal information.

2. Security Program: Eli Lilly shall establish and maintain a security program for the protection of its collected personally identifiable information.

3. Requirements of Security Program: The program shall include:
   a. Designation of personnel to coordinate and oversee the program;
   b. Identification of risks to the security, confidentiality and integrity of personal information;
   c. An annual written review conducted by qualified persons to evaluate the effectiveness of the program and recommended changes; and,
   d. Adjustments to the program based on the reviews, monitoring or any material changes in operations of Eli Lilly that affect the security program.

4. Third Party Audit: Not specified in the FTC order. However, Eli Lilly is required to have its annual internal written review examined and certified by an independent auditor. Additionally, per the multi-state voluntary assurance agreement with certain state attorneys general, Eli Lilly must undergo five annual, independent compliance reviews and report the findings of those reviews to the states.

5. Maintenance of Relevant Documents: For a period of five years, Eli Lilly shall provide (upon request):
   a. A copy of each representation made to consumers regarding the collection, use and security of collected information;
   b. All plans, reports or other materials relating to, Eli Lilly's compliance with the order; and,
   c. Any document that contradicts, qualifies or questions, Eli Lilly's compliance with the order.

6. Delivery of Order: Eli Lilly shall deliver to each current and future director, employee, agent or representative a copy of the FTC order.

7. Reporting: Eli Lilly shall notify the FTC of any change which may affect its compliance with the order. Within 120 days after service of the order and thereafter as requested, file a report with the FTC setting forth Eli Lilly's compliance with the order.

Duration of the FTC Order and Penalties for Violations
Except as otherwise indicated in the final order, the final order terminates in 20 years. Each violation of the final order may result in a civil penalty of $11,000.

Fine Imposed
None

International Laws Protecting Employee Privacy

Europe

The European Union's legal system gives more privacy rights to employees than in existence today across the United States. Under the E.U. system, privacy concerns generally predominate over competing concerns such as workplace safety and security, monitoring legal compliance by individual employees, and efficient business practices. Monitoring is restricted to a scope that has been disclosed in detail to the employees and is tailored to be "proportionate" to the harms that the employer is seeking to prevent. Only limited background checks are permitted. Employees across the European Union have fairly broad privacy expectations and rights.

E.U. Directives Applying to HR Data. The European Union can make a variety of different legislative statements including regulations, opinions, and directives. A European Union directive is the collective decision made by the member states, acting through their national Government Ministers in the Council of the European Union and Parliament. Directives themselves do not act as enforceable laws. Instead, they require member states to adopt laws that comply with the directive.[249]

Employee data are protected by a variety of directives. Under the directives, employers must comply with requirements for registration and processing, such as notice and choice, data transfers of employee data are heavily restricted, and there are even more stringent rules for sensitive data.

The most prominent directive in employee data protection is Directive 95/46/EC on the Protection of Individuals With Regard to the Processing of Personal Data and on the

Free Movement of Such Data. This directive requires each member state to pass a law that "protect[s] the fundamental rights and freedoms of natural persons, and in particular their right to privacy with respect to the processing of personal data."[250] This directive has a long reach in that it restricts corporations based in Europe, but it also applies to corporations that are not based in Europe but which collect personal data there. Therefore, multinational corporations based in the United States are frequently forced to comply with this directive. Also, due to a provision in the directive that prohibits transfers of personal data to jurisdictions that have "inadequate" privacy laws (which includes most non-E.U. jurisdictions) unless the party exporting the data has put in place "adequate protections" through contracts with the importing party or some other means, the rules of the directive are often extended to data processing outside the E.U.

E.U. Works Councils. On September 22, 1994, legislation was adopted by the European Union requiring the establishment of European Works Councils ("EWC"s) as mandated by the European Works Council Directive. This directive was adopted after a twenty-year drive to compel multinational companies to disclose information and to consult with their employees on a Europe-wide basis.[251] An EWC is a council that transmits information from management to employees. Under this system, it is the company's obligation to supply relevant information to its employees.[252] The information will then be communicated to all workers in all participating states.

EWCs are mandatory for certain corporations. They must be established and funded by the central management of a "community-scale undertaking." A "community-scale undertaking" is a company with at least 1000 employees within the participating states, and with at least 150 employees in each of two or more participating states.

This directive does not affect only the corporations based within the European Union. The EWC directive applies to any companies that operate in member nations, regardless of whether the central management is inside or outside the member nations. Therefore, the establishment of EWCs affects American companies that have employees in Europe.[253]

E.U. Collective Bargaining on Privacy Issues. Collective bargaining remains separate and distinct in each European country, despite the efforts of the European Union to encourage dialogue on a continental level.[254] In general, collective bargaining is more highly regulated on mainland Europe than in Britain and Ireland. Collective bargaining decisions throughout Europe apply to employees who are not unionized.

The European Trade Union Confederation ("ETUC") is working to make collective bargaining occur continentally rather than nationally. With the advent of the Euro, the ETUC is hopeful that bargaining will move in this direction.[255]

Canada

As described in Chapter Two, Canada has an E.U.-style privacy law in the *Personal Information Protection and Electronic Documents Act ("PIPEDA")*. However, this federal law provides no protection for business contact information, limited protection for employee data, and no special prohibition whatsoever on the export of employee data. Thus, employee protections are rather thin in Canadian jurisdictions—a closer parallel to the U.S. regulatory approach to workplace privacy rather than the European regime.

Asia Pacific

Japan's federal privacy law covers all employee data and requires employee consent for many types of sharing and processing, but does not have restrictions on cross border transfer. However, other countries in the Asia Pacific region with existing privacy laws (such as Hong Kong, Australia and New Zealand) have taken a more business-friendly approach, with lots of "reasonableness standards" and exceptions built into the rules, including many exceptions that apply to employee information. As discussed in Chapter Two, the Asia Pacific Economic Cooperation ("APEC") has published a "Privacy Framework" that its members have been encouraged to adopt, and it is significantly less strict than the European approach in many respects.[256]

Latin America

Latin American countries have privacy schemes that are more similar to Europe's than to the United States'. Argentina has a European-style privacy law, as it is influenced by the law of Spain, and Spain is also promoting this approach in other "Ibero-American" countries, including Colombia, Costa Rica, El Salvador, Mexico, Nicaragua, Uruguay, and Venezuela.

Workforce Hiring Considerations

Employers today consider more than whether a job candidate is simply qualified for an employment opportunity. With increasing frequency, employers are making extensive personal inquiries—whether through application forms, pre-hiring interviews, candidate testing exercises or background checks—to verify an applicant's ability to function in the working environment as well as to ensure the safety and security of existing workers. Some view these checks as invasive while others have grown accustomed to them or expect to undergo such scrutiny.

Employers in the United States and Europe require different levels of screening and are under different legal restrictions as to what they can ask, test, and investigate in a candidate for employment.

United States

Applicants for jobs in the United States often encounter extensive application forms and interviews and thorough background checks. There are several reasons why American employers are so careful in hiring employees. First and foremost, the marked rise in negligent hiring lawsuits. The threat of liability makes employers more cautious in hiring employees. Under this cause of action, the employer is liable for damages caused by the employee to other employees when it should have known of the employee's propensity to cause this type of damage.

Current events have stimulated an increase in applicant screening activities in the U.S. workplace. For example:

- Recent rises in child abuse and child abductions have led to new laws in almost every state requiring criminal background checks for people who work with children.

- The terrorist attacks of September 11, 2001 have resulted in heightened needs for security and stricter identity-verification requirements.

- Business governance scandals in the U.S. (such as Enron, Worldcom, Global Crossing, Adelphia and others) have forced corporate executives, officers, and directors to face a higher degree of scrutiny, so there are more thorough background checks on people in positions of power.[257]

These current events have led to an increase in laws mandating background checks. There are currently over 165 statutes in 39 states that require some form of employment-related background investigation.

Many states require criminal background checks by law for certain professions. Typically, anyone who works with the elderly, children, or the disabled must undergo applicant screening. Furthermore, the federal National Child Protection Act authorizes state officials to access the FBI's National Crime Information Center database for some positions that work with children. Also, many state and federal government jobs require rigorous background checks to obtain a security clearance.[258] Other groups that are targeted in background checks include emergency medical service personnel, county coroners, humane society investigators, euthanasia technicians in animal shelters, bus and truck drivers, athletic trainers, in-home repair services, firefighters, gaming industry employees, real estate brokers, and information technology workers.

There is also an increase in false or inflated information by job applicants. Estimates indicate that 30-40% of all job applicants and resumes have some false or inflated facts. These reports make employers wary to accept an applicant's word without some sort of background check.

Finally, the information age itself may have led employers to increase the extent of background checks. The availability of computer databases and the low cost have made it easier for employers to conduct background checks on its employees, and have also made it more reasonable to expect employers to do this type of checking to avoid liability for negligent hiring.

The following lists typical employer inquiries and what may and may not be inquired into during pre-hire applicant screening (these rules are a composite of various U.S. state and federal restrictions):

• *Name and Address*. An employer generally may ask for the applicant's name and contact information. An employer may also ask whether the applicant has worked under a different name and the name by which the applicant is known to his references. An employer may not ask about an applicant's name before it was changed by court order or marriage. An employer is also barred from asking about a name in a way that would divulge marital status, lineage, ancestry, or national origin. An employer may not ask the names or relationships of people with whom the applicant resides. Finally, an employer may not ask the applicant if he/she owns or rents a home.

• *Age*. An employer may ask for a date of birth and require proof of age when it relates to a job requirement. However, an employer may not ask any questions that imply a preference for persons under the age of 40 years.

• *Height and Weight*. An employer may only ask about height and weight if the employer can show that all or substantially all employees who fail to meet a height or weight requirement would be unable to perform the job with reasonable safety and efficiency.

• *Marital Status, Spouse, Relatives, and Family.* An employer may ask the applicant to divulge the names of the applicant's relatives that are already employed by the company or a competitor. An employer may also ask whether the applicant can meet certain work schedules or if the applicant has previous commitments and responsibilities. Most other questions about family are not allowed, including questions as to whether the applicant has (or has had) a spouse, children or other dependents.

• *Pregnancy*. An employer may ask an applicant questions about intended duration of stay on the job or anticipated absences. However, these questions must be made to males and females alike. Employers may not inquire into pregnancy or medical history concerning pregnancy and related matters.

- **Disabilities**. An employer may ask an applicant whether the applicant is able to perform the essential functions of the job for which they are applying. An employer may not ask questions about the nature, severity, extent or, or treatment of a disability or illness, including mental illness. Employers also may not ask whether the applicant requires reasonable accommodations prior to an offer of employment. However, this question may be asked after the job is offered. Finally, an employer may not ask whether the applicant has applied for or received worker's compensation.

- **Citizenship and National Identity.** An employer may ask if the applicant has the ability to read, write, and speak foreign languages when it relates to the job requirements. An employer may also ask whether the applicant is prevented from lawfully working in the United States because of visa or immigration status. Finally, an employer may ask whether the applicant can provide proof of a legal right to work in the country after being hired. An employer may not ask any questions about national origin, lineage, ancestry, descent, birthplace, native language, or the applicant's spouse or family. An employer may not ask whether the applicant is a citizen. Finally, the employer may not require the applicant to present a birth certificate, naturalization certificate, or a baptismal certificate before the job is offered.

- **Military Service and Organizations**. An employer may ask questions concerning education, training, or work experience in the armed forces of the United States. An employer may ask questions about membership in organizations, except for when the organization indicates race, color, creed, gender, marital status, religion, or national origin of the applicant. An employer may not ask about military experience outside of the United States or the type or condition of the applicant's military discharge, whether in the United States or outside. An employer also may not require that the applicant list all organizations that he/she belongs to.

- **Gender, Race, Religion**. An employer may not ask any questions concerning these topics. An employer may not ask questions concerning the color of skin, hair, and eyes. An employer may not ask questions concerning church memberships or religious holidays observed.

- **Photographs**. An employer should not request an applicant to submit their photograph before making an offer of employment, even if the submission would be voluntary, because it may appear to be asking for information about one of the prohibited issues that a photograph may reveal. However, an employer may request a photograph for identification purposes after the offer is made. The posting of photographs on public Web sites or internal intranet sites should only be done with employee consent.

• **_Arrests and Convictions._** An employer may ask an applicant about convictions within the last 10 years for crimes involving behavior that would adversely affect job performance. An employer may not make any other inquiries about criminal convictions. Employers also may not ask about arrests that were not followed by a conviction. However, there are a few exemptions to this for organizations that provide care for vulnerable groups such as children, the mentally ill, and other industries such as financial services.

• **_Alcohol and Drug Use._** An employer may ask questions about current illegal drug use. An employer may also ask questions about past illegal use of drugs and alcohol use, as long as the questions are not with the intent to elicit information about a disability such as addiction. An employer may not ask questions about legal drug use, questions about past addictions to drugs, legal or illegal, and the treatments received. An employer may not ask any questions about alcoholism or treatments received.

• **_References and Emergency Contact Information._** An employer may ask who referred the applicant to the employer and the names or persons willing to provide professional or character references. An employer may also ask the name and address of the person to be contacted in case of an emergency. An employer may not ask questions about former employers or acquaintances which elicit information about the applicant's race, creed, color, national origin, ancestry, physical handicap, medical condition, marital status, age, or sex. An employer also may not ask any questions about the relationship of the emergency contact to the applicant. An employer may not require that the emergency contact be a relative to the applicant.

FCRA Restrictions on Background Checks

The Fair Credit Reporting Act ("FCRA") imposes conditions on the obtaining and use by employers of job applicants' and employees' credit reports and other "consumer reports" from a "consumer reporting agency." A "Consumer reporting agency" includes any organization that regularly engages in assembling or evaluating consumer credit information or other information on consumers for the purpose of furnishing of consumer reports to third parties for a fee.[259] Under FCRA, "consumer reports" include all written, oral, or other communications bearing on the consumer's credit-worthiness, credit standing, credit capacity, character, general reputation, personal characteristics, or mode of living. Examples of inquiries covered by FCRA include a credit report obtained from a credit bureau and a driving history report obtained from an information aggregator.

FCRA prohibits obtaining a consumer report unless a "permissible purpose" exists. Permissible purposes include "employment purposes" which in turn include:

1. Pre-employment screening for the purpose of evaluating the candidate for employment; and,

2. Determining if an existing employee qualifies for promotion, reassignment or retention. FCRA also permits obtaining an "investigative consumer report" (a report in which some of the information is obtained through interviews with neighbors, friends, associates or acquaintances of the employee) if a permissible purpose exists. However, to obtain the investigative consumer report under FCRA, employers must meet additional protective standards.

In order for an employer to be able to obtain or use these reports under FCRA, the employer must:

• Provide written notice to the applicant that it is obtaining a consumer report for employment purposes;

• Obtain written consent from the applicant;

• Obtain data only from a qualified consumer reporting agency, an entity that has taken steps to assure the accuracy and currency of the data;

• Certify to the consumer reporting agency that the employer has a permissible purpose and has obtained consent from the employee;

• Before taking an adverse action, such as denial of employment, provide notice to the applicant with a copy for the consumer report; and,

• After taking adverse action, provide additional notice.

If there is non-compliance with the requirements, there are civil and criminal penalties that can be imposed on the employer.

U.S. State Law Counterparts to FCRA

State law versions of FCRA are often even more stringent. The *California Investigative Consumer Reporting Agencies Act* ("ICRA")[260] is quite similar to FCRA, but it has some additional requirements. Under ICRA, applicants and employees can "check the box" on the "notice and authorization form" to receive a copy of the report that the employer receives. However, in California, ICRA also requires that if the employer plans on taking adverse action on the basis of the report, the applicant must receive a copy of the report, whether the employee waived the right or not. This exception does not apply to employees suspected of wrongdoing or misconduct.

Under FCRA, an employer can use the original written consent to get updates to the employee's credit report as needed. However, under ICRA, the employer must provide written consent every time that a background check is requested.

FCRA requires that an employer get written consent only if a third-party does the background check. If the employer does the background check itself (without use of a consumer reporting agency), it does not need written consent under FCRA. ICRA, on the other hand, requires that if the employer does an in-house background check, the employer is required to give the employee or applicant any public records resulting from such a check unless the employee waives that right. If the investigation results in an adverse action, then the employer must give the employee or applicant a copy of the public records whether he or she waived that right or not. If the employer conducts an in-house reference check, it does not have to give that information to the applicant or employee.[261]

A job applicant may undergo a variety of testing types. Employers can use personality and psychological tests, polygraph ("lie detector") tests, substance abuse tests, and genetic tests, but there are some restrictions on the use of these tests and their results.

Testing of Job Applicants

Several varieties and methods for testing and evaluating applicants for employment exist in the United States today. These include attitudinal and behavioral evaluations such as personality and psychological testing and polygraph ("lie detector") testing to more elaborate physiological and biological assessments such as drug/substance abuse testing and genetic testing. The legal basis for any such testing to occur in the United States relies largely upon the context of the test and its relevance to the job task required of the testing subject in the working environment.

Personality and Psychological Testing includes cognitive ability tests, honesty and integrity tests, and interest inventories. Three major types of psychological tests exist today:

1. "Performance" tests in which the test taker is asked to react to a real-life situation and is assessed in their response;

2. "Projective" tests in which the test taker is asked to interpret ambiguous stimuli and respond in an open-ended manner; and,

3. "Objective" tests in which the test taker is asked to answer a series of multiple choice or true-false questions.

An employer takes a significant risk when it issues a personality or psychological test to job applicants. When an employer issues one of these tests, it runs the risk of the test being construed as a "medical examination," which is barred under the Americans with Disabilities Act ("ADA"). Projective and objective tests are especially risky because they were originally created to identify clinical conditions such as depression and paranoia. If an employer issues a personality or psychological test, they also could be sued for a state law tort claim. These torts include a violation of anti-testing laws or an invasion of privacy or intrusion upon seclusion. Finally, if the employer publicizes or leaks the test results, it can be sued for such torts as public exposure of private facts, publicity placing a person in false light, defamation, and intentional infliction of emotional distress.

To avoid the risks of personality or psychological tests, an employer should not use these tests at all during pre-employment screening. If an employer wants to use these tests, it can minimize potential liability by issuing these tests after there has been an offer of employment. If the tests are used, the employer should make sure that five requirements are met: (1) the test only asks job-related questions, (2) the test does not ask overly-intrusive questions, (3) the test is professionally designed with established reliability and validity, (4) the test is administered and interpreted by trained professionals, and (5) the results are limited to those with a need to know and used only for purposes for which the test was designed and validated. The safest practice in using these tests is to obtain the employee's consent to the test and to the specific uses of the results prior to administering the test.

Polygraph Testing. **The Employee Polygraph Protection Act of 1988** bars employers from using polygraphs in many situations.[262] The Act applies to "lie detectors," or polygraphs and other devices which render a diagnostic opinion on a person's honesty. The Act prohibits employers from requiring, requesting, or even suggesting that a prospective or current employee take a lie detector test. It also prohibits employers from using, accepting, referring to, or inquiring about lie detector test results. It also prohibits employers from taking adverse action against an employee who refuses to take a test. Lie detector tests are allowed under a narrow exemption for investigations of economic loss or injury in certain industries. The Act requires that employers post the Act's essential provisions in a conspicuous place so that employees know of its existence. If the Act is violated, employers can be subject to a $10,000 fine as well as private law suits by individuals involved. Also, state laws are not preempted, so a tort action could be brought.

Substance Abuse Testing includes pre-employment screening, routine testing, reasonable suspicion testing, post-accident testing, random testing, and rehabilitation/post-rehabilitation testing. Generally, no drug testing program is immune from legal attack. However, some are more acceptable than others.

Pre-employment Drug Testing is generally allowed in the United States if it is not designed to identify legal use of drugs or past or present addiction to illegal drugs, which is barred under the Americans with Disabilities Act. Routine drug testing is generally allowed in the United States as well if the employees are notified at the time of hiring.

Random Drug Testing. The legality of random drug tests (e.g., tests conducted after the employment relationship is underway and at any point thereafter prior to departure or termination) remains very questionable in the United States except where required by law. Cases upholding random drug testing usually involve existing employees in specific, narrowly-defined jobs that are either part of a highly regulated industry where the employee has severely diminished expectations of privacy or the jobs are critical to public safety or the protection of life, property, or national security. If an employer uses random drug testing, the testing should be part of a systematic testing program that does not target certain employees or classes of employees.

Alcohol Testing. Tests for alcohol levels generally are subject to the same rules as drug tests. Generally, tests for blood alcohol levels are better indicators of current impairment than tests for drugs, which can give positive results when there are only trace amounts remaining from past drug use. Less invasive tests, such as a breathalyzer, are more likely to be approved than are more invasive tests, such as collecting a blood sample.

Reasonable Suspicion Testing is also generally acceptable in the United States to test as a condition of continued employment if there is a reasonable suspicion of drug or alcohol use based upon specific, objective facts (such as appearance, behavior, speech, and body odors) and rational inference from those facts. There does not, however, have to be probable cause to conduct reasonable suspicion drug testing.

Post-Accident Testing is generally allowed in the United States to test as a condition of continued employment if there is a reasonable suspicion that the employee involved in the accident was under the influence of drugs or alcohol.

Rehabilitation and Post-Rehabilitation Testing is commonly used as a condition of continued employment during or after rehabilitation of an individual for substance abuse. These tests are generally allowed in the United States. To minimize the company's risk, the employer should make the terms of the testing clear to the employee. The employer and the employee should enter into a contract addressing the terms of the rehabilitation and the testing.

Genetic Screening involves examining the genetic makeup of employees or job applicants for certain inherited characteristics. Generally, employers screen for a trait that makes an employee susceptible to illness if exposed to certain agents or to detect general inheritable conditions.

On the other hand, genetic monitoring involves periodic testing to identify modifications of genetic material, such as chromosome damage that may have resulted from hazardous workplace materials.

Genetic Testing has a high chance of being abused because it can be used to screen out individuals who are at a higher risk of disabilities under the Americans with Disabilities Act ("ADA"). Genetic testing could also be used to screen out individuals who are at a higher risk of developing non-occupational conditions that impact group insurance rates. There are several potential legal attacks for genetic testing including violations of the ADA, specific state anti-testing laws, and common law tort claims.

The best practice for employers is to use genetic testing only where it is really related to job performance or to benefit the employee (for example, to detect damage due to hazards). The employer should also obtain specific consent for the test from the employee, not just consent to a general medical exam, to avoid liability.

Restrictions Under ADA

Prior to the enactment of the *Americans with Disabilities Act ("ADA")*, employers routinely asked questions on job applications and during interviews about prior injuries and illnesses.[263] However, the ADA has banned these types of questions before an offer of employment has been extended.[264] The ADA also bars the use of genetic tests to discriminate against job applicants. If genetic tests are used as a reason to deny employment, it is considered illegal discrimination.[265]

After an offer of employment has been extended, however, the employer can require a physical examination and withdraw the offer of employment if two conditions are met: (1) the examination reveals that the employee's condition will prevent him or her from performing one or more of the "essential functions," and (2) no reasonable accommodation can be made that would allow the employee to perform the essential functions without undue hardship to the employer.[266] If a person can perform the essential functions of their job after reasonable accommodations have been made, an employer may not discriminate against that person under the ADA.[267] The ADA, however, does not bar employers from performing routine physical examinations or drug tests on employees.[268]

The ADA does not protect certain conditions that may disable a person. The ADA does not cover the use of drugs or alcohol, although it does cover recovered drug addicts and alcoholics.[269] It also does not cover kleptomania, pyromania, or compulsive gambling.[270] Finally, the Act protects against discrimination because of homosexuality, pedophilia, or gender identity disorders.[271]

Europe

In general, European laws restrict the collection of data for applicants and employees much more than the laws of the United States. In 1995, the European Union passed the *E.U. Data Protection Directive (95/46/EC).*[272] This law was developed to protect the privacy of applicants and employees and their personal data. When it was enacted, the directive was seen as the "most important international development in data protection in the last decade."[273]

As described in Chapter Two, the Directive's goal is to "protect the fundamental rights and freedoms of natural persons, and in particular their right to privacy with respect to the processing of personal data."[274] The Directive achieves this goal, in part, through limiting the amount of information that employers may collect about their job applicants and employees, and limiting the sharing and purposes of processing of the data collected.

The E.U. Directive bars employers from collecting and processing personal data from any person in the E.U., including job applicants, unless a notice is provided to the applicant prior to collecting the data that:

1. Identifies the "controller" of the data (the employer or other entity that will be controlling the use of the data);

2. Identifies the controller's representative, if any;

3. Identifies the intended recipients or categories of recipients of the data;

4. Describes the purposes of the processing for which the data are intended;

5. Discloses whether replies to the requests for data are obligatory or voluntary, as well as the possible consequences of failure to reply;

6. Discloses the fact that the candidate will have the right to access and rectify the data; and,

7. Discloses any data that will be collected from any source other than the candidate.[275]

The Directive also prohibits any processing of the data unless the applicant unambiguously given his consent,[276] unless an exception applies such as:

1. The processing is necessary for the performance of a contract to which the data subject is party or in order to take steps at the request of the data subject prior to entering into a contract; or,

2. The processing is necessary for compliance with a legal obligation to which the controller is subject; or,

3. The processing is necessary in order to protect the vital interests of the data subject; or,

4. The processing is necessary for the performance of a task carried out in the public interest or in the exercise of official authority vested in the controller or in a third party to whom the data are disclosed; or,

5. The processing is necessary for the purposes of the legitimate interests pursued by the controller or by the third party or parties to whom the data are disclosed, except where such interests are overridden by the interests for fundamental rights and freedoms of the data subject.

As a practical matter, these exceptions are unlikely to be deemed applicable in most situations and it will be safest to obtain consent from the applicant after giving him a detailed notice. The exception for "legal obligations" may be applicable if local labor laws require the collection and processing of certain data.

If the data about the applicant are "sensitive data," which include information that reveals racial or ethnic origin, political opinions, religious or philosophical beliefs, trade-union memberships, and data concerning health or sex life, the "explicit" consent of the applicant must be obtained (meaning that he must specifically know that this type of data is being collected and exactly how it will be used in order for the consent to be effective), unless one of a handful of narrowly construed exceptions applies:

1. The processing is necessary for the purposes of carrying out the obligations and specific rights of the controller in the field of employment law insofar as it is authorized by national law providing for adequate safeguards; or,

2. The processing is necessary to protect the vital interests of the data subject or of another person where the data subject is physically or legally incapable of giving his consent; or,

3. The processing is carried out in the course of its legitimate activities with appropriate guarantees by a foundation, association or any other non-profit-seeking body with a political, philosophical, religious or trade-union aim and on condition that the processing relates solely to the members of the body or to persons who have regular contact with it in connection with its purposes and that the data are not disclosed to a third party without the consent of the data subjects; or,

4. The processing relates to data which are manifestly made public by the data subject or are necessary for the establishment, exercise or defense of legal claims.[277]

The Directive also prohibits the transfer of the candidate's personal data to the U.S. or to any other country with privacy protections that have not been declared "adequate" by the European Commission,[278] unless the applicant has "unambiguously" consented to the transfer, or adequate protections have been put in place for the data by an approved method (such as a "model contract" between the exporting and importing entities, or implementation of Binding Corporate Rules (for transfers to the U.S.), or if the company importing the data to the U.S. has certified to the U.S. Dept of Commerce that it is meeting all of the requirements of the "Safe Harbor" program) or one a narrow list of exemptions applies, including the following:

1. The transfer is necessary for the performance of a contract between the data subject and the controller or the implementation of pre-contractual measures taken in response to the data subject's request; or,

2. The transfer is necessary for the conclusion or performance of a contract concluded in the interest of the data subject between the controller and a third party; or,

3. The transfer is necessary or legally required on important public interest grounds, or for the establishment, exercise or defense of legal claims; or,

4. The transfer is necessary in order to protect the vital interests of the data subject.[279]

Individual member states are empowered to provide by law that the applicant's consent is not an adequate basis for transfer, and in fact some Data Protection Authorities take a critical view of the effectiveness of consent obtained by a prospective employer from a job candidate (due to the leverage in the relationship), and an even more critical view on the effectiveness of consent obtained by a current employer from an employee.

Human Resources Data Management

Human resources ("HR") data management encompasses many different considerations including legal compliance with the many laws that regulate employee data and the employment relationship, protection of human resources data from unauthorized use and authorized misuse, proper documentation to manage any potential claims against the company or that the company may have against its employees, and compliance with other corporate policies including substantive training, workplace liability management, and document retention.

United States

Human resources professionals must consider reporting obligations to a variety of U.S. governmental organizations and must meet specific privacy obligations from laws such as the *Health Insurance Portability and Accountability Act ("HIPAA")* and the *Fair Credit Reporting Act ("FCRA")*, such as handling sensitive information in a way that maintains privacy.

In the United States, employee data are widely collected and openly used. Unlike the European Union, which restricts employee data collection and use, the United States encourages its corporations to keep records on their employees through several federal laws. Other United States laws require that this information be periodically reported to the government. As a result, organizations under U.S. jurisdiction have a variety of reporting obligations to various U.S. regulatory bodies including the Department of Labor, the Securities and Exchange Commission ("SEC") and the Equal Employment Opportunity Commission ("EEOC"), among others.

The U.S. Department of Labor oversees and enforces most of the federal employment laws. The laws include, but are not limited to, the Fair Labor Standards Act ("FLSA"), The Occupational Safety and Health Act ("OSHA"), and the Employee Retirement Income Security Act ("ERISA").[280] Many of these laws require that employers maintain employee records and, in some cases, report employee information to the Department of Labor.

The Fair Labor Standards Act ("FLSA") requires that all employers subject to the provisions of the Act make, keep, and preserve records of employees and of the wages, hours, and other conditions and practices of employment.[281] However, it is not required that these reports be submitted to the Department of Labor. The provision requiring reports be sent to the Secretary of Labor expired August 6, 1998.[282]

The Occupational Health and Safety Act ("OSHA") also requires that employers maintain records on work-related deaths, injuries, and illnesses other than those requiring only first-aid treatment.[283] Employers are required to make periodic reporting of this data to Occupational Safety and Health Administration ("OSHA").[284] Furthermore, employers are required to maintain records on employee exposure to potentially toxic or harmful agents.[285]

The Employee Retirement Income Security Act ("ERISA") requires that employers maintain records on employees with information regarding when his or her benefits will come due and what benefits will be due.[286] This information is available only to the employee.[287]

The Securities and Exchange Commission ("SEC") oversees and enforces many laws regarding the sale of securities.[288] These laws include the Securities Act of 1933, and the

Securities Exchange Act of 1934.[289] These Acts require that employers maintain records and report periodically to the SEC.

The Securities Act of 1933, otherwise known as the "truth in securities law," was created to provide investors with accurate financial and other information regarding the company and the sale of the company's securities and to prohibit fraud, misrepresentation, or deceit in the sale of securities.[290] The Act accomplishes these goals through mandatory registration of securities.[291] In the registration, the company must disclose: (1) a description of the company's properties and business, (2) a description of the security to be offered for sale, (3) information about the management of the company, and (4) financial statements certified by independent accountants.[292] Although these disclosures are invasive to corporate entities, very little employee data must be gathered or disclosed. However, data about the company's management must be disclosed to the SEC.

The Securities Exchange Act of 1934, among other things, requires public corporations to make periodic reports to the SEC.[293] Corporations with more than $10 million in assets whose securities are held by more than 500 owners are required to file annual reports and other periodic filings.[294] These reports are made public to investors through an online system known as EDGAR.[295] The Securities Exchange Act of 1934 also requires that corporations disclose materials and information used in soliciting shareholders' votes.[296] The Act requires that all information pertinent to the vote be disclosed to all shareholders.[297] The Securities Exchange Act of 1934 also requires that certain information be disclosed by a party trying to acquire more than 5% of a corporation through direct purchase or a tender offer.[298] Finally, the Securities Exchange Act of 1934 requires that exchanges, broker-dealers, clearing agencies, and transfer agents register with the SEC.[299] Registration requires that these market participants file disclosure documents and update them regularly.[300] These detailed registrations and filings require employers to keep detailed records and therefore, may require employers to invade employee privacy.

The Equal Employment Opportunity Commission ("EEOC") oversees a variety of laws including Title VII of the Civil Rights Act, and the Equal Pay Act of 1963.[301] These laws require employers to collect and report employee information to the EEOC.

Title VII of the Civil Rights Act requires that employers keep records relevant to the determination of whether unlawful discrimination has occurred or is being committed.[302] These records must be reported to the EEOC annually.[303] These records will contain employee information.

The Equal Pay Act of 1963 requires employers to make, keep, and preserve records of employees' wages, hours, and other conditions of employment.[304] The Act also requires employers to periodically report this information to the EEOC.[305]

Reporting Obligations Under HIPAA. The Health Insurance Portability and Accountability Act of 1996 ("HIPAA") applies to any "covered entity" such as a health care provider that conducts certain transactions in electronic form, like a health care clearinghouse, and/or a health plan.[306] However, health care plan sponsors are not considered covered entities under HIPAA within certain guidelines (below).

Employers must consider several human resources issues such as employee benefits programs and employee health information. The key HR obligations under HIPAA are that:

• Employers must require individual confidentiality/user agreements from all personnel with electronic access to protected health information ("PHI").[307]

• Employers must implement data access controls where feasible to limit access to protected health information. Employers must have discrete employee-by-employee authorization to access the information only when it relates to job duties.[308]

• Employers must implement a monitoring and auditing plan to detect unauthorized access and impose accountability. Enforcement of violations must be consistent.[309]

• Employers must have confidentiality of protected health information within the organization, with no spillover of information from one function to another. For example, HR departments cannot access clinical records created by the entity as a health care provider to make employment-related decisions.[310]

• Employers must have whistleblower exceptions for when there are certain external disclosures of personal health information for whistleblower reasons.[311]

HIPAA and "Hybrid Entities." Hybrid entities are a single legal entity that is a covered entity whose covered functions are not its primary functions.[312] Some examples of hybrid entities are a factory which has an employee health clinic and transmits protected health information in electronic form with a request for an insurance payment and a health center at an academic institution which transmits protected health information electronically in connection with claims requests.[313] The effect of the hybrid entity classification is that many non-health care enterprises are directly regulated by HIPAA as health care providers and must comply with the previously listed HR issues. In hybrid entities, the following considerations must be addressed:

• HIPAA applies only to the health care component of the organization, however, at times, it can be difficult deciding where the health care component starts and ends.[314]

• The organization must assure compliance by the covered health care component, but it is responsible for noncompliance elsewhere in the organization.[315]

• The corporation must install firewalls between covered components and the rest of the organization.[316]

HIPAA most commonly affects employers who are health care plan sponsors. Employers who are health care plan sponsors are not considered covered entities. However, a health care plan, governed by ERISA, which provides medical care is considered a covered entity if there are 50 or more employees or the plan is administered by a 3rd party administrator.[317] The group health plan is subject to the same requirements as any other health plan under HIPAA. The employer is not.

Frequently, employers must gain access to the protected health information held by the group health plan in order to obtain premium bids, and to modify, amend, or terminate the group health plan. To protect the health information, HIPAA requires that the group health plans bar employer-access to this information unless two specific requirements are met:

1. The plan documents specify permitted uses and disclosures that the employer can make of the information; and,

2. The employer certifies in writing that it accepts and will comply with nine limitations.[318] The nine limitations that the employer must make before it can gain access to the information are:

   a. Not to further use or disclose the information except as required by the plan documents or by law;

   b. Ensure that its agents and subcontractors will comply;

   c. Not to use or disclose the information for employment-related actions or decisions;

   d. Not to use or disclose the information in connection with any other benefit or employee benefit plan of the employer;

   e. Self-report any disclosure violations to the plan;

   f. Meet certain administrative requirements applicable to health plans;

   g. Take its internal practices, books, and records related to use and disclosure of personal health information received from the plan available to the Secretary for compliance review, and, where feasible, return or destroy all personal health information received from the plan when done with it, and maintain adequate separation between the group health plan and the employer.[319] The group health plan can rely on the employer's certification and disclose the information unless the health plan knows or should know that the employer cannot meet the limitations. This is especially important where the parties administering the plan are part of the employer's workforce because the plan will have knowledge of the deficiencies in many cases. If the group health care plan knows of a deficiency and still releases the information to the employer, the group health care plan has violated HIPAA.

FCRA and HR Decision-Making. The Fair Credit Reporting Act ("FCRA") requires that an employer must provide applicants and employees with notice that it intends to obtain a consumer report from an outside consumer reporting agency regarding the applicant or employee for employment-related purposes. FCRA also requires that the employer gain the applicant's or employee's authorization to obtain such a report.[320]

FCRA affects human resources departments when they need to conduct undercover investigations using outside private investigators for allegations of employee misconduct, such as sexual discrimination. According to an opinion letter issued for the Federal Trade Commission ("FTC") known as the "Vail Letter," the FTC stated that when an employer hired an outside organization like a private investigator or background research firm to conduct these investigations, the outside organization constituted a "consumer reporting agency" under the FCRA and any reports furnished to the employer by the outside organization were "investigative consumer reports." Therefore, an employer that received these reports had to comply with the FCRA by providing notice to the suspected employee and obtain the employee's consent before the investigation could occur. This did not allow the employer to maintain a discreet investigation.[321]

This changed when Congress enacted the ***Fair and Accurate Credit Transactions Act of 2003 ("FACT Act").***[322] This law, among other things, amended FCRA so that an employer no longer has to notify an employee that it was obtaining an investigative report on the employee from an outside organization.

The FACT Act changed the definition of "consumer report" under FCRA to exclude communications relating to employee investigations from the definition if three requirements are met:

1. The communication is made to an employer in connection with the investigation of: (i) suspected misconduct related to employment, or (ii) compliance with federal, state, or local laws and/or regulations, the rules of a self-regulatory organization, or any pre-existing written employment policies;

2. The communication is not made for the purpose of investigating a consumer's creditworthiness, credit standing, or credit capacity; and,

3. The communication is not provided to any person except: (i) the employer or agent of the employer, (ii) a federal or state officer, agency, or department, or an officer, agency, or department of a unit of the local government, (iii) a self-regulating organization with authority over the activities of the employer or employee, (iv) as otherwise required by law, or (v) pursuant to 15 U.S.C. § 1681f, which addresses disclosures to government agencies.[323]

If the employer takes adverse action on the basis of these reports, the FACT Act requires that the employer disclose a summary of the nature and substance of the communication or report to the employee to avoid liability under the FCRA. This report can be issued after the investigation has been conducted and allows employers to maintain the secrecy of the investigation.[324]

Employee Access to Information. Even though United States laws generally impose less protection for privacy of employee data than some other jurisdictions, American corporations should still reasonably limit access to employee information to avoid potential liability in tort, to prepare for future changes in law that may be more restrictive, and to secure the trust of employees. This can be achieved through the classification of employees, role-based controls, and careful management of sensitive data.

Classification of Employees. To protect employee data, companies should classify employees according to their need for information about other employees. Only the classes of employees with a reasonable business need for specific classes of information should be allowed access to the information.

Role-Based Controls. Company information should be kept private through role-based controls. For example, the company directory may be made available to all employees, but the social security number of employees should be made available only on a need-to-know basis. There should also be special controls on data related to performance reviews and workplace investigations.

Management of Sensitive Data. Certain employee data should be classified to avoid disclosure and to preserve privacy. Factors to consider in classifying data include:

- *Data Sensitivity.* The more sensitive or personal the employee data, the fewer people should have access to it. Data that are sensitive and should be classified and include employee social security numbers and medical information. The E.U. definitions of what is considered "sensitive" data are instructive and should be considered: personal data revealing racial or ethnic origin, political opinions, religious or philosophical beliefs, trade-union membership, and personal data concerning health or sexual activities.

- *Country of Origin.* Different countries have different privacy laws and these should be taken into account when considering whether to classify data.

- Other legal restrictions and employee input.

When managing sensitive data, an employer should understand where its data flows. The employer should know where the data are collected, what data are collected, how the data are stored and secured, who has access to the data internally, what third parties have access to the data and why, and how and when the data are destroyed. It is also vital that employers understand their vendors' data flow system because management of sensitive data is frequently outsourced. Common vendors include service providers (benefits providers, for example), outsourcers (such as payroll processing), and IT and other corporate suppliers.

The HR department handles some of the corporation's most sensitive data. For this reason, companies should have a written procedure that establishes administrative security, technical security, and physical security of the data. To gain administrative security, the procedure should have a program definition and administration, manage workforce risks, and have thorough employee training. For technical security, the procedure should discuss the computer systems, networks, and applications, access controls, and encryption. Finally, for physical security, the procedure should describe the facilities, environmental safeguards, and how to recover in the event of a disaster.

Frequently, U.S. companies outsource management of important human resources data. United State's privacy laws generally anticipate the use of vendors and service providers in processing this data and do not restrict transfers of data based on geography (in other words, you can outsource your data to a service provider over-seas). However, recent anti-outsourcing bills are attempting to limit outsourcing and require more disclosures about it. Even when data are outsourced, companies always remain accountable for their outsourcer's actions, so security should be a huge consideration when outsourcing sensitive information.

If a company chooses to outsource sensitive human resources data, it should establish a formal vendor security qualification protocol and audit against it to ensure that the data remain secure. The company should also have established vendor contractual provisions such as limiting the scope and use of the data, mandating reasonable security, mandating confidentiality, mandating notice of any security or confidentiality breach, and providing for audit rights, insurance, and indemnification.

Human resources databases are prime targets for identity thieves because of the easy access to social security numbers and date of birth information. If a company's database is breached, then the corporation should notify the affected individuals immediately. Under the California data breach notification law (SB 1386), and over two dozen additional state laws passed in 2005, it is legally required to notify employees of security breaches involving certain types of data.[325] However, even if the employees are not residents of one of these states, the corporation should notify the affected individuals to avoid potential tort liability should the individuals become victims of identity theft.

Europe

The E.U. Directive (95/46/EC) states that the processing of personal data should be carried out "with the consent of the data subject" unless the processing can be justified under one of the exemptions provided in the Directive.[326] The Directive also requires that certain sensitive data "which are capable by their nature of infringing fundamental freedoms or privacy") should not be processed unless the data subject gives his explicit consent, unless certain "derogations" from this prohibition apply.[327] However, E.U. officials have expressed reservations about the validity of consent as a basis for the processing of employee data, because they believe that the employer has too much leverage in the employer/employee relationship, and that the consent of the employee may not be freely given. Therefore, in a given situation, Data Protection Authorities may require that other grounds for sharing, processing and transferring the data be established, such as model contracts between the importing and exporting parties, contracts between the controller and processor, certification to the U.S. Safe Harbor program, or adoption of Binding Corporate Rules within the corporate group.

Management of Sensitive Employee Data. The E.U. Directive bars the processing of certain types of sensitive data including data that would reveal racial or ethnic origin, political opinions, religious or philosophical beliefs, trade-union membership, and data concerning health or sex life.[328] This means that employers must not collect, store, or use data of these types that are collected within the E.U.

Exceptions to Data Collection. This processing rule has a variety of exceptions, although they are narrowly construed. Sensitive data can be collected and used when the data subject has given his explicit consent to the processing of the data.[329] Sensitive data can also be processed when it is mandated by the state.[330] For example, if the data are required to be reported by the state, then the corporation can collect the data. Sensitive data can also be processed if the processing is necessary to protect the vital interests of the data subject or to protect a substantial public interest.[331] This data can also be processed where they are necessary for medical treatment.[332] Finally, data that involve criminal offenses or security measures may be processed under the control of official authorities.[333]

Workforce and Workplace Monitoring Activities

In today's global marketplace, a variety of different employee monitoring approaches and technologies exist and different legal issues and considerations apply to such monitoring.

Generally, employers have the ability to monitor the workplace or specifically monitor an individual employee. General monitoring occurs when employers monitor their workplaces for general activity and or a specific employee or activity is targeted. This can be achieved through workplace surveillance, close-caption television, and access controls like badge cards and readers. Virus filters and spam filters may also arguably be considered as a form of general monitoring, because the contents and attachments of employee messages are screened.

Employers may choose to employ one or more of the methods and technologies described below to monitor their employees' activities. The reasons for such monitoring include risk management, quality control, productivity, public health and safety, corporate compliance, and investigation of theft. However, specific legal guidelines apply to such methods and technologies, in both the United States and across Europe.

Workplace Surveillance

A recent survey reveals that two-thirds of major U.S. companies monitor their employees through some sort of electronic surveillance.[334] For example, some companies elect to monitor their employees through "keystroke detector" programs that log everything typed on the computer keyboard. Others do so through interception of email messages sent or received on the corporate mail server or network.

The most common form of monitoring, however, is through the logging of telephone numbers and call durations for telephone calls that employees make or receive while in the workplace. Some experts argue, under tort law theory, that monitoring employees could expose employers to liability for invasion of privacy in the U.S. In Europe, employees can complain to an E.U. Works Council or data protection authority ("DPA"), and the DPAs can impose fines and order monitoring to be curtailed. To avoid this potential liability, employers should inform employees of the logging, investigations, and surveillance techniques that they use. If this notice is given, the monitoring may be considered a normal condition of employment and, therefore, the employee will not have an invasion of privacy claim in the U.S.[335] This notice is also important (and generally required) in the E.U., but employee monitoring and investigations must also be limited to that which is "proportionate" to the harm that the employer is seeking to prevent.

Closed-Circuit Television ("CCTV") is widely used by U.S. employers to monitor their employees and work spaces and is especially common in Europe—not just in company settings such as manufacturing floors but in public spaces such as train stations and street plazas. Many employers assert that the installation of video cameras deter employees from stealing (studies have demonstrated that 83% of employees steal from their employers).[336] Other reasons cited for use of these systems. are to deter shoplifting, armed robbery, and burglary.[337] Risk Control, Inc. has found that the installation of CCTV will improve customer service and employee productivity.[338] Finally, many insurance companies will give companies a discount once they have installed CCTV systems in their stores and warehouses.[339]

Under U.S. law, employers are free to monitor employees using closed circuit television. However, if employers record sound along with images, they may encounter problems with the Federal Wiretapping Statute.

Access Controls as Monitoring Devices. As will be described further in Chapter Three, "access controls" are physical security mechanisms that restrict entrance to a facility or property to only authorized persons. Such physical security access controls can also be used to monitor and record who enters and exits the building or other controlled facility. Physical security access control devices include visitor's logs, security cameras, gates, electronic locks, and biometric devices.

Access controls also can include information technology access controls, such as log-in procedures and passwords, hidden paths, digital signatures, encryption, and biometric scans. These methods of IT access control can also be used to monitor and record who enters the protected computer and communications systems.

Badge cards and readers are perhaps the most common examples to employees. These electronically-enabled devices control access to buildings and restricted areas, and may also be used to control access to computer systems. Badge card systems can also be used to keep records of when employees arrive and leave work and when they enter and leave restricted areas.

Message Filtering and Anti-Virus Applications. Many employers monitor their online systems, including incoming email, for unsolicited messages ("spam") and potential software viruses. There is some debate as to whether this type of filtering should be considered "employee monitoring" of a type that should be disclosed, and, under E.U. law, notified to the data protection authorities. Such filtering is more likely to be treated as reportable employee monitoring if: (a) human beings are given access to the contents of messages or files, as opposed to purely automatic screening, and (b) records are kept in which particular messages, files or events can be correlated to particular users.

Viruses can cause employer computer systems to slow down and valuable and confidential information to be stolen. Viruses most commonly enter employer computer systems through employee email accounts. Generally, there is no limit under U.S. law on an employer's ability to scan employee email for viruses. However, if records are keptin which particular messages or files containing viruses can be correlated to particular users, E.U. authorities may consider this a collection of "personal data" that should be disclosed to the employees, data protection authorities, and works councils.

According to a survey in 2003, the average employee received 7500 pieces of spam email in a year. Spam can reduce employee morale, clog email systems, reduce productivity, and defraud recipients.[340] Furthermore, there is a legal movement for holding an employer reponsible for creating a "hostile work environment" under Title VII for receipt of pornographic spam emails through the company email system.[341] Therefore, employers have good reasons to implement filters to rid their systems of spam.

Currently, no restrictions exist in the U.S. regarding employers' ability to implement spam filters on their company email systems. However, there are some problems with spam filters. Some legitimate email can be blocked ("false positives") and some spam email can pass through as ("false negatives"). Employers must implement processes for dealing with the false positives that balance the employees' right to privacy against a safe and productive work environment. If filtered emails are "quarantined" and then reviewed by people to try to identify and forward false positives, this may be run afoul of the Electronic Communications Privacy Act unless the employees have been properly notified that they will have no reasonable expectation of privacy in their messages. The safer approach for employers is to notify employees that the spam filtering is being done and that it may result in some lost messages due to false positives, and then to let the false positives go abandoned.

Postal Mail Monitoring. Although U.S. federal law generally prohibits interference with mail delivery,[342] mail is considered to be "delivered" when it reaches a business, so opening of business letters and packages by a representative of the business (even if he is not the party on the mailing label) does not violate that statute. There is always some risk in monitoring activities under state common law. Employers can mitigate their risks by advising employees not to receive personal mail at work, declining to read mail once it is clear that it is personal in nature, and maintaining confidentiality for any personal information obtained in the course of monitoring. Note that for unionized workers it will be necessary under many collective bargaining agreements to inform union representatives of monitoring activities.

Monitoring and Investigation of Specific Employees. Occasionally, employers will want to monitor one specific employee, perhaps because some evidence has been obtained that the employee has been engaging in behavior that violates computer usage policies, other company policies, or law. Employers often monitor the employee's telephone and computer usage in these situations.

Computer Use Monitoring. More companies are implementing software to monitor employees' computer usage. There are a variety of reasons why companies are feeling pressure to install these systems. Software can monitor the number of keystrokes logged, the number of Web sites visited, or the time spent on Web sites or in specific software applications, in order to monitor productivity. Software can also scan the content of incoming and outgoing email to identify whether personal data or proprietary company information are being leaked. Software can also monitor for security breaches and unauthorized access to personal data or confidential information. Security analysts suggest that 70% to 90% of security breaches come from inside corporations, rather than hackers.[343]

Email Monitoring. In the U.S., employers are generally free to scan and read all employee emails as long as they have a legitimate business reason for doing so. Employers often have a legitimate business reason for scanning or reading emails because not only does it allow the employer to assess the employee's productivity, but careless business-related emails can open the employer up to allegations of fraud, lawsuits, loss of confidential data, sexism, racism, pornography, as well as reputation damage and loss of business. [344]

Currently, U.S. federal law does not give employees much protection from employers monitoring their emails. There have been three major streams of attack, all of which have been unsuccessful.

Employer monitoring of email has been attacked under the federal Wiretapping Act (addressed below). However, this has been found either not to apply to email monitoring or because the way in which the employer monitors the email is outside the scope of the statute. Most companies that monitor employee emails do so by methods that involve the retrieval of a "stored" communication rather than actual "interception" that is covered by the Wiretapping Act.

Internet Access Monitoring. Employers frequently want to monitor employee Internet usage to increase productivity in the workplace. Internet usage monitoring can also stop unwanted pop-ups, reduce viruses, and optimize network bandwidth. Employers also are concerned with reducing their liability from pornography or racist material in the workplace. Finally, employers are concerned with employees leaking trade secrets through the Internet.

The first step that the employer should take in implementing an Internet monitoring system is to develop and articulate an "acceptable use policy." These guidelines should specifically describe what constitutes acceptable behavior on the Internet and the repercussions for violating the organization's policy on Internet use. Employees should be asked to read and sign this policy.

Some employers implement the use policy through monitoring employees Internet usage. Other employers choose to block access to certain Internet site in order to preempt any bad behavior.[345] Generally, employers can legally use either method in the U.S.

Challenges by U.S. employees to employer monitoring of computer usage have usually been based on privacy rights under state and federal constitutions, and employers have typically prevailed. Most of these constitutional claims apply only to state and federal public employers, but California has a constitutional right of privacy that applies to private employment relationships. Note that for unionized workers it will be necessary under many collective bargaining agreements to inform union representatives of monitoring activities.

In the E.U., blocking of sites is generally acceptable, but monitoring will be subject to the same types of scrutiny that are described for email monitoring in the section above.

As will be discussed further into this chapter, risk remains for the employer in monitoring these activities under state common law, and some states have passed specific statutes that require notice prior to electronic monitoring in the workplace.[346]

Risk Management

One key reason why employers monitor their employees is to reduce their risk of liability in a lawsuit. Several varieties of lawsuits can arise from workplace monitoring activities on the part of the employer. These can include hostile environment and workplace violence claims as well as product liability and workplace health and safety claims.

Hostile Environment Claims. Employers may want to monitor their employees to reduce hostile environment sexual harassment claims. These claims generally arise when unwelcome sexual conduct unreasonably interferes with an individual's job performance or creates a hostile, intimidating, or offensive work environment. To raise a hostile work environment claim, an employee does not have to have a tangible or economic job consequence (for example, they do not have to have been fired to be able to sue). Employers, supervisors, coworkers, customers, or clients can create a hostile work environment.

Hostile environment sexual harassment can include demeaning sexual inquiries and vulgarities, offensive language, repeated requests for sexual favors, and offensive verbal or physical conduct of a sexual nature.

An employer can be held liable for a hostile environment sexual harassment claim if the employer "knew or should have known" of the harassment and the employer failed to take appropriate action to correct it. If an employer monitors its employees, then it can reduce its liability for hostile environment sexual harassment claims.

Workplace Violence. An employer may also want to monitor its employees to reduce workplace violence. Homicide is the Third-most common workplace death.[347] There are four major types of workplace violence:

1. Disgruntled employees;
2. Crimes by unknown assailants;
3. Sexual harassment; and,
4. Displaced domestic violence.[348]

Employers can be held liable in all four of the examples described above.

When assessing a case of injury due to a disgruntled employee, courts generally evaluate what the employer could have done and should have done to decrease the risk. Steps that an employer can take to reduce the risk of violence due to a disgruntled employee include pre-employment screening, implementing and using progressive discipline in the workplace, issuing performance evaluations, and implementing policies and programs to treat alcohol and drug abuse, marital problems, and stress management. Employers can be held directly liable for negligent hiring, training, supervising, or retaining violent employees, and authorizing or ratifying an employee's violent behavior. An employer can also be held vicariously liable for acts committed by employees that are within the scope of their employment.[349]

Employers can also be held liable for workplace violence from unknown assailants. Employers have a duty to provide a safe workplace for employees. Under this theory, employers can be held civilly liable for the injuries resulting from an robbery or assault. Employers in industries that frequently encounter workplace violence should take the following steps to protect their employees: increase staff during high-risk periods, reduce store hours, install adequate lighting, drop safes, and silent alarms, and install bullet-safe shields to protect clerks.

Finally, employers can be held liable for injuries that occur due to displaced domestic violence. Seventy-four percent of women who are victims of domestic violence are harassed at work, either by phone or in person.[350] An employer has a duty to protect not only the victim of the harassment, but the other employees. If an employer does not take steps to stop the harassment, they could be held liable for any injuries that occur.

Because employers can be held liable for workplace violence, employers have an interest in monitoring their employees' actions.

Product Liability Lawsuits. Employers may want to monitor their employees to assure quality control of the products that they make. Not only will employers get a bad reputation for making defective goods, they could be held liable in a products liability suit.

Products liability suits arise when a company's product causes injury or harm because of a flaw or defect. To win a products liability suit, the plaintiff does not have to show that the employer was at fault. They only must prove 4 elements: (1) that the product was defective, (2) that the plaintiff was injured during its intended use, (3) that the defective product caused the injury, and (4) there was no substantial alteration to the product after its receipt.[351] Therefore, employers have a substantial interest in monitoring the quality of the products that their employees produce.

Productivity Metrics. Employers may also want to monitor their employees to increase their productivity. Employers lose billions of dollars annually because of employees wasting time or not doing their jobs. Monitoring employees can help remedy this problem.

Public Health and Safety. An employer may want to monitor its employees and workplace to ensure public health and safety. The Occupational Health and Safety Act ("OSHA") requires that employers furnish their employees with a place of employment that is free from recognized hazards and complies with the occupational health and safety standards.[352] If the employer does not do this, it could be exposed to liability under OSHA.

Furthermore, if the employer is engaged in a "dangerous" industry (for example, a nuclear power plant) the employer will want to monitor its employees to avoid injuring people outside the workplace and further employer liability.

Workplace Monitoring

United States

In general, U.S. laws exert very few restrictions on monitoring by employers. This is attributed to a very low employee expectation of privacy in the American workplace (especially if notice is given). However, U.S. law does prescribe some situations when employers must monitor their employees and when employers cannot monitor their employees.

Although there are many reasons for an employer to want to monitor its employees, an employer must monitor them in some situations. One of these situations is under the *Occupational Health and Safety Act ("OSHA")*. OSHA requires that employers provide a safe workplace that complies with occupational health and safety standards. Frequently, these standards require that employees perform tasks in a certain way to avoid injury. In this case, employers must monitor their employees to comply with OSHA.

State and federal wiretap statutes also can limit employers from collecting employee conversations. Under these laws, the employer must get the consent of at least one party that is being monitored. Twelve states require that all the parties being monitored give consent. A recorded message that says that the call may be monitored has generally been held to be adequate notice in most jurisdictions. Employers must be careful of *ad hoc* monitoring. The general rule is that employers cannot listen to employees' personal conversations and the employer must discontinue monitoring as soon as it is apparent that the conversation is personal.

The U.S. Wiretap Act, 18 U.S.C. §§2510-2522, contains general prohibitions on monitoring telephone calls, but has several exceptions that essentially allow employers to monitor employee telephone calls with employees, or with clients or customers for quality control reasons. The "business use exception"[353] can be invoked to monitor business calls "in the ordinary course of business" (such as, for example, help desk or call center employee calls). However, if a call turns from business to personal, and the employer becomes aware of its personal nature, it is required to stop monitoring immediately, if that is the only exception being relied upon.

A "prior consent"[354] exception also exists under the Act, which justifies call monitoring to the extent that the consent obtained from the employee (or other party) covered the monitoring. It is best to have this consent in writing to avoid issues with proof. If a party on the other end of the call has not consented, there are potential state law issues, as some states require both parties on the call to consent to a call being monitored or recorded. When monitoring incoming calls to company call centers, it is a standard corporate practice to play a recorded message in the greeting that "calls may be monitored for quality control purposes" in order to put the caller on notice that the call is being monitored, after which his continuation of the call at least arguably constitutes his consent. There is always some risk in monitoring activities under state common law, under which an employee or other person can bring a claim under the common law right of privacy and the torts of invasion of privacy, public disclosure of private facts, and intrusion upon seclusion. However, these often come out in favor of the employer if the employer is being reasonable in the scope and purposes of the monitoring.

Electronic spaces are even less protected than physical spaces in the United States. Computer systems are said to belong to the employer and employees generally have no expectation of privacy in use of employer equipment. However, some key laws enforce computer privacy in the U.S. workplace.

The Electronic Communications Privacy Act of 1986 ("ECPA") prohibits employers from intercepting electronic communications and unauthorized access to stored communications, but includes a business use exception and an employee consent exception. Some states do require notice of electronic monitoring. Delaware requires advance and acknowledged notice to employees of monitoring of the telephone, electronic mail, and Internet usage.

Interestingly, many U.S. employers have managed to escape liability under ECPA because there is a "provider authorization" exception (authorization by "the person or entity providing a wire or electronic communications service"; in this case, the employer itself)[355] to the bar on accessing stored communications. There is also a "user consent" exception allowing access to stored communications with the consent of the sender or the recipient of the message.[356] Therefore, employers generally can establish a "provider authorization" exception or obtain consent of the employee and can avoid liability under this statute.

Employers cannot monitor every location on their premises. For example, employee monitoring cannot occur in "private spaces." Private spaces develop when the employee has a reasonable expectation of privacy. The expectation of privacy develops through the employer's policies and the location of the space. If the space is used by multiple people and the employer clearly reserves the right to search at any time, an employee does not have a reasonable expectation of privacy. On the other hand, if a space has a lock and only one person uses the space, the employee does have a legitimate expectation of privacy unless he has been expressly notified by the employer that he does not. Common private spaces include desks, lockers, and offices. If an employer wants to conduct a search of a private space, the employer should give advance written notice to the employee to avoid a lawsuit for invasion of privacy. The notice should disclose the methods for searching the employees and their possessions, define the scope and intent of the search, and inform the employees about the employer's exact concerns and interests. The search must occur only if there is a justifiable, job-related reason. The search also must be properly authorized and conducted according to the company's policies. Furthermore, only certain upper-management level employees should be allowed to conduct the search to minimize the invasiveness.[357]

Many areas of the law of employer monitoring are not yet fully defined in the U.S. In fact, some areas have not even been addressed. For this reason, employers should protect themselves by providing employees notices and obtaining written and signed consent forms. Notice and consent to monitoring establishes that an employee has no expectation of privacy while at work. In most situations, this should protect employers from invasion of privacy lawsuits.

Employee monitoring has a variety of legal issues on either side, monitoring too much or monitoring too little. In the case of monitoring too little, an employer can be exposed to many different lawsuits including products liability claims for producing defective products, Occupational Health and Safety Act claims for not monitoring employees to assure that they perform their jobs properly, claims resulting from workplace violence, hostile work environment sexual harassment claims, and any number of claims resulting from vicarious liability or *respondeat superior*.

On the other hand, if a U.S. employer monitors its employees too much or in an improper fashion, the employer can be exposed to multiple claims including Federal Wiretapping Statute claims, invasion of privacy claims under state tort law and constitutional law (if the employee works for the public sector), and claims of violations of the National Labor Relations act.

Europe

Employee monitoring is much more limited in the European Union than in the United States. Employee monitoring is likely to run afoul of either privacy laws or employment laws unless:

1. The employer notifies the employees, the Works Councils, and the local Data Protection Authority in some detail of the types of monitoring it will be doing (and in some countries obtain approval from the employee, Works Council and/or DPA); and,

2. The monitoring is "proportionate" to a "legitimate harm" that the employer is trying to prevent; and,

3. The monitoring is justified by being (a) "necessary for compliance with a legal obligation to which the employer is subject," or (b) "necessary in order to protect the vital interests of the data subject," or (c) "necessary for the performance of a task carried out in the public interest," or (d) necessary for the establishment, exercise or defense of legal claims, or (e) necessary for the performance of a contract to which the data subject is a

party (arguably including the contract of employment, which may justify monitoring to ensure compliance with company policies).[358]

The personal data collected in monitoring *may not be transferred* to the U.S. or to any other country with privacy protections that have not been declared "adequate" by the European Commission,[359] unless the applicant has "unambiguously" consented to the transfer (which, in the case of employees, may not be deemed adequate), or adequate protections have been put in place for the data by an approved method (such as a "model contract" between the exporting and importing entities, or implementation of Binding Corporate Rules, or if the company importing the data to the U.S. has certified to the U.S. Dept of Commerce that it is meeting all of the requirements of the "Safe Harbor" program) or one of a narrow list of exemptions applies, including the following:

1. The transfer is necessary for the performance of a contract between the data subject and the controller or the implementation of pre-contractual measures taken in response to the data subject's request; or,

2. The transfer is necessary for the conclusion or performance of a contract concluded in the interest of the data subject between the controller and a third party; or,

3. The transfer is necessary or legally required on important public interest grounds, or for the establishment, exercise or defense of legal claims; or,

4. The transfer is necessary in order to protect the vital interests of the data subject.[360] Individual member states are empowered to provide by law that the applicant's consent is not an adequate basis for transfer, and in fact some Data Protection Authorities take a critical view of the effectiveness of consent obtained by a current employer from an employee.

The Directive also requires that:

1. The personal data be kept accurate and current;[361]

2. The data subject will have the right to make corrections to the data,[362]

3. The personal data must be kept in a form which permits identification of data subjects for no longer than is necessary for the purposes for which the data were collected;[363]

4. The controller must implement appropriate technical and organizational measures to protect personal data against accidental or unlawful destruction or accidental loss, alteration, unauthorized disclosure or access;[364]

5. The controller must ensure that appropriate technical and organization measures are also used by its third party processors, and must bind them by contract or other legally binding act (in writing or other equivalent form) to do so and to process the data only on instructions from the controller;[365]

6. The personal data may not be used for "automated decision-making" except in certain narrowly defined circumstances;[366]

7. The data subject (employee) will have the right to object to the processing for purposes other than direct marketing on "compelling legitimate grounds relating to his particular situation" except where otherwise provided by national legislation;[367] and,

8. The data subject shall have the right to obtain from the controller, at reasonable intervals and without excessive delay or expense, information regarding the categories of data being processed about him, the sources of the data, the purposes of the processing, and the recipients or categories of recipients to whom the data are disclosed, and a description of the logic involved in any automatic processing of data concerning him.[368]

Data protection authorities and courts in the E.U are very restrictive on the "proportionate" issue, and require very specific forms of notice. If records of the monitoring are kept in which particular messages can be correlated to particular senders or recipients, E.U. authorities will likely consider this a collection of "personal data" that should be disclosed to the data protection authorities and works councils as well as the employees.

In E.U. labor law, "covert monitoring" is distinguished from "overt monitoring." Overt monitoring is generally allowed where the employee is aware of the recording. Customers must also be informed that calls are being monitored. Covert monitoring is generally not allowed. It can be carried out only when an employer is investigating a criminal offense. Employees must be warned when hired that if they are suspected of a criminal offense, they can be monitored in this way. Data obtained through covert monitoring can only be used to investigate criminal activity.

Lastly, with regard to electronic communications privacy in the workplace, E.U. laws are decidedly different from those in the U.S. The scanning and recording of email content is likely to be run afoul of either privacy laws or employment laws unless: (a) the scanning is "proportionate" to the harm that the employer is trying to prevent, and (b) the employer notifies the employees that it will be doing this type of monitoring. Data protection authorities and courts in the E.U. are very restrictive on the "proportionate" issue, and require very specific forms of notice.

Employee Misconduct

When employee misconduct occurs, special concerns must be addressed by the employer. The employer must be careful to avoid liability or loss because of failure to take the allegations seriously. Under the due process clause, the employee must be reasonably protected during the investigation. The employer must be sure to ensure compliance with other corporate policies during the investigation. The employer must also be sure to ensure compliance with external obligations such as laws and collective bargaining agreements during the investigation. The investigation and misconduct must be documented to minimize the likelihood of successful employee claims against the employer. Finally, the employer must be careful to balance the rights of other people who may be involved in the investigation.

In the event of employee misconduct, it is paramount for employers to document the problem and retain this written summary as a record. This will help demonstrate that the employer has engaged in progressive discipline with the employee; also it will help minimize the likelihood of successful employee claims against the employer.

In an employee misconduct situation involving multiple employees, the rights of each employee must be balanced. In the case of a sexual harassment allegation, the complainant's allegations must be taken seriously and investigated thoroughly. However, the alleged harasser cannot be persecuted.[370]

Data Handling in Misconduct Investigations

There are essentially eight steps that an employer must take to properly document employee misconduct:

1. Record the employee's name, job title, supervisor's name, subject and any other introductory information.

2. Describe the employee's misconduct in specific details, including all dates and times, as well as a complete description of the disciplinary problem.
3. Record any rule, regulation, policy, protocol, work standard or law that the employee violated and place a copy of the rule in the file.

4. Look through previous files and reference all prior attempts by management to gain employee compliance with the applicable rules.

5. Issue a clear, unambiguous directive to the employee that his or her behavior must improve.

6. Inform the employee of the probable disciplinary consequences that will occur if his or her behavior does not improve.

7. Inform the employee that the disciplinary document will be placed in his or her personnel file and that there is a right to respond in writing.

8. Provide a line for the employee to sign and date receipt of the document.[371]

Use of Third Parties in Misconduct Investigations

After the investigation has been documented, it is crucial that the files remain confidential. If the employer tells other employees of the misconduct, it could expose itself to suits for defamation or invasion of privacy.

Frequently, employers use third-parties to investigate employee misconduct. Formerly, this exposed corporations to liability under the *Fair Credit Reporting Act ("FCRA")*. FCRA requires employers to give employees notice that they are obtaining a consumer report on them and requires that the employer get the employee's consent before it can be issued. According to an opinion letter issued for the Federal Trade Commission ("FTC") known as the "Vail Letter," if an employer hired an outside organization like a private investigator or background research firm to conduct these investigations, the outside organization constituted a "consumer reporting agency" under the FCRA and any reports furnished to the employer by the outside organization was an "investigative consumer report." Because of this opinion, an employer that received these reports had to comply with the FCRA by providing notice to the suspected employee and obtain consent. This destroyed the undercover aspect of any investigation.[372]

This was changed by Congress when it enacted the *Fair and Accurate Credit Transactions Act of 2003 ("FACT Act")*.[372] Among other things, this law amended the employment-related provisions of FCRA so that an employer is no longer required to notify an employee that it is obtaining an investigative report on the employee from an outside organization. Specifically, the FACT Act changed the definition of "consumer report" under FCRA to exclude communications relating to employee investigations from the definition if three requirements are met:

1. The communication is made to an employer in connection with the investigation of: (i) suspected misconduct related to employment, or (ii) compliance with federal, state, or local laws and/or regulations, the rules of a self-regulatory organization, or any pre-existing written employment policies;

2. The communication is not made for the purpose of investigating a consumer's credit-worthiness, credit standing, or credit capacity; and,

3. The communication is not provided to any person except: (i) the employer or agent of the employer, (ii) a federal or state officer, agency, or department, or an officer, agency, or department of a unit of general local government, (iii) a self-regulating organization

with authority over the activities of the employer or employee, (iv) as otherwise required by law, or (v) pursuant to 15 U.S.C. § 1681f, which addresses disclosures to government agencies.[374]

If the employer takes adverse action on the basis of these reports, the FACT Act requires that the employer disclose a summary of the nature and substance of the communication or report to the employee to avoid liability under FCRA. This report can be issued after the investigation has been conducted and allows employers to maintain the secrecy of the investigation.[375]

Notification of Authorities and Employee Rights of Notification

Certain events of employee misconduct must be reported to the authorities under federal statute. For example, OSHA requires that the employer report events that affect health and safety. However, other federal statutes do not mandate the employer to report the incident to the authorities. Title VII of OSHA for example, can be handled internally and does not require the employer to report the incident to the authorities.

An employee has a right of notification when his or her employer is making note of his or her misconduct. If an employee is not notified of his or her misconduct and the company has a policy of progressive discipline, the company could be held liable for wrongful discharge.

Termination of the Employment Relationship

At the end of the employer-employee relationship, there are many privacy issues that an employer must confront. An employer must follow the correct termination procedures, minimize risks of post-termination claims, help management to transition after the termination, and address any privacy claims that arise.

Once a company has terminated an employee, a company should be sure to follow specific termination procedures to avoid any breaches of privacy. To ensure a smooth transition and avoid any privacy implications, employers should ensure that former employee's access to company information is curtailed and retrieve any personal data that the former employee had access to.

Ensure that employee access to company information is curtailed.
At the end of the employee-employer relationship, employee access to company information must be curtailed to protect the company and other employees within the company. To do this, there are two basic steps that must be taken:

1. Computer accounts must be disabled; and,

2. Access devices must be repossessed. Also, it is useful to remind the former employee of his obligation to maintain confidentiality of employer data.

Ensure return of personal data that employee may have access to.
To ensure a smooth ending to the employer-employee relationship, the employer should seek to retrieve personal data that the employee may have had (i.e., company directories and computer storage devices). This will make relations between the employer and the former employee much better.

A variety of steps can be taken to minimize risks of post-termination privacy claims. The employer should document the reason for the termination and classify it as sensitive data. This will balance the employee's privacy concerns against the employer's need to maintain records.

The employer also should be careful in providing references for the former employee. The employer should consider the privacy interests of the employee and the risk of a defamation suit before disclosing information. However, the employer should also try to be honest, especially if health or safety is at risk.

Transition Management

Once an employee has been terminated, the company must be careful to transition. The company must carefully handle any external communications to the former employee and carefully handle mail received for the former employee.

External communications to former employees should be carefully crafted especially if the relationship was terminated as a result of misconduct. Internal messages to remaining employees and messages to customers should be constructed carefully. Messages to regulatory agencies, if applicable, should also be written so that they do not violate the employee's right to privacy. The employer should not say anything that would expose itself to liability. The employer should also be careful to not communicate any private company information to the former employee.

When an employer provides references for the former employer, the employer should consider the employee's privacy interests and applicable defamation risks, but still remain honest, especially if health or safety is at risk.

Employers should carefully handle the former employee's postal mail. Mail that is clearly marked as personal should be forwarded to the former employee. However, mail that is work-related should be kept by the employer to avoid leaking private information.

Finally, employers can take many steps to avoid invasion of privacy claims, such as establishing clear policies. Once a privacy claim arises, an employer should be careful to gather information about the event, document it, and change policies or implement new ones to avoid future privacy claims. If an employer has handled the employee termination properly, there is a good chance that the employer will be held not liable or there will be a reduction in damages awarded.

Conclusion

Personal information comes into play at virtually every phase of the employment relationship—from evaluation and hiring to employee management, monitoring and termination or departure. As organizations grow in size, expand to new geographies and involve larger numbers of outside partners and vendors, the employment privacy challenges become more acute. Global employers must navigate through a complex patchwork of applicable U.S, E.U. and international workplace privacy laws.

Effective legal compliance and thoughtful management of employee personal information can help reduce the risk of any potential legal claims as well as offer many benefits to both employer and employee. These benefits include minimizing the risk of information mishandling, disclosure or theft; increased employee morale; and an improved working relationship between employer and employee.

Chapter Four

INFORMATION SECURITY

Introduction and Learning Objectives

Information security is an essential component of information privacy: it is often said that privacy is not possible without security.

For privacy purposes, information security systems, procedures and tools help to ensure the protection of personally identifiable information ("PII") by preventing unauthorized or uncontrolled access to that information. An effective privacy plan must appropriately link both privacy and security within the overarching business and operational goals of the organization.

"Information Security" describes the systems, policies and controls within a typical, enterprise-level information security operation. It provides a high-level view into methods for managing, maintaining and protecting the privacy of sensitive or personal information.

The CIPP will understand:

- The role of privacy in ensuring effective security within an organization;

- Information controls such as classification, encryption, authentication and authorization;

- Maintaining information integrity, confidentiality and availability through system monitoring and auditing; and,

- Strategies for intrusion prevention including incident handling and disaster recovery.

Information Auditing and Monitoring

Information security is the protection of information in order to prevent loss, access or misuse. It is also the process of assessing threats and risks to information and the procedures and controls to preserve the integrity of information across three key attributes:

1. *Confidentiality*. Access to data is limited to authorized parties;

2. *Integrity*. Assurance that the data are authentic and complete; and,

3. *Availability*. Knowledge that the data are accessible, as needed, by those who are authorized to access them.

An effective information security system begins with an auditing process. In general terms, an audit is simply an assessment of the current state of the information technology ("IT") infrastructure including an inventory of all data assets and the identification of processes used for entering, changing, and accessing the data in these systems. From a privacy perspective, auditing is an essential first step because a privacy professional cannot determine how secure a system is until he or she has complete knowledge of what the system contains and how the system operates.[376]

A thorough audit can be quite complex and involve many people, but it is very important that the process not be abbreviated. Without a complete understanding of the IT infrastructure and the data control processes, any future attempts to increase security may be, at best, ineffective or, at worst, detrimental to the basic business functions of the organization. A good audit will provide the auditor with not only a technical schematic of the infrastructure and processes but also provide insight into how individuals actually use these systems on a real day-to-day basis. In the end, an audit should provide a full and complete picture of how data systems are used and operate in reality and not just theory.[377]

While auditing is essentially backward-looking (i.e., determining how things have been done previously), monitoring is used to provide current or even real-time information about the system. Without monitoring, it is impossible to know what is occurring on the system on an ongoing basis.

The most common form of monitoring is system logs. Systems logs capture a current record of changes to the system and other important events. At a minimum, system logs need to record the presence of new and unauthorized accounts, the running of unauthorized programs, and the access privileges of those operating on the system. And it is also important that logs are checked regularly for gaps that may indicate that they have been altered to conceal a security breach.[378] Logs should have some form of access control measures applied to prevent unauthorized tampering.

Information Security Controls

Security controls are the actual processes used to ensure the security of an information system. It is imperative that these controls are in place and functioning as intended. It is also important that a control monitoring process be in place to provide immediate notification in the event that any of the controls fails.

At a high level, there are three main types of information security controls:

1. **Preventive** security controls are intended to stop incidents before they can impact operations. Preventive controls are the most common and include password verifiers, and firewall systems, among other approaches.

2. **Detective** security controls are comparatively more effective than preventive controls but also more complex. Detective controls are aware of normal operations and look for system anomalies such as unusual activities or events. Where preventive controls are static, detective controls are dynamic and able to watch for new and previously unknown security threats. Detective security controls most commonly come in the form of Intrusion Detection Systems ("IDS"), which are defined further into this chapter.

3. **Corrective.** After a preventive or detective control becomes aware of a security threat, a corrective security control can take automatic actions to manage or mitigate that threat. Corrective controls are generally integrated into other controls, such as Intrusion Prevention Systems ("IPS") which are defined further into this chapter.

One can also consider each of these controls as hybrids of procedure and technology. Each approach above includes elements of established process to anticipate or prevent errors, irregularities or unauthorized access. In addition, each approach includes the hardware and software technologies required to maintain technical security. These can include system diagnostic devices, software patches and other tools. Lastly, these controls can include facets of physical security such as facility oversight or environmental management.

Encryption

Encryption is yet another method for ensuring effective system security and is a means to prevent unauthorized access of private information: it can take all of the data that one computer is sending to another and encode it into a form that only the other computer will be able to decode and read. Generally, encryption is a good means of ensuring confidentiality but not authentication. Thus, encryption by itself (the protected state of the data) does not verify that the person who claims to have sent the message is the true sender. Digital signatures are most often used to address this problem and are covered further into this chapter.[379]

Encryption. The process of obscuring information often through the use of a cryptographic scheme in order to make the information unreadable without special knowledge (e.g., the use of code keys).

Information Infrastructure

Data Storage and Recovery

Regular data backups are an important part of information security: they create an unalterable system record that can be an invaluable forensic tool in determining the timing, origin and nature of a data event (access, breach or loss).

While most people consider information security in terms of hackers and exploits, data can be lost just as easily through more mundane means such as lack of personnel oversight or mis-located documents and electronic files. In the event of data loss from any cause, backups are essential to maintaining business functionality. They also provide a base line in the event of a security breach to better gauge what data may have been lost and thus require recovery. Backups can be used to determine if any data have been altered or even aid in tracking an attacker who has erased system logs.

The data contained on backups must be protected from unauthorized access. The actual storage files backups should be maintained in a physically secure location; if the data are sensitive, they should be encrypted. Additionally, it must be understood and accepted by the organization that any person who has authorization to make data backups has authorization to access all the data backed-up. Therefore, such ability must be tightly controlled. [380]

A backup is only as good as its recoverability. Emergency data recovery plans should be made and tested by the organization and backups should be evaluated regularly in order to verify the efficacy of data recoverability. Data recovery procedures are typically integrated with other disaster contingency and business continuity plans that an organization may have in place.

Most PII data are stored within databases. Therefore, proper database management is central to ensuring effective privacy. The process of determining who should have access to the information stored in these databases should take into consideration that database administrators ("DBAs") do not need access to the information in order to manage the database. The use of "database views" is valuable in restricting access to sensitive data contained within databases.

Computer Hardware

Knowledge of the computer hardware and the physical IT infrastructure are important elements of information security. One must understand where the information physically resides on a network before the information can be secured. For example, if a person has physical access to a server computer's data drives, buses, serial ports, or any other accessible parts of the computer, many security controls are easily subverted. Controlling physical access to network switching and routing devices is equally important in this context as will be discussed further below. [381]

A wide variety of computer hardware devices are in use at any given moment in an average-sized organization. These varieties include mainframe computers, server computers, network computers, desktop computers, laptop computers, handheld devices (such as personal digital assistants, pagers and smart phones) and portable storage media (such as auxiliary data devices or "flash" drives). Each of these hardware varieties has the ability to receive, store and accept access to, personal information. Yet as the size, power, capacity and extensibility of the hardware increases, the levels of control and protection of the personal information are further challenged.

Laptop and handheld computers offer two compelling examples. Each presents two distinct types of information security problems.

The first involves information legitimately stored on these devices. While it is often convenient to keep information such as contacts, addresses and personal schedules on a personal digital assistant ("PDA"), the very mobility of the device is also its greatest security weakness. PDA devices are easily lost or stolen, making any information stored on the device susceptible to loss or abuse. If information is stored on a mobile or handheld device, it should always be encrypted so that, if lost or stolen, any data would remain inaccessible.

The second problem involves data theft. As handheld devices become more sophisticated, they pose a greater threat to information security. Apple Computer's ubiquitous iPod music player and similar handheld mass storage devices can be easily modified so that when connected to any machine equipped with a USB data port they automatically copy the contents of the connected hard drive. [382] Once the storage devices is detected, the operating system of the hard drive will automatically mount the drive, which allows a data thief to bypass many of the standard system security controls. While not as sophisticated, portable storage media (such as the popular "flash" memory drives, memory sticks or "thumb" drives) pose a similar threat. These devices can store a gigabyte or more of data on digital media that is less than the size of a stick of gum. This sort of availability and simplicity offers an inviting opportunity for hacker or exploit artist. A data thief can easily use a flash drive to remove sensitive information without detection. [383]

Desktop workstations (office personal computers) are often called "thin clients" for their reliance on a central computer or server. From a best practices standpoint, these machines should not store PII because it is very difficult to control access to the information stored on desktops. Ideally, desktops should have no mass storage devices or other peripherals connected to them.

Network Hardware

Network Hardware is often the most enigmatic of IT equipment because it comes in sealed boxes without the interfaces of a keyboard and monitor that most end users are accustomed to—though these systems are almost always managed by networking systems professionals. Network hardware is extremely powerful and is the linchpin of network security. If one of these devices is compromised, it is easy for an attacker to gain access to the entire network. Because of this, these devices have been designed with security in mind and a good network engineer can use these devices to enhance data security.

Network Servers are centralized hubs that contain business information and are accessible to many users often simultaneously. These machines are the heart of business functionality and the key to data flows across an organization as well as to outside partners and users. Information security starts with server security. An organization's network architecture needs to be designed such that server operating systems are stripped of non-essential services and "hardened" for security.

Two types of network systems are:

1. *Local Area Networks ("LANs")* exist within an operational facility, are considered within local operational control and are relatively easy to manage; and,

2. *Wide Area Networks ("WANs")* may involve coordination between several groups, are considered outside of local operational control and are relatively difficult to manage.

Ethernet is the most common type of LAN connection. It is based on a broadcast model and trusts the responses it receives. Thus, Ethernet has some inherent security vulnerabilities related to reliability, interception, and spoofing. However, with proper network design and management Ethernet can be made very safe.[384] Optical connections are increasingly common in connecting WANs. Optical networks use complex light wave patterns to transmit information rather than electrical impulses. The network protocols used over optical (such as ATM, FDDI, and HPPI) are much more modern and are more robust and incorporate much more security than Ethernet.

The following are additional network systems that need to be managed in order to ensure effective information security.

Internet. Managing and securing information accessible to the Internet is extremely important. Since it is difficult, if not impossible, to completely secure any Internet-connected machine, privacy professionals should consider creating "PII only networks" that are separate from Internet-connected networks. For example, the U.S. Department of Defense maintains three physically separate networks: (1) an Internet-connected network; (2) a general internal network; and, (3) a classified data network. No machine or device is connected to more than one of these networks at any time so it is physically impossible to gain access one network from another. While this practice offers the most information security, similar feasibility in a business environment has to be determined.

Extranet. Many businesses find it both practical and expedient to share internal information, directly and in real time, with external business partners, vendors, customers and/or subsidiary businesses. Extranets are just such a network system formed through the connection of two corporate intranets. Arguably necessary—but extremely practical—these external networks create inherent security risks. An extranet opens a backdoor into the internal network and provides a third party with a level of trust. While these risks cannot be eliminated, they can be assessed, managed, and mitigated.[385] The foundation of this management is a thorough and detailed e-business contract that specifies who may access data, what data will be accessed, and what security controls the partner has in place. It should also detail how shared devices will be managed, procedures for cooperating with technical staff in the event of problems, and escalation procedures for resolving difficult technical problems.

Private Branch Exchange ("PBX"). Standard telecommunications equipment is often under-protected in comparison to more advanced networking systems. Most office telephone systems are controlled by a Private Branch Exchange ("PBX") system. These systems control telephone numbers, store voicemails, and perform many other functions related to telephony. PBX systems are often connected to the internal network for management and monitoring and many run on standard Windows-based servers. However, infiltration and manipulation of a company's telephone system can pose serious information security risks. Therefore, steps should be taken to protect PBX systems and telecommunications equipment.

Remote Access Connectivity is an important business function today but also introduces pronounced security risks. Mobile connectivity should be allowed only through a Virtual Private Network ("VPN"),[386] a system that incorporates authentication and encryption schemes in order to create a secure connection to a corporate LAN that is made available to authorized users over the Internet. This type of connectivity is most familiar to telecommuters who log on to corporate networks from a home office or remote location through a secure connection.

Mobile and Wireless Network Connectivity are accomplished through software protocols that travel over standard radio waves. These software protocols negotiate connections between laptops or devices and/or laptops/devices and land-line networks. Often known as "wireless fidelity" or "WiFi," the radio waves that carry the wireless data are relatively easy to intercept and emulate and thus pose number of information security threats. The first is data interception. This can be avoided easily through the use of an encrypted network signal. The second problem is data emulation and this is more difficult to combat. In this scenario, certain devices can imitate a wireless base transceiver and hijack a network session, leading to the interception of passwords and other sensitive information that may pass over the network during the session. Technologies are still in development to combat this risk, but having a mobile device with properly configured network settings can be a significant first step in reducing the scope of this risk before stronger, more robust solutions are publicly available.

Voice Over Internet Protocol ("VoIP") allows telephone calls to be made over a private WAN or even the Internet itself. This system poses the same risk as network-connected PBX systems but also poses the additional risk of data interception when such data travel over an unsecured connection. It is paramount that VOIP equipment be locked down, placed behind firewalls, patched against vulnerabilities, and monitored with intrusion-detection systems in much the same way as a WAN (above).

Electronic Mail. By default, email is sent over the network in plain text format. Anyone who has access to the network traffic then has the ability to see the data contained in text email. Similar to a standard postcard sent through the mail, the electronic message can just as easily be read in transit, changed and then sent on to its intended recipient without the recipient's being aware of any alteration. Email encryption at either the network or application layer, or both, can prevent either of these eventualities. However, encryption by itself does not ensure that the person sending the mail is the person he/she claims to be. This raises the issue of non-repudiation. Digital signatures and public keys can be used to solve this problem and are discussed further into this chapter. [387]

Computer Platforms

Mainframe Computers. Many enterprises, especially banks and government agencies, continue to rely on mainframe computers as a key part of their IT infrastructure. Mainframes are very large computing hardware installations, hail from the very earliest days of information technology, and are generally housed within a physically secure mainframe building area. They present equally daunting challenges from an information security perspective by virtue of their sheer size and scope. System administrators are reluctant to make changes on these large machines and this often means there are equally large security holes present. The impact of any exploitation or breach of these machines can be enormous.

Server Computers are smaller and less powerful than mainframes, but satisfy many of the same enterprise functions. Servers may often even work in conjunction with a mainframe.

By design, servers are broadly distributed and can be physically located anywhere—not just within the same facility but at remote sites. However, such distribution of tasks makes these machines more difficult to secure both logically and physically.

Desktop Computers. As discussed above, desktops are powerful and able to store large amounts of information. However, for security purposes, no business-critical information should ever be stored on a desktop. All business-critical information should be stored in a centralized location where it can be secured and backed up.

The IT Organization

Effective project management is an often overlooked but crucial component in creating a secure information infrastructure. Without competent project management—and importantly, the skilled and experienced personnel to drive such management—complex IT projects often languish without the direction and leadership necessary to complete them. Even for relatively simple projects, a good project manager will anticipate problems ans ensure that projects are implemented according to design and will work with technical and non-technical staff to ensure that the project is used to its full potential.

Figure Four: Information Technology Roles and Responsibilities (Source IAPP)

Roles and Responsibilities

To maintain security within an organization, roles and responsibilities must be clearly understood

Chief Executive Officer and Executive Committee
- Oversee overall corporate security strategy
- Lead by example and sponsor adoption of security

Chief Security Officer
- Sets security strategy and policies
- Facilitates the implementation of security controls
- Undertakes security risk assessments
- Designs risk management strategy
- Coordinates independent audits

Security Personnel
- Implement, audit, enforce and assess compliance
- Advise and validate security designs and maintenance
- Keep abreast of new security developments (vulnerabilities, exploits, patches, etc.)
- Communicate policies, programs and training
- Monitor for security incidents
- Respond to security breaches

Outsourced Security Functions
- Supplements internal security personnel
- Should be overseen by internal security personnel

Managers and Employees
- Implement security controls
- Report security vulnerabilities and breaches
- Maintain awareness of security in action

Every organization should have a defined information security ("IS") department—whether in the form of an individual, group, team or entire division. Within this department, IS management should ensure that there are adequate knowledge and experience for managing the operation. Hiring only qualified professionals such as those certified in information systems security ("CISSP"), information management ("CISM") and/or information auditing ("CISA") is a prudent way to ensure an objective, validated standard of expertise. Additionally, companies should provide for ongoing training in technologies, policies and methods in order to keep the entire information security team knowledgeable and current.

The security department should also develop comprehensive security policies and procedures and communicate these to the organization as a whole—not just the immediate privacy and security groups concerned. These policies should incorporate industry-standard best practices such as those espoused by the National Institute of Standards in Technology ("NIST"), the IT Governance Institute's "Control Objectives for Information and Related Technology ("COBIT") and the International Standards Organization ("ISO") ISO 17799 standard.

It is important that the security department have a role in overseeing system administration groups when it comes to validating and communicating system maintenance. Regular system maintenance is one of the simplest and most important security functions. Security patches come out often for operating systems, and it is important that these patches are applied in a timely way.[388] However, system administrators are often reluctant to make changes to a system because they can see their role more as ensuring system uptime than security. Since patches can sometimes create system instability, administrators will often try to wait as long as possible to apply them.

Figure Five: Information Technology Training (Source: IAPP)

Security Awareness Training

Technology alone cannot provide information security — education and awareness among employees are key

Ensure that all employees understand:
- The value of security and the importance of recognizing and reporting incidents
- Their roles and responsibilities in fulfilling their security responsibilities
- Security policies and procedures including password protection, information sensitivity and information protection
- Basic security issues such as virus, hacking and social engineering
- The importance of compliance with legal/regulatory requirements

Ultimately, security is about people—not technology. The information security department should help the company understand that security is everyone's job. With that in mind, security training must become an integral part of every employee's knowledge base.

It is important that all employees are trained to recognize security incidents and know the process for reporting them. Employees should know and be expected to follow security policies and procedures. Finally, all employees should understand essential security basics such as not sharing passwords, not talking business in public, and avoiding social engineering. Employees should also be familiar with regulated requirements, policies, standards and procedures that affect their industry (e.g., HIPAA, Gramm-Leach-Bliley and other applicable laws).

Information Asset Oversight

Information security systems must be designed and implemented with the dual purpose of providing access to the end-user while protecting the data from the end user.[390] Misuse of systems by authorized users is the single largest cause of data loss and data compromise in the marketplace today.[391] Users must be provided access only to data required for their specific job.[392] All high-level access (e.g., ROOT or administrator-level privileges) should be reserved for technical or security professionals. A privacy professional must always work with the user in mind, both to keep the user's system secure and to secure the system from the user.[393]

The first step in protecting information is to understand what data your organization holds, and who—both within, and without the organization—owns such data. This means not only identifying what the information is but also where the information is physically located. Once the information is identified, it is also important to create an asset-tracking process so that machines containing PII can be repaired, maintained, re-used, and retired securely. Again, this tracking principle applies to information that is owned by the organization as well as information that is owned by others, but used by the organization.

Retention of Records

Retaining sensitive data—including personal information—is imperative for a variety of reasons. Aside from the obvious concerns about organizational integrity, there are business and legal factors that must be considered.

Retention schedules should address record types (level of sensitivity) and retention periods (duration of storage) and should be based on demonstrated business needs as well as any of the regulatory requirements as described in Chapter Two. Process controls should be implemented that protect essential data from loss, falsification or inadvertent destruction.

A recommended minimum period of record retention is six years. One reason is the audit power retained by the U.S. Internal Revenue Service ("IRS") for purposes of tax fraud investigations. Other powers of inquiry may come into play such as the U.S. Securities and Exchange Commission ("SEC"), Equal Employment Opportunity Commission ("EEOC"), Federal Trade Commission ("FTC") and state attorneys general. All of these regulators hold oversight and enforcement powers for information privacy as articulated in Chapter Two. Ultimately, your organization should work with its own corporate counsel or attorney to determine what legal aspects should be considered in creating a viable and defensible data retention policy.[394]

Duplication of Records

Duplicates of important records should be maintained in case one copy is displaced or lost entirely. However, maintaining multiple sets of sensitive data compounds the difficulty of keeping such data private. These factors must all be weighed when evaluating the costs and benefits of maintaining multiple record copies.

Once it is determined that records are no longer needed, they should be deliberately and securely destroyed. While paper records are easily shredded and disposed of, electronic records are more difficult to completely eliminate. Even when electronic records are deleted from a computer system's file directory, the record itself is not necessarily eliminated and the "deleted" data may be easily recoverable.[395] Computer operating systems function much like the traditional library card catalog: when a new file is created, the operating system creates a record showing where the file is located on the drive. When the file is "deleted," the operating system deletes the record from the drive and then indicates that the physical space is free to accommodate a new file. However, the file itself is never deleted, though it eventually may be overwritten with new data. Yet, even when the old data are overwritten with new data, the old data are still not gone completely.

Computer hard drives work by using a magnet to change the polarity of charged particles on the surface of the magnetic disc. This process is inexact at the atomic level, so that even after the drive head writes new data in an area, a magnetic "shadow" of the previous data remains. That is why, for example, security experts were able to recover readable sensitive information off the hard drives purchased from resellers on Ebay using readily available software even after the drives had been reformatted and over-written many times.[396] From 158 drives, the team recovered 5,000 credit card numbers, and one drive, apparently from an ATM machine, contained a year's worth of transactions including account numbers and other sensitive bank information.

It remains essential that persons involved in information security have a full understanding of the data structures of computer operating systems, the physical properties of computer hard drives, and the level of security required to protect data across both systems and drives.

Information Classification

Information directories and the records they contain may be quantified according to their value to the organization, as well as by ownership, and how critical such information is to the operations of the organization. Generally speaking, the higher the value of the information the greater the security required. For example, an employee directory may not be as highly valued as a customer database which includes sensitive PII—depending upon the country within which the organization operates and the corresponding legal requirements in that jurisdiction regarding acquisition, storage, use and/or disclosure of personal information. Once a value has been given to the information asset then a classification can be established and corresponding security level can be identified and implemented.

Figure Six: Information Asset Classification (Source: IAPP)

Asset Classification

Information should be protected in accordance with the value of the asset... The higher the value, the greater the security needed.

Asset value should be evaluated based on:
• Sensitivity and confidentiality
• Potential liability
• Intelligence value
• Criticality to the business

Effective risk management balances the potential for loss with the cost of security protection and management.

An information classification scheme provides the basis for managing access to, and protection of, information assets as well as for establishing a clear understanding of the relative sensitivity of the information. Asset value can be evaluated based upon a number of factors including confidentiality, potential liability, intelligence value (for government or business) and criticality to the organization. Effective information security—and risk management generally—balances the potential for loss of these assets with the cost of their security protection and management.

Three of the most common information classification levels are:

- *Confidential:* Information, which, if disclosed, would cause the business to be seriously compromised or outright fail (e.g., a customer databases that include large amount of sensitive PII). It is absolutely essential that this class of information remain secure and private;

- *Sensitive:* Important business information intended for internal use only (e.g., company contact directories, strategic business plans or sales revenue forecasts); and,

- *Public:* Information that may be safely shared with the public at large (e.g., marketing materials or a company's address—though in some cases, the latter is considered sensitive for security purposes).

Outsourcing IT Functions

Outsourcing in everything from software design to hardware construction to call centers is an increasingly popular option for businesses looking to reduce their IT costs. While businesses generally do a good job in ensuring that outsourcing will function and produce a quality work product, they often do much less to ensure that outsourced data will remain secure. Even if IT systems are outsourced, the management and security of these systems must remain internal.[397]

The security requirements of an organization that is engaging in outsourcing should be addressed in a contract that is agreed upon between the parties. This contract should reflect:

- Security roles and responsibilities;
- Requirements for information protection in order to achieve levels of security with the third party that are equivalent to those of the organization;
- Information ownership and appropriate use;
- Physical and logical access controls;
- Security control testing of the third party;
- Continuity of services in the event of a disaster;
- An incident coordination process;
- The right to conduct audits; and,
- A clear statement of respective liabilities.

In addition to the agreement initiating the data relationship, sound operational practices should be implemented and supported by the underlying agreement. For example, one U.S. insurance company that outsources work to India has the following security procedures in place for the outsourced employees:[398]

- Employees and their belongings are subject to search when arriving and leaving the workplace
- Cell phones are checked-in and held until the day is over
- Papers are shredded on a daily basis
- Computer security prevents files from being moved or copied
- Phone privileges are limited to calls to the help desk
- The Internet and email are similarly "locked down"

Again, effective business contracts with liability clauses are both advisable and necessary.

Information Systems Security

Access by an individual employee to an organization's information systems should be tied to the role the employee plays and should require further management approval at the departmental (IS/IT), operational (CIO/CTO) and, if necessary, executive (CEO) levels of the organization.

> *No employee should have greater information access than is necessary to capably perform his or her job function.*

These types of precautions are known as "Role-Based Access Controls" ("RBAC"). They are built on the basic security principle of "least privilege" (e.g., access is granted on the basis of the lowest possible level of access required to perform the function). Most commonly, job role/responsibility and executive clearance are the measures that determine the level of access control for a particular employee.

While stringently assigned and controlled, individual system access accounts are also necessary in order to ensure system accountability. The alternative—a shared or group account—is essentially anonymous and poses acute security risks. Organizations must know who is accessing information and when—down to the individual level. This keeps end users—whether employees, partners, suppliers or customers—accountable and facilitates quicker and easier identification when an account is being compromised.

> ***Non-repudiation*** *is the ability to ensure that neither the originator nor the receiver can dispute the validity of a transaction or access request. An independent verification takes place which allows the sender's identity to be verified by a third party, and also allows the sender to know that the intended recipient of the message actually received it. Non-repudiation of origin proves that data have been sent and non-repudiation of delivery proves that the data have been reviewed.*

Authentication

Once individual access accounts have been identified, approved and established, information security professionals employ methods of authentication and authorization to monitor access and thus ensure system security over time.

Authentication identifies an individual account user based upon a known credential (log-in, password, digital certificate, identity card, etc.) and/or biometric identifier (fingerprint, voice recording, iris scan, etc.). Often a combination of two such attributes (credential and biometric) will be required—a process known as "two-factor" authentication.

Security Case Study:
ChoicePoint

The ChoicePoint case involved the appropriation of sensitive personal information by disingenuous third parties through a vulnerability in the organization's credentialing process.

In late 2004, ChoicePoint, a Georgia-based data broker, reported the event of a data breach to law enforcement in the state of California. After a delay in notification at the request of law enforcement, the company then notified individuals living within the state of California beginning in February, 2005, as they were obligated to do under SB 1386, the state's data breach notification law. Shortly thereafter, ChoicePoint notified potentially affected individuals who resided outside of California despite the lack (at the time) of any state law, federal law or other precedent that may have compelled such action.

The FTC, following its own investigation alleged that ChoicePoint was in violation of relevant sections of the FTC Act and the Fair Credit Reporting Act (FCRA). The FTC Act, FCRA and SB 1386 are all described in detail under Chapter Two.

Facts and Allegations

ChoicePoint is a Georgia-based company that collects and sells consumer reports and other consumer data to businesses, professionals and government agencies that use the data for risk management, FCRA permissible purposes such as insurance underwriting and employment and other purposes. These entities must apply to become ChoicePoint subscribers. The applications are processed in order to establish that the applicant is a legitimate organization and has an appropriate permissible purpose for purchasing the consumer data. Once the applicant is approved as a subscriber, they may access consumer data from ChoicePoint.

In late 2004, ChoicePoint discovered that sensitive personal information of approximately 145,000 consumers had been disclosed to persons who lacked a proper purpose to obtain such information. According to the FTC, the information was obtained by criminals who had been approved as subscribers based on applications containing false information and other misrepresentations.

The FTC alleged that ChoicePoint failed to have reasonable procedures in place to screen potential subscribers and therefore failed to detect the false information and other misrepresentations in the applications. As a result, the FTC alleged that ChoicePoint violated the Fair Credit Reporting Act by:

- Furnishing consumer reports to subscribers who did not have a permissible purpose,
- Failing to first make a reasonable effort to verify the identity of the prospective user and its intended uses of the consumer reports,
- Continuing to furnish consumer reports when it had reasonable grounds for believing the consumer reports would not be used for a permissible purpose, and
- Failing to monitor and identify unauthorized activity after being alerted of fraudulent activity from authorities between 2001 and 2005.

The FTC alleged that ChoicePoint also violated the FTC Act by failing to use reasonable and appropriate measures to protect the security of sensitive personal information and that this failure caused or is likely to cause substantial injury to consumers. The FTC classified these acts and practices as unfair or deceptive under Section 5 of the FTC Act.

Privacy and Security Promises

ChoicePoint had adopted privacy principles since at least 1999, and publicized them through its Web sites, in contracts, in annual reports and other documents. It made the following representations regarding the security and privacy of personal information it collects and sells:

1. "ChoicePoint allows access to your consumer reports only by those authorized under the FCRA. In addition, each ChoicePoint customer must verify that he/she has a 'permissible purpose' before receiving a consumer report."

2. "Every ChoicePoint customer must successfully complete a rigorous credentialing process."

3. "ChoicePoint does not distribute information to the general public and monitors the use of its public record information to ensure appropriate use."

4. "ChoicePoint uses administrative, technical, personnel, and physical safeguards to protect the confidentiality and security of personally identifiable information in our possession. These safeguards are designed to ensure a level of security appropriate to the nature of the data being processed and the risks of confidentiality violations involved."

FTC Stipulated Order with ChoicePoint

1. *Bar on Misrepresentation:* ChoicePoint shall not misrepresent the manner or extent to which it maintains and protects the privacy, confidentiality or security of the personal information it collects.

2. *FCRA-related Provisions*: ChoicePoint is permanently restrained from furnishing consumer reports to persons who do not have a permissible purpose; therefore it must maintain reasonable procedures to ensure that consumer reports are provided only to those with a permissible purpose. These procedures include obtaining written certification from each subscriber describing the nature of its business and specific intended permissible purpose for using consumer data, and following that with verification of the subscriber's identity, the legitimacy of its business and determining whether each subscriber has a permissible purpose. In addition, ChoicePoint must use various means to alert subscribers to the penalties for violating FCRA.

3. *Security Program*: ChoicePoint shall establish, implement and maintain a well-documented, comprehensive information security program reasonably (a) designed to protect the security, confidentiality, and integrity of consumers' personal information, and (b) contain administrative, technical and physical safeguards appropriate for the size, complexity, nature, and scope of its business.

4. *Requirements of Security Program:* The program shall include:
   a. Designation of an employee responsible for the security program;
   b. Identification of internal and external threats to security, confidentiality, and integrity of personal information through an assessment focusing on employee training, information systems, and potential system failures;
   c. Design and implementation of reasonable safeguards to identified risks; and,
   d. Evaluation and adjustment of the information security program according to assessment and any material changes in business.

5. *Third Party Audit:* Within 180 days after service of order and thereafter biannually for 20 years, ChoicePoint must obtain an assessment and report from an independent, third party within 60 days after the end of the reporting period that:
   a. Sets forth the specific safeguards implemented and maintained by ChoicePoint;
   b. Explains how such safeguards are appropriate for the size and complexity of ChoicePoint, the nature and scope of ChoicePoint's activities and the sensitivity of the consumers' information;
   c. Explains how the implemented safeguards meet or exceed the protections required above; and,
   d. Certifies that ChoicePoint's security program is operating with sufficient effectiveness to provide reasonable assurances that consumer information is protected.

6. *Maintenance of Relevant Documents:* For a period of six years, ChoicePoint shall create and retain the following:
   a. Subscriber files containing all materials used in the verification of the identity of subscribers;
   b. Consumer complaints and responses to complaints;

c. Copies of all training materials;

d. Copies of all subpoenas and communications with law enforcement personnel; and,

e. Copies of all records or documents that show full compliance with the order.

For a period of three years after the preparation of each biennial assessment, ChoicePoint shall retain all plans, reports, studies, reviews, audits, audit trails, policies, training materials, work papers and assessments.

7. *Delivery of Order.* For a period of five years after service of order, ChoicePoint shall deliver a copy of the FTC order to all officers and directors, and managers who have responsibility related to this order. Within 10 days after service of order, ChoicePoint shall deliver an accurate summary of the order to all current employees who are engaged in conduct related to ChoicePoint's compliance with the order or the required information security program and assessments. Future employees engaging in the above conduct should receive the summary no later than the date they assume job responsibilities. Within 30 days of delivery of the order, ChoicePoint shall obtain signed and dated statements acknowledging receipt of the order from each person.

8. *Reporting.* For a period of 20 years after service of order, ChoicePoint shall notify the FTC at least 30 days prior to any corporate change that may affect compliance with the order. Within 180 days after service of order and thereafter as requested, ChoicePoint shall file a report with the FTC setting forth its compliance with the order.

Duration of the FTC Order
Not specified

Fine Imposed
$10 million in civil penalties plus an additional $5 million for consumer redress.

Conclusion
In the days and weeks following ChoicePoint's data breach incident, the company undertook a series of steps to identify and address the areas of its security, privacy and credentialing that needed to be enhanced. With this came an unprecedented level of internal and external scrutiny, not just of the company's business practices but of the customers of the company as well: ChoicePoint's customers were asked to undergo a re-certification process that included site visits to their primary places of business. This effort involved ChoicePoint's senior leadership and resulted in a vastly improved public perception of the company's commitment to protecting personally identifiable information from misuse.

Password Management

The most basic level of end user authentication is a password scheme—although such schemes can become complex. A password is an example of *"one-factor" authentication* such that it relies on one input (the password sequence) to validate the end user.

Administrative passwords that allow broad access to information systems are particularly crucial to keep password-protected. In addition, system administrators should keep different passwords for their personal accounts and administrative privileges.

Some of the industry-standard password conventions in use today include the following:

- System passwords should be independently assigned and used (not shared);

- Blank-field passwords should never be used;

- Passwords should consist of at least 8 characters in length (if the system supports such length; if not, then as many as the system does support);

- A combination of upper and lower case letters, numbers, and at least one special character should be used in composing the password;

- Passwords should be actively cycled at least once every 30 days: existing passwords retired and replaced with new passwords; inactive passwords or passwords of departed or terminated employees disabled completely;

- Password schemes should not be associated with anything that may be broadly familiar to the individual or others at the organization such as nicknames, pet names or known interest such as a favorite sports team; and,

- Common dictionary words, a well-known string of numbers, or birthdates should be avoided in any password scheme.

Repeating or reusing existing passwords does not offer a viable alternative since a previous password can become compromised. However, maintaining a strong password scheme is often difficult because the more complex the password the more difficult it often is for end users to fully memorize the scheme and use the password in a practical manner. When password aging is added to the complexity requirement, users will generally resort to writing down passwords or storing them in some other insecure manner.

Though passwords should never be stored in any location that is within plain view of a casual observer (both virtually and physically), sometimes this is not practicable. Password storage policies must be made with the strong understanding that access to a password is equivalent to access to the system itself.

The intent of a complex password scheme is to prevent "brute force" password attacks. These are exploits that attempt to undermine an individual password or group of passwords by running all possible word and number combinations against the system. Obviously, the simpler the password scheme the more likely such an exploit will accurately determine the password and then emulate the password in order to gain access to the system. With every extra character and character set in the password, the difficulty in guessing a password through a brute force attack or other exploit becomes exponentially more difficult.

Implementing a strong but user-friendly policy an important part of ensuring a functional and effective one-factor (password-based) security framework.

Two-factor authentication schemes combine the same password requirements and process articulated above with a second credential. This can include any one of the following:

- *Pass-card:* an identity instrument that can range from a magnetic strip (similar to a credit card) to more sophisticated device embedded with computer chips;

- *Smart-card:* a small, electronic device that contains a certain capacity for digital memory as well as, possibly, an integrated circuit for active data processing; and/or,

- *Biometric:* a biological identifier such as a fingerprint, palmprint, voice scan, iris scan or other unique physiological attribute that can be identified and evaluated dynamically through an available technology.

The two-factor process will analyze both the password and the additional credential as well as determine the validity of both attributes before authenticating the access request.

Digital Signatures

Digital signatures provide a means for ensuring the authenticity of an electronic document—whether an email, text file, document, spreadsheet or image file. If anything is changed in the electronic document after the digital signature is attached, it also changes the value associated with the document and this renders the signature invalid.

The Digital Signature Standard ("DSS") is the certificate protocol most commonly used in connection with electronic documents. It is based upon a type of public-key encryption (defined below) that uses the Digital Signature Algorithm ("DSA") endorsed by many U.S. government agencies for the purpose of securing sensitive information. The DSA consists of a private key, known only by the originator of the document (the signer) plus a public key that is offered to select recipients of the document.

Public Key Infrastructure ("PKI")

PKI is a system of digital certificates, certificate authorities and other registration entities that verifies the validity of each party involved in an electronic transaction through the use of cryptographic (coded or encrypted) signatures. PKI enables users of insecure public networks (such as the Internet) to privately and securely exchange electronic data and/or digital money with other parties.

The term PKI represents a set of security ideals and the means to accomplish them. It can be applied to a number of different source technologies rather than any single technology.[399]

PKI schemes permit a sender to create two unique tokens (identifiers) similar to the DSA algorithm described above:

1. A "public key" which allows anyone to encrypt data and send it securely to the recipient; and,

2. A "private key" which allows the recipient to unlock the data signature and view the contents of the message in a readable format such as plain text.

PKI implementations use encryption to guarantee the safety and reliability of data transmitted over an insecure network. This yields a number of security assurances:

1. That the data have not been altered or corrupted in transit;

2. That the source of the data is who or what it claims to be;

3. That the transmitted data have remained private and secure while in transit; and,

4. That the transmitted data may be introduced as evidence in a court or law.[400]

PKI implementations use public key encryption to fulfill these goals. The public key allows anyone to encrypt data and send them securely; the recipient then uses his or her private key to unlock the data, the only key that will return the data to plain text.[401]

Authorization

Authorization is the process of determining if the end user, once authenticated, is permitted to have access to the desired resource such as the information asset or the information system containing the asset. Authorization criteria may be based upon organizational role, job function, group or departmental membership, level of security clearance, executive order, any combination of these factors or all of these factors.

The process, when effective, validates that the person or entity requesting access is in fact who or what they claim to be.

Even with appropriate safeguards in place, on principle, no one person should have complete access to all business systems. The duties of systems and security administrators should be segregated. This provides accountability, oversight, and mitigation of damages. Also, from a business continuity standpoint, no one person should be the only person who can perform any single, essential function. If that person is suddenly lost, then operations stop.

Changes in employee position, responsibility level or even employment status are some of the more common workplace events from an organizational perspective. System access levels need to be adjusted just as an employee's role changes. Since these factors tend to be neglected, information systems must be reviewed periodically to ensure that accounts and access levels accurately reflect employment level and status. Where necessary, system access accounts should be deleted—particularly those of former employees.

Intrusion Prevention

Based on the premise that prevention is the best possible cure, information security professionals strive to prevent any unauthorized access to data assets before the access even occurs. This is accomplished through a variety of means from modest hardware and software implementations (such as firewalls and anti-virus solution suites) to the more intricate methods of cryptographic schemes (such as the examples of public key encryption described above).

Some of the most dangerous system vulnerabilities are the simplest. For example, an empty, logged-on workstation is the equivalent of an openly available user ID and password. Desktops should be configured to time-out after a certain period of inactivity and revert to a locked screen-saver or other automated mechanism that prevents unauthorized access while the workstation user is away.

Improper Internet and email use also offers an easy way for users to create network vulnerabilities. Incoming and outgoing email should be scanned for viruses, suspect documents, and executable software attachments such as spyware or adware applications.

Information Security Case Study:
Visa

One real-world example of a successful information security program in the banking industry is the Cardholder Information Security Program ("CISP") developed and managed by bank card issuer, Visa. To comply with this program, merchants must meet the following requirements under the Payment Card Interface ("PCI") Data Security Standard that Visa developed in conjunction with another card issuer, MasterCard:[402]

1. Build and Maintain a Secure Network
   a. Install and maintain a firewall configuration to protect data
   b. Do not use vendor-supplied defaults for system passwords and other security parameters

2. Protect Cardholder Data
   a. Protect stored data
   b. Encrypt transmission of cardholder data and sensitive information across public networks

3. Maintain a Vulnerability Management Program
   a. Use and regularly update anti-virus software
   b. Develop and maintain secure systems and applications

4. Implement Strong Access Control Measures
   a. Restrict access to data by business need-to-know
   b. Assign a unique ID to each person with computer access
   c. Restrict physical access to cardholder data

5. Regularly Monitor and Test Networks
   a. Track and monitor all access to network resources and cardholder data
   b. Regularly test security systems and processes

6. Maintain an Information Security Policy
   a. Maintain a policy that addresses information security

Anti-virus solutions offer a straightforward and relatively easy-to-implement protection against system intrusions of the software variety. Virus programs developed and deployed by "hackers" and other exploit artists from inside or outside the organization, are often used to create specific vulnerabilities in the organization's network systems. These include "back-doors" that allow immediate and open access as well as "Trojan" programs that masquerade as ineffectual programs but which in fact mutate into far more nefarious, barrier-breaking tools that also allow unauthorized access to the network.

Other viruses exist in the form of "key-loggers" that record everything that is typed into a computer through a keyboard or other input device (personal information that may include names, user IDs, passwords and other data). The key-logger program monitors and records these data and transmits them back to the hacker.

Anti-virus protection can be deployed against these system intrusions in several ways. The easiest is maintaining a centralized mail server with anti-virus capabilities that scan all incoming and outgoing messages.

The most effective anti-virus method is also the most complex and expensive: vectoring anti-virus software works within a network "firewall" solution (defined separately, below) and scans all incoming data for virus signatures in the data streams.[403] If there is a large volume of network traffic, the machines handling vectoring anti-virus software must be very powerful to make this solution completely effective.

Firewalls are generally used as means of protecting internal networks from external networks. A firewall is a software program that resides at the network router or server level and is configured with a policy that allows only certain types of traffic to move in certain directions. Firewall policies can be very detailed and can be designated based on user, type of use, machine, time of day, and/or application variety, among a multitude of other factors. The more specific the policy the more security it can provide—but also the more difficult the firewall is to manage and maintain.

Firewalls should block access to potentially dangerous sites (e.g. hacker and porn sites often contain browser exploit code). These systems should also articulate clear use policies on email and Internet access and these policies should be consistent with the organizational security philosophy described in the employee manual or privacy policy.

Perimeter Controls

Information security professionals also manage technologies and processes that are designed to secure an entire network environment by preventing penetration from the outside. This is called "controlling the perimeter" of the network and the different methods include:

- Network and host-based firewalls;
- "Malware" (bad software) detection and anti-virus application suites;
- Access control lists (with anti-spoofing) that reside on networks;
- Host and network-based Intrusion Detection Systems ("IDS");
- Host and network-based Intrusion Prevention Systems ("IPS");
- Connection encryption schemes such as Virtual Private Networks ("VPN"), Secure Sockets Layer ("SSL") and Internet Protocol Security ("IPSEC") protocols; and,
- Strong user, email and device encryption.

Anti-virus, firewall and encryption-based solutions have already been addressed in this chapter. The Web-based security protocols of SSL and IPSEC are defined in Chapter Five.

Intrusion Detection Systems ("IDS") inspect network activity and identify suspicious patterns that may indicate a network or system attack from someone attempting to penetrate or compromise a system. Such systems provide policies and rules for network traffic along with an intrusion detection system for alerting system or network administrators to suspicious traffic.

An IDS:
* May be network-based or host-based
* May be signature-based or anomaly-based
* Requires human intervention in order to respond to the attack

Intrusion Prevention Systems ("IPS") are often considered to be extensions of IDS but are actually another form of access control. An IPS is much like an application layer firewall:
* Its intent is not only to detect a network attack but to prevent it
* It neither requires nor involves human intervention in order to respond to a system attack.

Security Monitoring

Information security professionals can monitor the success of IDS, IPS and other perimeter controls through the use and analysis of log files. These are essentially "event reports" that are generated automatically based on the originating system, computer, software application or software tool.

Many computer operating systems such as Unix, Linux, and Windows record natural as well as suspect events ("anomalies") in any one or all of three different log types: application logs, system logs, and security logs.

* ***The Application Log*** contains events logged by applications or programs. For example, a database program might record a file error in the Application Log. The program developer decides which events to record.

* ***The System Log*** contains events logged by the operating system components. For example, the failure of a driver or other system component to load during startup is recorded in the System Log. The event types logged by system components are predetermined for the operating system.

* ***The Security Log*** can record security events, such as valid and invalid logon attempts as well as events related to resource use, such as creating, opening, or deleting files.

An administrator can specify what events are recorded in the Security Log. For example, if you have enabled logon auditing, attempts to log on to the system are recorded in the Security Log.[404]

In order to minimize risk to an information system, many factors need to be considered, managed and minimized to the best of an organization's abilities. One industry-standard risk assessment formula is:

$$Risk = Threat \; x \; Vulnerability \; x \; Expected \; Loss$$

Security metrics help evaluate the effectiveness of security policies, processes and products as well as help to calculate the risk and determine the value of reducing or mitigating the risk.

Some of the metrics that contribute to a risk/threat/vulnerability/loss matrix are the number of security breaches, the number of system outages and the number of lost information assets. Additional factors include the presence of software viruses and the use of investigations such as computer auditing and forensics (described further under "Incident Handling" below).

Number of breaches. A breach is defined as any time an attacker enters into the organization's system, even if no information is altered or stolen. Breaches are common and expected. The essential feature is how well an organization reacts. The National Strategy to Secure Cyberspace reported that while 90% of companies had security systems installed, 90% had also experienced a breach.[405] Often, one breach is intended to allow others to happen more easily. Therefore, the breach must be remedied as soon after detection as possible.

Number of outages. An outage occurs when a component of the information system is taken offline as the result of an attack. Outages are a frightening—but not cataclysmic—outcome of a security breach. If an organization retains cached information, the users may never know that there has been an outage in the system at all.[406] At a much higher level, the United States could be devastatingly affected if it became the successful target of a terrorist attack to the power grid or other central system or utility. As interoperable entities, both public and private security systems need to be in place and include an integrated plan for how to react should an outage occur on such a massive scale.[407]

Unauthorized access occurs when an individual who does not have proper authorization to view information does so. It may lead to improper modifications, disclosures, or deletions.[408] This may apply to email, databases, or confidential reports. Often, unauthorized access may be detected by noting unusual access patterns to a system.[409]

Lost assets can be in the form of money or data, occurring through theft or a breach or improper disposal techniques.

Software Viruses. According to an ICSA Labs 2003 Virus Prevalence Survey, in 2003 nine of the Top 10 reported viruses were "mass mailers."[410] The only virus that did not contain a mass-mailing functionality was Blaster.[411] Emails are also the most common way to be infected with a virus, and its dominance as a source is increasing.[412] One is five times more likely to be infected through an email than the next common form, Internet downloads.[413] As ICSA concludes in the 2003 report, "The impact of viruses on organizations is huge. The impact goes far beyond money, resources, and effort required to recover from such incidents. It also includes loss of productivity, corrupt and/or lost data, and loss of user confidence."[414]

Investigations are aided through an organization's audit and monitoring controls. The administrator should be able to work backwards through the logs, reports, and forensics to determine the nature and extent of the attack. The investigation should occur both during and after the attack to ensure the shortest response time and least data loss.

Contingency Planning

Threats to an information system can take many different forms and arrive through different channels—external and internal. The Internet, with its wide and unregulated expanse, poses a significant danger to any organization and remains a continued threat source with its preponderance of software viruses, spyware applications, phishing exploits and unsolicited ("spam") email.

As intimated earlier, the greatest security threat to an organization originates from inside the organization. The U.S. Federal Bureau of Investigation ("FBI") confirms that employees are the number one source of unauthorized data access as well as outright data theft and data destruction.[415] While most security is aimed outward to protect against attacks from the public, many businesses fail to design their information security systems and policies to protect against an internal compromise. Data loss caused intentionally or inadvertently is still data loss—irrespective of source.

Exploit Tools

As acute as internal threats can be to an organization's data assets, external threats remain quite real. One reason is the easy availability of automated exploit tools: the largely home-made software programs that hackers develop and openly exchange with other exploit artists. They deploy these programs against information systems in various combinations, both in individual and combined attacks, with relative abandon and ruthless frequency.

Automated exploit tools are easily accessible, but, luckily, are also recognizable and relatively easy to defend against. Typically, these exploit tools are developed by sophisticated hackers in order to maximize or take advantage of a known and common vulnerability in a particular system. However, since the vulnerability is common (i.e., widely known), software patches (fixes) from legitimate software developers become rapidly and widely available at about the same time the exploit tool is distributed. Thus, for a prepared and vigilant security administrator, exploit tools pose little threat. However, for a company that does not apply security patches regularly and in a timely manner, these simple tools can become devastating.

Malicious Code

"Malware" is software whose purpose is to harm the system that loads it. Generally, it is considered a type of computer virus and may often take the form of a "Trojan horse" (bad software masquerading as good software). Malware applications can arrive as file attachments to emails or as executable software that is initiated through some form of network connection. Invariably, these applications hijack the computer and make it a "zombie" machine under the control of the external party. Files can be read or stolen and additional software attacks can be launched with the coordination of the malware application.

Currently, there is a very thin line between online threats (such as "spyware" and "adware" applications, defined further under Chapter Five) and truly destructive "malware." All of these will, at best, consume system resources, provide a means for outsiders to "view" a portion of a machine's contents and even track the activities of the machines' users.

Layered Attacks

A threat can be designed and deployed to attack an information system at any number of layers—from the network to the system to any of the applications that reside in between.

Network-Layer Attacks are those attacks that exploit the basic network protocol in order to gain any available advantage. These attacks generally involve "spoofing" a network address so that a computer sends data to an intruder rather than their proper recipient or destination. Other attacks can involve service disruptions through a denial of service ("DOS") attack—a brute force method that overloads the capacity of a Web site's domain such that it renders the server inoperable.

Applications that "listen" to Internet server ports in order to track suspicious activity often themselves contain vulnerabilities that may allow a hacker to gain access. A good preventive strategy is to deactivate all unnecessary network services and block any and all unused or idle network ports so that the scope of any vulnerability is drastically minimized.

Firewalls, located on both network perimeters and hosts, are generally fairly effective at preventing network layer attacks.

Application-Layer Attacks exploit flaws in the network applications that are installed on the network servers. Such weaknesses exist in Web browsers, email server software, network routing software and other standard enterprise applications. This constitutes the most common type of exploit because there are so many different possibilities for the hacker to consider.[416] The best way to prevent application attacks is to regularly apply all relevant and current patches and updates to all applications.

Disaster Recovery

Information security threats also can originate from beyond the human or technical realms—such as from catastrophes, unforeseen events and acts of nature.

Localized emergencies such as fires can pose a significant risk for data loss. Backup tapes should be stored in location away from the organization in order to ensure greater protection. Additionally, business machines should be kept in a off-site, data storage center designed for mission critical systems. These centers are continuously monitored, environmentally controlled with backup systems, and contain advanced fire suppression systems. Should a fire occur in a data center, the server is more likely to be destroyed by the sprinkler system than the fire.

Tornados, earthquakes, and hurricanes are admittedly very difficult to prepare for. These natural emergencies can affect a geographically significant area and bring considerable destruction. If an organization is located in an area prone to these types of events, it may be advisable to consider geographical co-location. Under this arrangement, the data center is exactly replicated in another location and contains data fail-over capacity. The challenge to co-location is keeping the data synchronized. Depending on the organization's business requirements, this may be a simple or extremely costly task.

When planning for catastrophic loss, an organization must provide for the eventuality that the physical systems (the facilities themselves and everything contained within) are completely destroyed. The remedial options range from simply purchasing new hardware to maintaining a replicated data center in another location that can be turned operational at a moment's notice. Obviously, these plans involve vastly different levels of cost and complexity. The business requirements will determine the type of contingency planning that is best for the organization.

While recovery of data and hardware is often planned for, application recovery is too often overlooked. This can become a significant problem if the organization uses custom applications. But even purchasing replacement "off the shelf" programs for installation may not be as simple as re-installing existing software. Many programs have very complex licensing procedures that may take days to process if not planned for in advance.

In summary, it is essential to have a business continuance strategy in place well in advance of any emergency. This strategy combines business contingency planning with IT recovery planning. A data security professional should work with business professionals to ensure that the core business functions will continue to operate after any emergency.

Incident Handling

Despite the strongest software tools, the most well developed contingency plan and the best communicated and rehearsed business continuance procedures, information security breaches can—and inevitably will—occur. It simply isn't possible to prevent them completely.

A detailed incident response plan should be developed that specifies how your enterprise will address a system compromise the moment it has been detected. This is especially important if that compromise causes a system-wide failure. Such a failure poses two, often competing concerns:

1. Securing other systems and beginning the process of identifying the nature of the intrusion as well as preventing future intrusions; and,

2. Getting production systems up and running in an effort to return to normal business operations.

A key first step to proper incident handling is a complete analysis and documentation of the incident. Computer forensics can offer the necessary details to troubleshoot a security breach.

> *Computer Forensics. The discipline of assessing and examining an information system for relevant clues even after it has been compromised by an exploit.*

The admissibility of computer forensic evidence is admittedly complex. For evidence to be admissible, it must be proven that the information presented has not been changed or altered. However, computers are constantly writing and re-writing data and a significant amount of forensic evidence can be altered or even lost entirely just by logging into a compromised system. A computer forensic expert should be consulted in constructing a policy or procedure so as to ensure that the integrity and lasting value of the forensics process are assured.

Assessing forensic information after a network intrusion also requires a trained professional. Even the most novice hacker will take steps to cover tracks, making it difficult to collect any relevant evidence along the network path.

It is absolutely essential that no one use a network or system after it has been compromised and until such time that forensic experts can analyze the system fully, and verify its condition. Most people do not know that even logging into a system can destroy important evidence. If a system has been compromised, the system should be immediately powered down (depending on the computer operating system), the hard drive should be removed, and data restored from backup onto a new drive. While not directly related to preservation of evidence, it also is important that a full system audit be performed to make sure that the vulnerability that was once exploited is not inadvertently restored or reactivated.

The methods employed by rogue employees, hackers and exploit artists are often revealed in basic behaviors that can be detected and observed by a discriminating information security professional. These behaviors include multiple failed system log-in attempts, use of long-idle or dormant access accounts, unexplained changes in access permissions, activity during non-business hours, use of unauthorized new accounts, files or applications and gaps in system logs.

- The presence of failed log in attempts may be an indication that someone is trying to access the system by guessing a password. The account should be monitored for further activity if not deactivated promptly.

- The sudden use of an idle or long-dormant access account may also indicate the compromise of a system. A dormant account may be an account that was created or modified by an intruder for later use. Usage should be monitored and dormant accounts deleted or verified as to why they are not in use.

- Hackers will often try to break into a system during non-work hours in hopes that they will not be detected until the next business day. Evidence of usage during unusual times of day is not a guarantee, but a strong indication of suspect system activity.

- The presence of an unauthorized access account (a new account not created by the system administrator) is itself strong evidence of a security compromise. Since only a "super-user" (system administrator) holds the authority to create an access account, the existence of an unauthorized account requires the presumption that such super-user privileges have been compromised and ought to be re-architected entirely.

- A key sign of a system compromise is the presence of unfamiliar programs or files. Hackers will often leave programs or files behind themselves in their virtual "travels" for the purpose of collecting data or permitting return access. However, the only real way to know that a file does not belong to a specific directory is to know what files do belong. This requires a full system audit with complete documentation that identifies all authorized files by name, variety and size. Programs are available that can automate this rather laborious process.[417]

- Hackers will often exploit vulnerabilities, such as weak user passwords or psychological manipulation (pre-texting or social engineering) in order to gain low-level access to a system. The hackers' job then is to elevate the privileges of that account to gain more access. Unexplained elevation of privileges is a sure sign of a system compromise.

- Changes in file permissions can be a very significant clue to unauthorized access. Only users with privileges equal to that of the file have the ability to make any such changes. Therefore, unauthorized changes to the permissions of a super-user file indicate a compromise of the super-user account.

- Discovering gaps in system logs is the most common way of discovering a system compromise. In an attempt to hide his/her tracks, a hacker will attempt to delete those logs that automatically record exploits. Since log files are generally very long transcripts of all system activities, it can be difficult to detect any discernable gaps. Scripts and programs can automate the task of log validation.

It also is considered good practice to establish a highly secure log host. This provides a secure location for logs to reside and single point for monitoring logs from all the systems on a network.[418] Additionally, system logs can be simultaneously written on the local system and on a remote system and then periodically compared. If the second log can be written to write-once media like a CD-ROM or a printer, then you can know for sure that the second source is valid.

Conclusion

Information security is a central business function precisely because it enables virtually every other type of business function within the organization to operate. Security ensures a high level of confidence in information management and must itself be considered a formal business function in order for the organization to be successful. Security-enabling technologies, policies and methods are integral parts of any successful privacy program and must be included in an organization's business life cycle from design through implementation to retirement.

Effective information security can also become a significant financial investment for an organization. It is important for privacy professionals to explain IT and information security expenditures in terms of Return on Investment ("ROI") and to demonstrate to executive management (and other stakeholders in the organization) that investments in security will reflect positively in the organization's bottom line.

Most importantly, effective information security reinforces the privacy programs and policies the organization implements. These serve as the bedrock of the consumer and stakeholder trust the organization has established and will continue to build over time.

Chapter Five

ONLINE PRIVACY

Introduction and Learning Objectives

The Internet and World Wide Web have enabled an ease and immediacy of information exchange that at one time was unimaginable. Online communications and electronic commerce are now common parts of contemporary life and business.

At the same time, the breadth and speed of Internet technologies has allowed new privacy risks to develop. While laws and regulations attempt to keep pace with these risks, the nature of online fraud and computer crime is becoming more sophisticated and threatening each day. Certain protections are essential in order to ensure the privacy and security of personal information online while building the confidence and integrity necessary to help revolutionary media like the Internet and World Wide Web to continue to grow and thrive.

"Online Privacy" describes the key platforms, protocols and enabling technologies that power the Internet and World Wide Web. It provides an overview of privacy and security considerations for an organization's external Web sites and other e-commerce channels such as electronic mail.

The CIPP will understand:

- The technical makeup of the Internet and World Wide Web from a privacy perspective;

- Privacy and security considerations for collecting personal information online, delivering online features and services based on preferential data and tracking end user activities online;

- The privacy concerns around children's online activities;

- The emerging online threats of spam email, spyware applications and phishing exploits;

- The importance of effective online disclosure mechanisms such as P3P and layered notices; and,

- A selection of online privacy standards and best practices that mitigate risk while building and maintaining the trust of end users and customers.

Overview of Web Technologies

The Internet is a global network that connects millions of computers around the world and allows these machines to exchange electronic information with each other nearly instantaneously.

The precursor to the Internet we know today was the ARPAnet, a military computer network developed in the early 1960s by the U.S. Advance Research Projects Agency ("ARPA"). The ARPAnet established a secure means for the exchange of military information[419] and grew to expand scientific research when the National Science Foundation ("NSF") became involved with the network in the early 1970s.

Far from its origins in usage—and in spite of the subsequent availability of expanded applications—the Internet today remains essentially the same as it was when it was first designed. Data on the vast network are transferred by shuttling small pieces of information known as data "packets" from one computer to the next. Packets are disassembled on transmission, scattered throughout the network while in transit and then dynamically reassembled upon arrival to the destination computer. This open and dynamic nature of the Internet enables its speed, functionality and continued growth but—as will be described further in to this chapter—also exposes it to certain information privacy vulnerabilities.

The World Wide Web is an information sharing model that is built on top of the Internet. It was first designed to facilitate the exchange not just of text-based information—as the Internet did primarily—but also graphic images, interactive document files and other "richer" information formats.

The Web functions entirely on two key software languages:

1. *Hypertext transfer protocol ("HTTP")*, a networking language that manages data packets over the Internet. HTTP defines how messages are formatted and transmitted over a TCP/IP network (defined below) for Web sites. Further, it defines what actions Web servers and Web browsers take in response to various commands; and,

2. *Hypertext markup language ("HTML")*, a content-authoring language used to create documents on the World Wide Web. Hundreds of document "tags" can be used to format and layout a Web page's content and to "hyperlink"—connect dynamically—to other Web content. Forms, links, pictures, and text may all be added with minimal commands. Headings are also imbedded into the text and are used by Web servers to process commands and return data with each request.[420]

Sir Tim Berners-Lee, a British physicist working out of the Switzerland-based particle physics laboratory known as CERN, developed the HTML authoring language in the early 1990s. Berners-Lee recognized the inherent limitations of the early Internet and advanced the HTML language as a means for research scientists such as himself to dynamically tie documents and files together—a capability he referred to as, "hyper-linking."

Also in the early 1990s, the U.S.-based National Center for Supercomputing Applications ("NCSA") developed the very first Web browser application, Mozilla. This browser software offered, for the first time, a user-friendly interface through which the ever-evolving Web documents and Web sites could be viewed from a personal computer. Mark Andreessen, an NSCA student and young author of Mozilla later went on to form Netscape Communications and create the product known today as the Netscape browser, a derivative of the earlier Mozilla.

The Web browser software is considered a "Web client" application in that it is used to navigate the Web and retrieve Web content from Web servers for viewing. Some Web server firewalls also function as a Web client.[421] In order to protect the inner system, the firewall will interact with the inner Web proxy as a client, and then relay the same request out to the Web server. By forcing a two-step process, the inner system is never forced to have a direct network connection with the external Web.

Two of the more common Web browser-level functions are URLs and hyperlinks.

- *A URL ("Uniform Resource Locator")* is the address of documents and other content that are located on a Web server; specifically, the letter and number coordinates that an end user submits to the Web browser to instruct it to connect with the desired Web server (Web site). A typical URL contains an HTTP prefix to indicate its use of the protocol, www to signify a location on the World Wide Web, a domain name (e.g., the Web server name), and an indicator of the top level domain ("TLD") (e.g., "com" for a commercial site, "org" for an organization, "gov" for government, or "edu" for an educational institution).[422] The number of possibilities for a URL continues to be expanded through options in each of the indicators.[423]

- *A hyperlink* is used to connect an end user to other Web sites, parts of Web sites and/or Web-enabled services. The URL of another site is imbedded in the HTML code of a site, so that when certain words or images are selected through the of the Web browser, the end user is transported to the destination Web site or page.

Web Infrastructure

The Web is built upon a conglomeration of hardware and software technologies that include server computers, client applications (such as browsers, discussed above) and various networking protocols.

A Web server is a computer that is connected to the Internet, hosts Web content and is configured to share that content. Documents that are viewed on the Web are actually located on individual servers and accessed by a browser.[424] Part of the President's National Security strategy includes ensuring that all Americans are aware of the configurations of their servers so that they face less of a security risk.[425] For example, a small business could quickly enhance their protection by ensuring that their Web server is not using a default password.[426]

A proxy server is an intermediary server that provides a gateway to the Web (e.g., employee access to the Web most often goes through a proxy). By using a proxy server, performance is improved through caching, and it filters the Web. The proxy server will also log each user interaction. By working behind a firewall to sort the incoming traffic to appropriate programs, a dedicated proxy server can ensure that the information gets to the correct proxy server that can safely handle the data.

Caching occurs when Web browsers and proxy servers save a local copy of the down-loaded content. To protect privacy, pages that display personal information should be set to prohibit caching. Caching allows firewall traffic to be reduced because certain pages are not as restricted.[427]

The following are additional terms that are essential in understanding the online privacy concepts to be addressed further in this chapter.

The Internet Protocol ("IP") specifies the format of data packets that travel over the Internet and also provides the appropriate addressing protocol. An IP address is a unique number assigned to each connected device. It is often assigned dynamically to users by an ISP on a session-by-session basis. This is referred to as a "dynamic" IP address. Conversely, a "static" IP address is the phenomenon that addresses are increasingly becoming dedicated, and are continuously offered by the computer to other users on a network.[428] A static IP may be considered personally identifiable information, as it can link data that are collected to a specific user.[429]

Transmission Control Protocol ("TCP") enables two devices to establish a connection and exchange data. Therefore, a combination of TCP and IP is used to send data over the Internet. Data are sent in the form of a packet. As discussed previously, a packet is a portion of a message that is sent over the TCP/IP network. It contains content and a heading which specifies the destination.

The Secure Sockets Layer ("SSL") is the protocol for establishing a secure connection for transmission and facilitates much of the online commerce (shopping and purchasing) that occurs on the Internet today. For example, HTTPS, a secure form of HTTP, is an SSL application used in password exchanges or e-commerce. "The primary goal of the SSL Protocol is to provide privacy and reliability between two communicating applications."[430] There are three properties to the protocol: (1) The connection is private, (2) the peer's identity can be authenticated using asymmetric, or public key, cryptography, and (3) tThe connection is reliable.[431]

Javascript is a scripting language used to produce a more interactive and dynamic Web site. By using it, one can create roll-over features and interact with HTML. However, the language should be used with the recognition that many browsers still do not support it.[432] Internet Explorer supports only a subset called Jscript.[433]

Javascript has many vulnerabilities and problems interacting with many programs and systems.[434] A common malicious practice is "Javascript bombing," which overloads older systems by rewriting Javascript code. Simple additions, like an infinite loop, can overwhelm the memory and impose a denial of service attack. Generally, one should be aware of the entity from which he is downloading a program to prevent attacks.

Flash is a bandwidth-friendly animation technology increasingly used to enliven Web pages and advertisements. Although no problems are currently obvious, researchers have predicted that a flash worm could take down the entire Internet in under 15 minutes.[435] This theory was tested by a lab simulation of a similar worm called the "Warhol worm" for its potential 15 minutes of fame.[436]

Online Data Collection

The most common mechanism for capturing end user information online is through the use of Web forms.

Figure Seven: Web Form (Source: IAPP)

A Web form is a portion of a Web page that contains blank fields, text boxes, check boxes or other input areas that end users complete by providing data (which may or may not include personal information).

- **One-line text boxes** in Web forms are used to capture specific pieces of information such as name, city, credit card number, or search terms. A label requesting a clear-cut entry is typically present. An important privacy consideration is that limitations should be placed on one-line text boxes to ensure that they are only used as intended (e.g., maximum of 14 characters for a first name). Otherwise, data could potentially be withdrawn from the database instead of entered.

- **Scrolling text boxes** in Web forms are used to capture a sentence or more of text. These are frequently used when an unspecified answer is desired. For instance, a common use is a request for support. Also, scrolling text boxes should be used with caution since little control exists over what information a user submits.

- **Check boxes and radio buttons** in Web forms are used to collect answers to structured questions. Check boxes allow multiple answers to be selected out of a list of items, while radio buttons limit the user to one answer. Both options are more secure, as the input is limited to the given options.

When the user completes and submits the Web form, it is sent to a Web server that processes and stores the submitted information in a database. This information may be used subsequently to process any number of user requests such as site entry, search queries or online transactions.

Active vs. Passive Collection

Web forms commonly employ two methods of data collection: active and passive.

Active data collection occurs when the end user deliberately provides information to the Web site through the use of one of the input types described above.

Conversely, *passive data collection* occurs when information is gathered automatically—often without the end user's knowledge—as the user navigates from page to page on a Web site. This is typically accomplished through the use of Web cookie files, Web beacons or other types of identification mechanisms. These will be defined further in this chapter.

As a best practice, Web forms should be designed to require only the information that is genuinely needed (and make it clear to the end user what, if anything, is optional). The end user is then forced to give personal information only that is absolutely necessary in order to complete the transaction.

Further, the form input should be accompanied by a functioning link to the privacy statement (known formally as "notice at the point of collection"). The privacy statement should give the user a clear idea of how the data are used, and who will have access to the information. The process that the user must undergo in order to view his data should be clear and explicit. One important consideration is that all collection of sensitive personal information should be protected by use of secure transmission (e.g., SSL).

The auto-complete function of most Web form submission processes should be disabled such that any sensitive personal information is not exposed on shared computers (such as a machine used jointly by multiple family members for surfing the Web). Passwords should never be pre-populated in the Web form to protect against the possibility that an account could be accessed by an unauthorized person.

A single sign-on service allows one universal authentication service to confirm user authentication.[437] Only one sign-on is required per Web session. This practice is risky if the user is on a public computer. Should he leave his station, another party could access information without proper authorization.

Desktop Products with Web Interfaces

Increasingly, client software applications (both business and consumer varieties) are supporting Web-friendly capabilities such as live hyperlinks and active file types that support live sound and video. From a privacy perspective, adequate notice and choice mechanisms need to be built into these products at the development phase in order for the applications to be used safely and appropriately.

- *Word processing programs* allow users to connect to the Internet in order to receive more extensive help desk services. When the link is made, these products should ensure that the transmission does not allow the data to leak into unprotected areas and risk capture by unauthorized persons.

- *Media player applications* allow music and video files to be played on a computer. However, the player software must be discriminating in terms of the file formats and sources it imports and stores. For example, a past vulnerability was allowing a false music file to be played that created a buffer overflow. Another concern has been the extent to which players allow the unauthorized distribution and enjoyment of copyrighted material. [438]

- *Financial software* and services contain substantial amounts of confidential information. Consequently, their protection is essential. When investigating reports of financial leaks in the past, the U.S. Government Accounting Office ("GAO") has evaluated features a company might use to control financial data. These include: protect data and application programs from unauthorized access; prevent the introduction of unauthorized changes to application and system software; provide segregation of duties involving application programming, system programming, computer operations, information security, and quality assurance; ensure recovery of computer processing operations in case of a disaster or other unexpected interruption; and ensure an adequate information security management program.[439]

Third Party Interactions

The boundaries between Web sites are becoming blurred through the emergence of syndicated content, Web services and co-branded online ventures. Privacy professionals need to understand these third-party interactions and ensure that the appropriate privacy protections are in place. It must also be exceedingly clear to end users which entities are capturing or receiving personal information in each of these scenarios—and that such entities accept accountability and fulfill their obligations under contract and applicable law.

Syndicated content is not actually created by the host site, but rather developed by and/or purchased or licensed from outside sources such as news organizations. The main concern associated with this type of Web content is that it might contain malicious code that is then unwittingly incorporated into the organization's own Web site source code. For example, cross-site scripting (XXS)[440] attacks attempt to take advantage of the trust that users have for a given site. The browser may have settings that accept cookies or downloads from certain sites and not from others.[441]

Web services facilitate direct communication between computers.[442] They make it possible for organizations to interconnect with their suppliers online. The linking organizations need to be particularly conscious of the information that is flowing between the computers, though, as the complexity of the system places both ends at a greater risk.

Co-branded sites are online partnerships between two or more content or service providers. Sharing of information is often allowed on co-branded sites, as long as it is disclosed in the notice statement. The U.S. Senate acknowledged the necessity of this in its proposed *Online Personal Privacy Act of 2002*.[443]

Agent and vendor contracts present a unique set of issues. Language in contracts holding software vendors liable for problems that lead to security breaches is becoming more common. Similarly, the contracts may contain provisions that require notification of breaches that take place or patches that are available to repair the software.

Onward Transfers

A final consideration in online data collection is onward transfer of information. This occurs when a host Web site conveys PII to a third-party Web site or service—such as a sweepstakes partner, payment processor or registration engine—for the purpose of additional handling, processing or distribution of that information.

Onward transfers are often problematic because consumers lose much of the control they had in the original Web-based transaction. The FTC considers onward transfer to be the sole responsibility of the host Web site—not the third party—and has issued guidance as well as enforced actions toward this end.

Protection of PII must be assured—contractually and procedurally—in data transfers between an organization's Web site and its partner sites. Moreover, consumers must be explicitly notified at the point at which such transfers occur that: (a) their PII will be in the custody of a third party engaged by the host site; and, (b) they have the ability to disengage (opt-out) of this process if they so desire in advance of any onward transfer.

Online Disclosure

The same principles around information security articulated in Chapter Four also extend to the Web information environment. Awareness of who has access to Web-based information, when they can access it, and for what reasons are all important considerations in constructing a defensible online disclosure scheme. As will be discussed further in this section, a Web privacy policy should lay out what sort of notice a customer will receive and when and how they can access their records.

Four approaches to customer access exist: [444]

1. **The total access approach** would allow a consumer to have access to all information that exists about him. This includes more than just personally identifiable information. Derived information that is work product of the company is also included.[445] Revealing such extensive amounts of information may be costly and expose company secrets. Also, it may go further than access needs to go in correcting errors and encouraging consumer confidence.

2. **The default rule approach** is limited to revealing information which is personally identifiable to the user.[446] This approach gives companies flexibility in how they want to make the data available, as long as they take steps to ensure accuracy and create reasonable terms.[447] "Individually identifiable information" includes "information that, when associated with an individual, can be used to identify him or her."[448] This information is both important to keep secure to prevent identity theft, and important to give users access to so that they can verify its accuracy. Options for access could include: requiring

the same information as the account (account name and password), requiring additional information about activity, requiring either option and send the information to the account, and require either option and send a one-time access code to the account.[449]

The approach presented by the default rule is similar to the BBB OnLine approach and the Safe Harbor proposed by the U.S. Department of Commerce, which was inspired by the European Union Directive on Data Protection.450

3. *A case-by-case approach* would evaluate whether the costs of providing access outweigh the goals of accuracy and customer trust. By specifically analyzing each type of data, no unnecessary leakage would occur, but users could be reassured that no inaccurate information was being stored about them. Costs would be greater for both firms and customers, however, since more processing resources would be utilized.

4. *Access for correction* provides access only to information that is used by the commercial Web site to grant or deny a significant benefit to the consumer, and then only if access is likely to produce an improvement in the accuracy of the information that justifies the costs.[451] This approach would minimize costs, however, it would not acknowledge that there is a greater purpose for access than merely error correction.[452]

Web Privacy Policies

A comprehensive privacy statement is the standard mechanism for organizations to both articulate and communicate their various information practices to the public. Such a statement is commonly—though not exclusively—made available on the organization's Web site. This statement will cover:

- Effective date;
- Scope of policy;
- Types of information collected (both actively and passively);
- Information uses and disclosures;
- Choices available to the end user;
- Methods for correcting or modifying information or preferences;
- Methods for contacting the organization, or registering a dispute; and,
- Processes for how any policy changes will be communicated to the public.

The online trust verification service TRUSTe recommends the following practices when developing a basic Web site privacy statement:

1. Say what you do; do what you say.
2. Tailor the Model Privacy Disclosures.
3. Privacy Statements are not Disclaimers.

4. Re-visit your privacy statement frequently.

5. Communicate your privacy practices to your entire company.[453]

Consumers have the right to know if their information can be sold to another company or used for a purpose beyond the scope of their relationship with the primary organization. This principle applies in equal measure to any information gathering that is conducting online. If consumers are aware that the information will be adequately safeguarded, then they can make informed decisions about allowing the secondary use of their information.[454] Limiting secondary use of personal information—unless consent is obtained—is one of the Fair Information Practices described in Chapter One. These practices are firmly embodied into the *U.S. Privacy Act of 1974* and also the *Organization for Economic Development and Cooperation ("OECD") Guidelines.*[455]

The Platform for Privacy Preferences Project (P3P)

In the late 1990s, the World Wide Web Consortium (W3C)—the international standards body behind many Web technologies—established the Platform for Privacy Preferences Project ("P3P"). This framework requires that privacy statements be produced in a standardized, machine-readable way (e.g., based on the long-established XML document format that any personal computer equipped with a Web browser could parse and translate).

At its most basic level, P3P is a standardized set of multiple-choice questions, covering all the major aspects of a Web site's privacy policy. Taken together, the answers to these questions present a complete view to the end user as to how the Web site handles the personal information of and about its visitors. Significantly, this enables standard Web browser software applications to communicate basic components of the Web site's privacy policy to the end user as well as facilitate the setting of particular usage preferences—as considered and set by the end user—based on that policy. P3P-enabled Web browsers can automatically review a Web site privacy policy and compare it to the consumer's set of privacy preferences."[456]

- *A Full P3P Policy* is referenced from a well known location on the Web server or from the server header data (the addressing information in its protocol) so Web browsers know where to locate it. Web browsers translate this into a human readable version in a standardized format that will be communicated upon user request. For example, Microsoft makes the information readable to users in the Internet Explorer menu options: View/Privacy Report/View Summary).

- *A Compact P3P Policy* is a shorter version of the policy constructed of a series of 3 or 4 letter "tokens" which are communicated with each Web page served.

Figure Eight: Compact P3P Policy (Source: IAPP)

```
<?xml version="1.0" ?>
- <POLICIES xmlns="http://www.w3.org/2002/01/P3Pv1">
  - <POLICY discuri="http://privacy.msn.com/privacyredir.asp" opturi="http://privacy.msn.com/choiceredir.asp"
    name="MSN_DRAFT_P3P_Policy">
    <!-- Description of the entity making this policy statement.  -->
    <TEST />
  - <ENTITY>
    - <DATA-GROUP>
      <DATA ref="#business.name">Microsoft Corporation</DATA>
      <DATA ref="#business.department">MSN Privacy</DATA>
      <DATA ref="#business.contact-info.postal.street">One Microsoft Way</DATA>
      <DATA ref="#business.contact-info.postal.city">Redmond</DATA>
      <DATA ref="#business.contact-info.postal.stateprov">WA</DATA>
      <DATA ref="#business.contact-info.postal.postalcode">98052</DATA>
      <DATA ref="#business.contact-info.postal.country">USA</DATA>
      <DATA ref="#business.contact-info.online.email">MSNPrivacy@MSN.com</DATA>
      <DATA ref="#business.contact-info.telecom.telephone.intcode">1</DATA>
      <DATA ref="#business.contact-info.telecom.telephone.loccode">425</DATA>
      <DATA ref="#business.contact-info.telecom.telephone.number">882-8080</DATA>
    </DATA-GROUP>
  </ENTITY>
  <!-- Access is given to identified online and physical contact information as well as to other personal
  information -->
  - <ACCESS>
    <contact-and-other />
  </ACCESS>
  <!-- Disputes  -->
  - <DISPUTES-GROUP>
    - <DISPUTES resolution-type="service" service="http://support.msn.com/contactus.aspx?productkey=privacy" short-
      description="Use this online form to contact MSN Privacy">
      <LONG-DESCRIPTION>MSN welcomes your comments regarding this Privacy Statement. If you believe that MSN has
      not adhered to this Statement please use the online form to contact MSN Privacy. You may also contact us by
      telephone or postal mail: +1 425 882-8080; MSN Privacy, Microsoft Corporation, One Microsoft Way, Redmond,
      Washington 98052.</LONG-DESCRIPTION>
```

Layered Notices

P3P offers a consistent and compelling means for organizations to communicate their privacy policies to end users over the Web. However, the framework does not solve all the challenges inherent in policy communication. The very "readability" of the written policy itself is a lingering challenge for many organizations who, in their vigilance for protection from potential claims, obscure the very meaning and intention of their practices in overwrought legal language. Complicating matters further is the strong evidence that end users, despite growing privacy concerns, rarely review published privacy policies if not disregard them entirely.

Layered notices are a recent industry initiative to provide privacy statements in a more succinct readable and comparable format that end users can be engaged to review and understand. The notices are constructed in two simple ways:

- *The short notice* is the top layer. Using a standard format, it summarizes the policy scope as well as basic points on the organization's practices for information notification, choice, use and disclosure. Details for contacting the organization on information privacy matters are also included along with links to the full statement (below).

- *The full notice* is the bottom layer. Often referenced from the short notice via a hyperlink, it is a comprehensive information disclosure that articulates the organization's privacy policy in its entirety.

Figure Nine: Short Notice Privacy Policy (Courtesy of Microsoft)

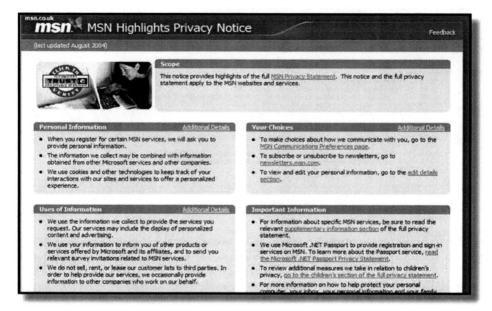

At a minimum, privacy statements should be accessible from the Web site home page to all possible data collection points across the Web site (e.g., any page that includes data inputs such as the Web form types described earlier). By following the principle of "at or before the point of information collection" many Web sites choose to provide a link on every page to cover passive information collection. The best choice is an easy to find location, in a font that is no less prominent than other links on the page.

Unsolicited Online Activities

Many Web sites rely on online advertising and sponsorship revenues in order to fund their services to customers. The very same technologies that power the delivery of personalized Web features are leveraged by online marketers to deliver messaging in the form of display advertising units such as banners, pop-ups, interstitials and sponsor tiles, among many other formats.

Targeted advertising can provide value to both the Web user and the Web site operator: it creates a more relevant, contextual experience for the Web user and the resulting ad revenues allow Web site operators to keep their businesses viable. However, such advertising may be considered privacy-invasive if it is performed without transparency or is based on sensitive information. Network advertising service providers—third parties that deliver paid advertising campaigns to Web sites that have contracted for such services—have the most sensitivity to privacy risks due to their ability to create broad profiles of user behavior. [457]

Pop-up ads are advertising messages that appear to the end user in a separate browser window in response to browsing behavior or viewing of a site. Pop-up ads can interfere with Internet usage, but also be a symptom of greater problems, such as spyware, which can inhibit a computer's performance.[458] Even though many consumers are not fond of the practice, it is not likely to be found unconstitutional, as was acknowledged in a recent court case.[459]

Adware

Adware is software that is frequently bundled with freeware (free software) such as peer-to-peer/file-sharing programs, online games and/or music players. Its purpose is to monitor the end users' online behavior so that additional advertising can be targeted to the end user based on the specific interests and behaviors of that end user.

Spyware

Spyware is software that is covertly downloaded (e.g., without the end user's knowledge or consent) and used to fraudulently collect and use sensitive PII such as bank account credentials and credit card numbers.

Marketing based on context (such as adware, above) is concerned with serving customers according to their interests. In response to a consumer's current browsing behavior, relevant categories of advertisements are displayed. Companies need a clear indication of which advertising practices are acceptable. Users should be protected from "drive-by" downloads. These programs fall dangerously close, if not within, the standard definition of spyware. A program is automatically installed on a user's computer, without his or her knowledge or consent, which later will prompt ads to appear.[460] In this case, the consumer has received no notice, and the information is covertly taken without consent.

Figure 10: False Security Warning (Source: IAPP)

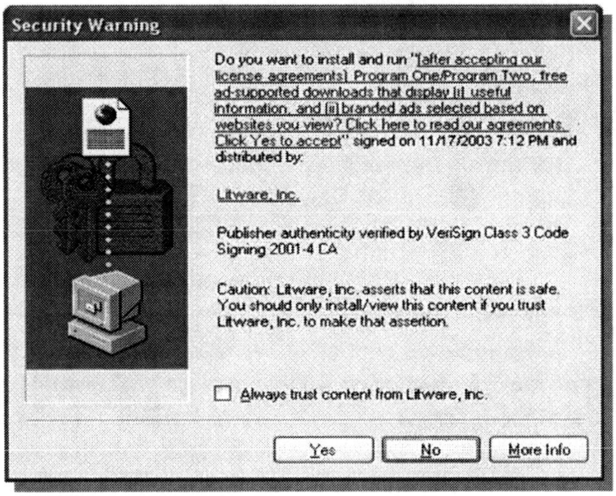

Figure 11A: 'Spyware' Application WIndow (Source: IAPP)

Figure 11B 'Spyware' Application WIndow (Source: IAPP)

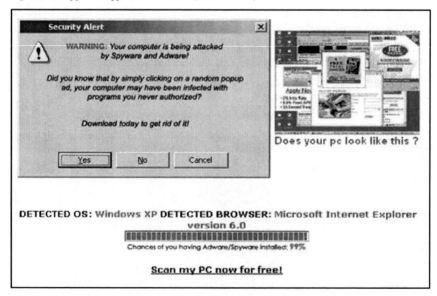

Protection from spyware or "drive-by" downloads is necessary, while general restrictions on monitoring would block parental controls or virus-detection programs. To find the appropriate balance, federal legislation is needed, but does not currently exist. If states continue to enact separate standards, compliance becomes difficult because there are too many conflicting rules and resources are wasted.

Spam Email

The popularity of the HTML authoring language has extended beyond the Web itself and into other online channels such as electronic mail. Thus, marketing emails have evolved quickly beyond simple text to include text-plus-hyperlinks and most recently, entire HTML pages enveloped in email messages. While these marketing emails do not always include Web forms, they can offer links to Web pages, enable third party interactions and track personal usage. Behavioral profiles are often built so that Web beacon and cookie protections apply. Spam and phishing remain key concerns.

Spam is unsolicited, commercial email. The euphemism was first coined in the early 1990s in response to an electronic mass marketing campaign. Cantor & Seigel, a U.S. immigration law firm, distributed to thousands of Internet users an email message promoting the firm's legal services. Long-time Internet users responded with understandable rage and likened these unsolicited, commercial messages to a mass-packaged meat product.

Beyond being an intrusive annoyance, spam emails can contain software viruses, malicious code, and other software exploits. The messages themselves can be deployed in sufficiently high volumes such that they overload an information system or mail server rendering such a system or machine unavailable to end users or inoperable entirely. As recently as 2005, fully a third of the email sent or received in North America was reported to be spam.[461]

Technical methods to combat spam include many of the anti-virus, firewall and network protection software that information security personnel install and which are defined under Chapter Four. On the legal front, many U.S. states have anti-spam laws in place and the federal CAN-SPAM Act has been in force since 2004. To date, CAN-SPAM has a successful track record in enforcement resulting in millions of dollars in fines and in some cases, imprisonment of violators. The CAN-SPAM Act and other marketing privacy laws are detailed further under Chapter Two.

Phishing

"Phishing" is the practice of luring users to a fake Web site in order to fraudulently capture sensitive PII via a spoofed spam email. Often, these emails will seem to originate from legitimate organizations—such as recognized banks or retailers—and may include seemingly legitimate trademarks, colors, logos or other corporate signatures. Users are asked to follow a link to confirm their account number, credit card details or other sensitive or personal information. The link takes the users to a forged Web site that then records the data that they enter to perpetrate subsequent illegitimate uses such as bank fraud or identity theft.

Phishing is a fairly recent online fraud phenomenon—and while the technique employs email as a key mechanism, it goes far beyond an annoyance or technical threat to become an actual crime. A May 2004 study by research firm Gartner Group estimates that

76 percent of all known phishing attacks occurred after December 2003 and that the direct cost to companies of phishing attacks has already totaled $1.2 billion in 2003.[462] This technique's usage continues to expand and be one of the primary means of identity theft in existence. According to the Gartner report:

> For the most part, a phishing attack is easy and cheap to engineer, is extremely hard to trace, and even if only a small percentage of recipients respond to requests for personal information—the return on investment can be very high. Sending an email costs a fraction of a cent, and minimal response can result in high returns.[463]

Online Verification and Certification

Verifying and certifying the privacy protections of Web sites provide a means for users to determine the level of trust that a Web site deserves. Third party organizations—known variously as accreditation/assurance services or trust seal providers—evaluate the practices of a given Web site against a set of pre-defined industry standards and best practices. These third parties then certify the Web site's policies and practices against these standards and award the Web site an approving, "trust" seal if, in their judgment, the Web site deserves such merit.

As outlined in Chapter One, TRUSTe, BBB Online and CPA WebTrust are three such examples of third parties that provide online verification and certification services. Each offers a self-regulatory regime that certifies Web sites with a trust mark and also provides an independent dispute resolution process in the event of a privacy abuse alleged by an online consumer.

Custom Attestations

Some organizations demand a more comprehensive audit of privacy compliance due to the sensitivity of certain matters or an internal drive for better competitive differentiation. In these examples, an independent third-party will test actual compliance with Web privacy policy and publish an audit report. Many leading corporate auditing and consulting firms offer these services, among them Ernst & Young, Deloitte & Touche, PricewaterhouseCoopers, KPMG, Booz Allen Hamilton and others. This comprehensive privacy audit is often tied to a broader corporate analysis that the firm may conduct for its clients.

Still other vendor companies offer services—and technologies—that address a long list of privacy concerns across a growing array of Web sites. Services such as Watchfire, Sonomos and Vontu (among other vendors) "crawl" over Web sites and report on Web privacy issues and compliance status. Clients can then make modifications or changes to Web site infrastructure or process in order to ensure better privacy compliance.

Web User Tracking

Web site operators have a number of technologies at their disposal to aid in the identification and tracking of visitors to their Web site(s). These technologies do not, in and of themselves, act as user tracking agents. However, in combination with other methods, these technologies can provide a fairly complete profile of Web user behavior—as well as enable a process known as "online preference marketing" to occur.

Every time a Web page is requested, the Web server may automatically log information connected to the request. These log files may include the IP address of the visitor, the date and time stamp of the page request, the URL of the requested page or file, the URL the visitor came from immediately prior to the visit (e.g., the referrer URL), the visitor's Web browser type version and the Web user's computer operating system.

As explained earlier in this chapter, when an end user arrives to a destination Web site, the end user's browser makes a Web page request through the Web browser. The destination Web site's server computer receives this page request and returns to the end user's computer the formatting information (the HTML) plus any attendant image or document files necessary to fulfill the page request.

The Web site's page server may also deliver—in advance of, along with, or after the Web page—a small text file to the end user's computer hard drive via the Web browser.

Web Cookies

Known rhetorically as "cookies" for their relatively small and innocuous size, Web cookie files are used to identify an end user as that individual navigates through a Web site and/or returns to the Web site at a later time. The Web cookie may include information such as the cookie's identification number, file name, Web site domain, and expiration date. These files enable a range of functions including authentication of Web visitors, delivery of personalized content and delivery of targeted advertising.

Figure 12: Cookie Prompt in Microsoft Internet Explorer (Courtesy of Microsoft)

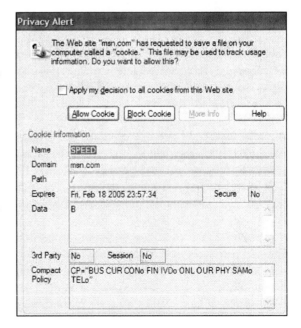

Whether or not Web cookies contain PII remains a topic of continued debate. Some privacy advocates contend that all Web cookie files used in connection with Web user tracking should be automatically classified as "tracking" cookies and be considered highly suspect. Still others are convinced that Web cookie files are used as mechanisms for triggering spyware attacks on unsuspecting Web users. However, it is worth noting that the same Web browser applications that facilitate the delivery of Web cookie files—along with all other Web content—also offer strong permissions controls to end users for managing such delivery. For example, end users can set specific usage preferences through their Web browsers that limit the number of Web cookie files delivered to them or prevent their delivery entirely. These same controls can prompt the end user prior to the download of any Web cookie file.

Certainly, Web cookies can contain detailed technical information and do introduce a number of privacy considerations. From a best practices standpoint, Web cookies should:

- Not store unencrypted personal information on them;

- Provide adequate notice of their usage;

- Only use a persistent variation if the need justifies it (see below);

- Not set long expiration dates; and,

- Disclose the involvement of a third-party cookie provider (if applicable) as well as an opt-out mechanism for delivery from that third party.

Several varieties of Web cookie files exist and enjoy broad use today across the Web. These include session-based and persistent cookies (relating to the time and duration of cookie deployment) as well as first-party and third-party cookies (relating to the origination point of cookie file delivery).

A session cookie is stored only while the user is connected to the particular Web server— the cookie is deleted when the user leaves that Web site or disconnects from the Web entirely by "closing" the Web browser application. For example, session cookies are often used by networking Web sites to manage online chat sessions as well as by online market research organizations to support interactive opinion surveys." [464]

A persistent cookie is set to expire at some point in the future: a few minutes or hours from initial delivery to many hours, days or even years from initial delivery. Persistent cookies are the standard mechanism for authenticating return visitors to Web sites that depend on real-time information such as sports scores, weather reports or stock updates. For example, an individual investor who maintains an online stock portfolio is able to revisit that Web site several times per day or week without having to re-enter company information because the persistent Web cookie allows the Web site to recognize the investor on each visit—as well as keep the investor's stock portfolio selections in an active state.

A first-party cookie is set and read by the Web server hosting the Web site the user is visiting. Conversely, *a third-party cookie* is set and read by a third-party Web server that is providing a service, such as advertising or analytics, to the Web site the user is visiting.

Web Beacons

Another online identification mechanism is called a Web beacon. Known alternately as a Web bug, pixel tag or clear GIF, a Web beacon is a clear graphic image of 1x1 pixel in size that is delivered through a Web browser or HTML-compliant email client application to an end user's computer—usually as part of a Web page request or in an HTML email message, respectively.

The Web beacon operates as a tag that records an end user's visit to a particular Web page. It is also often used in conjunction with a Web cookie and provided as part of a third-party tracking service. Web beacons provide an ability to produce specific profiles of user behavior in combination with Web server logs. Common usage scenarios for Web beacons include online ad impression counting, file download monitoring, and ad campaign performance management (click through rates, ad frequency limitation, etc.).

Uses include hit counter, ad campaign performance measurement, and email readership.

Privacy considerations for Web beacons include the need for notice (the clear pixel state of Web beacons make them quite literally, invisible to the end user), implementing without the use of PII, and the requirement of choice when used in a personally identifiable manner.

Online Preference Marketing

In 2000, the Network Advertising Initiative ("NAI"), currently a cooperative of network advertisers, ad serving vendors, Web analytics companies and online measurement services published a set of self-regulatory standards for online preference marketing—including appropriate uses for Web cookies and Web beacons.

The NAI Principles received the unanimous support of all the acting FTC Commissioners and remain today the benchmark for responsible online marketing practices. These principles declare that network advertisers will:

1. Adhere to the Online Privacy Alliance ("OPA") Privacy Policies guidelines for personally identifiable information;

2. Not use sensitive personally identifiable data for online preference marketing;

3. Not, without prior affirmative consent ("opt-in"), merge personally identifiable information with information previously collected as non-personally identifiable information;

4. Provide consumers with robust notice and choice regarding the merger of personally identifiable information with non-personally identifiable information collected on a going forward basis for online preference marketing;

5. Not use personally identifiable information ("PII") consisting of PII collected offline merged with PII collected online for online preference marketing unless the consumer has been afforded robust notice and choice about such merger before it occurs;

6. Require Web publishers with which they have contractual relationships to provide notice and choice regarding the collection of non-personally identifiable information for online preference marketing.[465]

The NAI Principles are mandatory for all members of the NAI itself but are broadly applicable to any company that engages in online marketing.

Web Security

Security administrators and hackers alike use software scripts to probe Web sites for security vulnerabilities—though with markedly different agendas.

A security administrator will use tools to identify system weaknesses so that these can be addressed and rectified.[466] However, an attacker can use these same tools to exploit weaknesses in order to gain unauthorized access to the Web server.[467] In many respects, this has led to an "arms race" of technical weapons and tactics that pits "white hats" (security practitioners) against "black hats" (hackers and exploit artists).

The Web facilitates information exchange between computers. While this gives further communication capability, it also exposes Web servers and computer to greater risks. An organization should ensure that proper precautions are taken when it connects its computers to the Internet and the Web:

• HTML-based account names and passwords should be formatted in such a way that they are not easily discernable or obtainable by a hacker;

- Account names should not allow symbols, so that entries in a field could result in unauthorized access; and,

- Passwords should not be dictionary words, but rather a combination of letters and numbers that cannot be derived from everyday English.

Web Access

As discussed in detail in Chapter Four, an organization should have a comprehensive defense plan and procedure in place to effectively address information security threats. All employees of the organization should be aware of the procedure, and the plan should extend to multiple areas and combat a variety of attack types. Also, the organization should anticipate that an attacker will utilize more than one method, so the design should have both the depth and the breadth to withstand sophisticated attacks.

These same information security principles apply in equal measure to an organization's Web site infrastructure. In many respects, Web sites are more vulnerable to compromise—both internal and external. Virtually every commercial entity in existence today employs at least one Web site as part of their business operations. These Web sites are, by design, externally facing and easily accessible through the use of a standard Web browser application.

This sort of easy external visibility underscores the need for stringent Web access policies. The more sensitive the Web site, the stronger the Web site authentication should be—requiring more than one form of access credential (e.g., two-factor authentication such as manual password plus token or ID card, also defined under Chapter Four). Further, Web forms should be built using the "password field" type in HTML. This masks the display of text—even as it is entered—so as to both respect and ensure privacy.

Despite their use by Web site operators as identification mechanisms, Web cookies and Web beacons offer imprecise means for authenticating and authorizing end user access. Consider multi-user platforms such as a personal computer used by many members of a single household or a workstation accessed by several scientists of a University research laboratory. In these scenarios, several users may access an external Web site based upon a single prior visit—when a Web cookie file is first deployed. The Web server—and thus the Web site operator—do not have an accurate means of differentiating individual users of a single machine.

Secure Sockets Layer (SSL)

The standard method for encrypting the transmission of PII over the Web—including the verification of end user information required for Web site access—is called Secure Sockets Layer (SSL).

SSL is a much stronger, higher-resolution scheme for data transmission. Though it does not rise to the security standard of PKI or other cryptographic schemes defined in

Chapter Four, SLL is well suited for handling transmission of sensitive online data such as passwords or bank account numbers between Web computers.

SSL gives the end user some level of comfort in the security of a Web page delivery process. It also provides actual security if the Web page hosting the Web form is secured in SSL and the resulting data transmission also supports the protocol.

Protecting Online Identity

Ultimately, end users are responsible for keeping their information private—and not disclosing it without appropriate consideration. Even if every Web site offers impeccable security, human error can lead to identity theft or data leaks. The following are standard practices to protect the privacy of information captured, stored or transmitted over the Web:

- *Login/Password/PINs*. Use unique passwords whenever possible; change passwords regularly; never set a system to "Remember My Password;" and memorize passwords rather than document them on paper or convey them to others;

- *Software*. Purchase anti-virus and firewall software and keep it up-to-date; also, keep the computer and server operating system (OS) software up-to-date.

- *Wireless Networks (Wi-Fi)*. Be particularly cautious when using wireless networks to connect to the Internet as they are prone to outside interception.

- *File Sharing*. Be wary of peer-to-peer Web sites or services as these may give hackers or exploit artists an entry point into your computer.

- *Public Computers (libraries, universities, etc.)*. Be cautious of the information you provide online since you are not personally aware of how these machines have been configured, who has used them previously or what software (suspect or legitimate) they may host.

- *Personal Information*. Do not provide any information unless you know the Web site is secure (look for verifiable proof)

As identity theft becomes more common, and companies face legal liability for breaches of inadequately protected databases, more organizations are developing standards for the secure storage of PII whether the data are stored internally or via third parties such as subsidiaries and vendors.

The privacy and security ramifications of outsourcing information handling to third parties—as well as across geographic borders—will be addressed in the next chapter.

Email Security

The principles of confidentiality, integrity, and availability are as important to protecting email as in any other areas of Web security or of information security generally. Confidentiality of email involves making sure it is protected from unauthorized access. Integrity of email involves a guarantee that it has not been modified or destroyed by an unauthorized individual. Availability of email requires that mail servers remain online and able to service the user community.[468]

Some of the common features in mail security products today include content filtering services such as antivirus, anti-spam, HTML tag removal, script removal, blocking of attachments by file type, scanning of inappropriate content, confidentiality checks, and disclaimer enforcement. Anti-spam methods supported by most products include real-time blackhole lists (RBL), heuristics, confirmation process, Bayesian filtering, open relay protection, size and bandwidth control, and encryption.[469]

Children's Online Privacy

Allowing online communications by and between children and collecting their information online are closely related activities. The privacy concern is that a child may be entirely unaware as to exactly how much information he/she reveals in a typical online "conversation." This is particularly apparent in the relaxed environments of online chat services and social networking Web sites where anonymity rules and strangers become all too familiar. To unsuspecting young Web user's, personal details such as their appearance, the name of their school, or the location of their home may be fairly innocuous information to share with another individual online—but a malicious Web user can appropriate such information to often criminal advantage.

While many consider it the parent's obligation to install filtering software on the household computer to block access to certain Web sites or even certain Web content topics, most Web sites require that a person be of a certain minimum age in order to access the Web site. For example, online retailers and adult entertainment sites often put restrictions on the abilities of minors to access their products or services by requiring additional consent or credit card information.

The U.S. *Children's Online Privacy Protection Act ("COPPA")* was passed with the expressed purpose of protecting children's use of the Internet—particularly Web sites and services targeted toward children.

As described in Chapter Two, COPPA requires Web site operators to provide clear and conspicuous notice of the data collection methods employed by the Web site including functioning hyperlinks to the Web site privacy policy on every Web page where PII is collected. It also mandates strict requirements on parental oversight and consent on behalf of children.

However, neither the safeguards described throughout this book nor the relevant privacy laws such as COPPA will function as a complete preventative against the potential abuse of children's personal information online. Parents are advised to have a frank and honest discussion with their children about the Web environment and basic online "do's and don'ts." Importantly, they should become positively engaged in their children's online activities as well as keep fluent on emerging online threats.

Online Privacy Case Study:
Ohio Art

Since COPPA was enacted in 2000, the FTC has taken a number of enforcement actions pursuant to the provisions of the Act. These include cases against Bonzi Software, the Education Research Center of America and the Hershey Company.

As of this writing, the Ohio Art case is the most recent FTC action taken under COPPA.

Facts and Allegations

The Ohio Art Company is a marketer of children's toys including the legendary "Etch A Sketch" drawing tool. In addition to its corporate Web site, the company maintained a Web site devoted to the Etch A Sketch. This Web site targeted children under the age of 13 through the use of a cartoon mascot (called "Etchy"), and featured games, coloring activities, and an interactive story in addition to a showcase of different drawings made using the Etch A Sketch.

Ohio Art also collected personal information from children though its "Etch A Sketch Birthday Club" whereby children submitted their name, address, email address, age, and date of birth.

The FTC alleged that Ohio Art violated the Children's Online Privacy Protection Act (COPPA) by failing to provide sufficient notice of its information collection practice, provide notice to parents of information collection practices, obtain parental consent, provide reasonable means to review/delete the personal information, and on conditioning participation in the birthday club upon providing more information than necessary.

Privacy and Security Promises

COPPA requires companies that collect personal information from children under 13 online to include certain disclosures in the privacy statements. Although Ohio Art posted a privacy policy on its Web sites, the FTC alleged that this statement, "did not clearly, understandably, or completely disclose all of its information collection, use and disclosure practices...."

FTC Consent Agreement with Ohio Art

a. Bar on Misrepresentation: Must fully disclose information collection, use, and disclosure policies on the Web site and in the COPPA-mandated parental notice.

b. Treatment of the Children's Personal Information: Within fivedays from the entry of the Consent Decree, Ohio Art, shall delete all personal information collected from every child through the Web site any time from April 21, 2000 to the date of the order.

c. Consumer Education Remedy: For five years, Ohio Art shall place on all Web sites a clear and conspicuous notice:

  1. Within the privacy policy required to be posted on its Web site;
  2. Within the direct notice required to be sent to parents in boldface type directing them to the privacy policy statement online; and,
  3. Boldface type at each location on its Web site(s) that collects personal information.

d. Maintenance of Relevant Documents: For a period of five years, Ohio Art shall provide (upon request):

  1. Copy of different information collection forms;
  2. Collection, use, and disclosure policies with regard to children;
  3. Any document that contradicts, qualifies or questions Ohio Art's compliance with the order.

e. Delivery of Order: Within 30 days, Ohio Art shall deliver and obtain signed receipt of the FTC order along with the FTC compliance guide entitled "How to Comply with the Children's Online Privacy Protection Rule" with respect to each current director, employee, agent, representative, or employee with managerial responsibility. Required delivery of the same for five years to all future directors, officers, agents, and managerial employees.

f. Reporting: For 20 years, Ohio Art shall notify the FTC within 30 days of any change which may affect its compliance with the order. Within 60 days after service of the order and thereafter as requested, Ohio Art shall file a report with the FTC setting forth Ohio Art's compliance with the order including:

  1. Registration process for the birthday club;
  2. Collection of all other registration information;
  3. Copy of privacy notices;
  4. Procedures for notifying parents, obtaining parental consent, and facilitating parental review of information; and,
  5. Procedures to assure security, confidentiality, and integrity of personal data.

Duration of the FTC Order

Not Specified

Fine Imposed

$35,000

Conclusion

The continued growth and success of the Internet and World Wide Web are due largely to their increasing popularity as a combined platform for electronic communications, commerce and information exchange. Not surprisingly, privacy and security considerations abound. Web consumers accustomed to submitting information to various service providers in order to obtain desired features and services must be more vigilant about the release of such information. Web site operators have a number of legal and practical obligations to ensure that they are capturing personal information for reasonable business purposes and with appropriate notice and choice to the consumer.

Chapter Six

DATA SHARING AND TRANSFER

Introduction and Learning Objectives

The Internet and World Wide Web offer two familiar examples of how easily and instantaneously many types of data—including personal information—are transported, managed, processed and stored electronically. As discussed in Chapter Four, organizations also employ proprietary mechanisms such as local access networks ("LANs"), virtual private networks ("VPNs"), extranets and other data relays where information flows with even greater regularity and complexity than on the Web.

"Data Sharing and Transfer" is the sixth and final chapter in this volume. It examines the practices and controls necessary for ensuring the integrity of information as it flows between and amongst business enterprises, institutions, governments, vendor companies and other organizations as well as across geographic boundaries.

The CIPP will understand:

- The impact of privacy policy development, review and implementation on data usage and data flow management;

- Effective inventory of data assets including the types of uses of PII;

- Management of customer preferences in relation to data sharing commitments, regulatory requirements and disclosure obligations;

- The privacy implications of vendor contracts and third-party activities including the outsourcing of information; and

- Considerations for trans-border data flows including global marketing programs and global HR privacy requirements.

Data Inventory

It is incumbent upon each organization to undertake an inventory of all the data that it collects, stores, uses or discloses—whether to other divisions of the organization or to outside entities such as subsidiaries, vendors or partners. This inventory should include both customer and employee data records. It should document data location and flow as well as evaluate how, when and with whom the organization shares such information— and the means for data transfer used.

Such attention to an inventory of personal data will benefit the organization by continuing, and possibly improving, the organization's reputation amongst customers. In the event that a legal claim is made against the organization in connection with its data handling policies or processes, the penalties are likely to be less severe if the company already has an established system of recording and organizing this inventory. The inventory should be reviewed and updated on an annual basis.

Figure 13: Sample Organization Flow Chart (Source: IAPP)

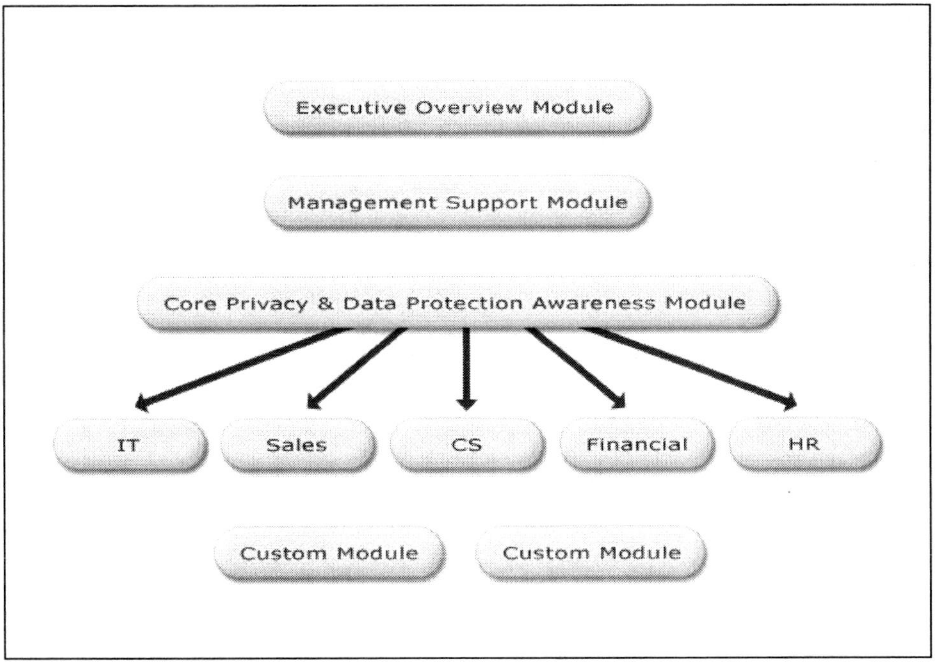

Documenting Data Flows

An organization chart can be used as a template to map and document the systems, applications and processes handling personally identifiable information. This document tracks the flow of personal data within the company and after it is transferred to a third party. This organization chart is instrumental in identifying sensitive areas where data is held and used and can help to identify mistakes in usage, theft or other errors. It should be readily available and regularly updated so as to ensure currency and accuracy as changes to the organization occur.

The location of the personal data that a company collects is important in determining the safeguarding procedures necessary to secure the information. Different countries and even different states may require varying security protocols.

If data is stored within the United States, a variety of laws may regulate its storage and security. HIPAA regulates the retention of personally identifiable health information while the GLBA regulates personally identifiable financial information. Other data may be subject to a variety of other federal laws.

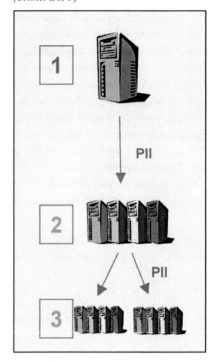

Figure 14: Organizational Data Flow (Source: IAPP)

Additionally, requirements may vary according to the state in which the data is stored. While HIPAA and the GLBA create a legal baseline in the U.S. for required privacy practices, states may individually require higher standards of the companies operating within their borders. Each organization must keep current on relevant state privacy requirements.

Personal information that is transferred to/from the U.S. and another country may be at a high risk of security breach. Extra measures, such as background checks of employees at the company being transferred to or encryption of data being transferred, should be taken as necessary to ensure the security of data. All of these steps are due diligence procedures in engaging any third party vendor—but are especially important in a privacy practices context.

Determining Data Accountability

As a privacy professional, you are always responsible for the actions of those who process data on behalf of your organization—in the interactions the organization conducts with vendors and business partners. Thus, your due diligence involves the active participation of these organizations in ensuring the secure status of the information you collect from your customers and/or employees.

Each type of PII has several attributes which need to be considered in creating an overall inventory scheme for all data types. The organization should seek answers to the following questions for all of its PII data:

Where is the personal information stored?

Whether in electronic or physical form, personally identifiable information should be stored in a secure area which is protected from destruction or potential hazards, such as fires or other emergencies. Such data should also be stored together and logically or physically separate from any publicly available information the company may collect. Separation will avoid any intermingling of information and possible confusion over the source of its contents.

How sensitive is the information?

It is widely understood that personally identifiable information must be kept secure and confidential. Though the data management cycle includes many participants— from the data owner to the privacy professional, the information security professional, the vendor (if applicable), the auditor (if applicable) and the end user—ultimately, the data owner is responsible for assigning the appropriate sensitivity level of the information. Common categories include: confidential, proprietary (e.g. property of the organization), restricted (e.g. available to select few) or public (e.g. generally available).

Should the information be encrypted?

Strong differences of opinion exist among information security professionals as to whether encryption should be implemented across all states of the data process (from collection and storage to transmission, use and disclosure). Such broad-scale implementation can prove prohibitively complex and expensive. In order to comply with legal requirements, organizations may be compelled to encrypt at least one state of the process for any sensitive data that is being transmitted electronically over networks or stored online.

Will the information be transferred to other countries, and if so, how will it be transferred?

Trans-border transfer of PII data calls for a high level of security. Different countries have a variety of privacy laws, many of which do not contain the same provisions as many U.S. privacy laws. For example, privacy laws across the E.U., Canada and Japan vary greatly from the U.S. Thus, data being transferred to and from other countries may be subject to stricter regulations than those imposed under the laws of the U.S. Before transferring PII, an organization should familiarize itself with the privacy requirements of both the originating and destination countries.

Who owns the information?

Personal data owned by an entity other than the storing entity may be subject to different storage and security requirements than the storing entity. If an organization must store data on behalf of another, the organization should expect to be required to meet the privacy policy guarantees of the other entity in the use and storage of such data. Most likely, a storing company will be required to sign a contract to this effect.

How is the information to be processed, and how will these processes be maintained?

The very processes through which personal information is processed also must be secured. Steps should be taken to train all staff involved and to secure the computers on which the information will be processed and minimize the risk of any data leak or breach. Any physical transfer of the data also should be secured.

Is the use of such data dependent upon other systems?

If the use of personal data depends upon the working condition of other systems, such as specialized computer programs, the condition of those systems must also be evaluated and updated if necessary. A system that is outdated may call for developing a new method or program for using the relevant data.

Privacy Policy and Disclosure

Policy Development

The organization should employ established privacy principles in designing and implementing its overall privacy policy, with careful attention to its collection and use of data. The fair information practices (such as the OECD Guidelines, APEC principles and other frameworks outlined in Chapters One and Two) can serve as a foundation for effective privacy and disclosure policies.

The development and approval of a organizational privacy policy is a strategic decision. When drafting a privacy policy, consider whether one policy is appropriate for all of the activities within the organization. If your organization engages in a wide variety of activities and has well-defined divisions of management, the use of multiple policies may be a logical strategy. This is particularly true if each division uses customer data in very different ways and does not often share that data with other divisions. For example, securities firms often use joint privacy notices. A fund and its adviser may wish to adopt a joint privacy policy and a joint form of notice.[470] This approach may benefit companies which cooperate significantly with another company in performing business.

If you decide to use multiple policies, clearly state in your privacy notices the existence of multiple policies and the division or function within your company that each policy covers.

Conversely, using multiple policies may create complications for an organization. If one division's privacy policy is more stringent than another division's, the two divisions may be unable to share customer information because the policies violate each other or are otherwise incompatible. If multiple policies are to be used, pay close attention to the drafting in order to allow the full amount of information to be shared within divisions that the company desires.

Whether you are developing a single company-wide policy or multiple policies, it is highly recommended that the executive stakeholders for the organization's divisions review and approve the policy(s). The organization's executive management and other business functionaries are vital to creating a policy that can be successfully implemented. This increases your ability to effectively communicate and enforce the policy throughout the company.

Policy Review and Approval

An organization should not finalize and post a privacy policy without legal consultation followed by executive approval. Otherwise, open-ended statements or overly ambitious security promises could result in penalties and litigation (including FTC inquiries) in addition to undesired media or public attention that could threaten the reputation of the organization.

If a privacy policy is subsequently revised after it has been published (physically and/or electronically), the organization should announce the change to both its current and former customers. The information provided should include a new notice that accurately reflects the change in policy and a new opt-out notice with reasonable means to opt-out.

Privacy Policy Case Study:
Tower Records

The FTC's seminal enforcement action against music retailer Tower Records serves a good example of the consequences engendered by unannounced revisions to an organization's privacy policy. The FTC successfully alleged that Tower Records exhibited unfair and deceptive trade practices for violating its privacy and security promises.

Facts and Allegations
Tower Records was a national retailer of recorded music, videos and books. It sold these goods through its stores as well as online. The Tower Records Web site collected personal

information from its online customers including name, billing address, shipping address, email address and telephone numbers. It also maintained a purchase history of all orders by each customer.

In December 2002, Tower Records redesigned the checkout portion of its Web site. The new Web site included an order history look-up feature, but it did not include any authentication controls in the to protect sensitive data. This vulnerability made it possible to view customers' personal information by entering a valid order number into the Tower Records checkout feature. As a result, the personal information of 5,225 consumers was accessed by unauthorized users.

The FTC complaint alleged that Tower Records failed to implement reasonable and appropriate procedures to maintain and protect the privacy and security of personal information obtained from or about consumers. The FTC classified such misrepresentations as deceptive under Section 5 of the FTC Act but it did not allege harm to consumers as a result of the breach.

Privacy and Security Promises

Tower Records made the following representations regarding the security and privacy of personal information collected on its Web site:

(2) "We will never share your personal information with anyone for any reason without your explicit permission."

(3) "We use state-of-the-art technology to safeguard your personal information. All TowerRecords.com employees are required to acknowledge that they understand and will comply with this privacy policy."

(4) "TowerRecords.com takes steps to ensure that your information is treated securely and in accordance with the relevant Terms of Service and this Privacy Policy.... Once we receive your transmission, we make our best effort to ensure its security on our systems."

FTC Consent Agreement with Tower Records

A. **Bar on Misrepresentation:** Tower Records shall not misrepresent the extent to which it maintains and protects the privacy, confidentiality, or security of any collected personal information.

B. **Security Program:** Tower Records shall establish and maintain a well-documented, comprehensive information security program reasonably (i) designed to protect the security, confidentiality, and integrity of consumers' personal information and (2) appropriate for the size, complexity, nature, and scope of its business.

C. Requirements of Security Program: The program shall include:

(1) Designation of an employee responsible for the security program;

(2) Identification of internal and external threats to security, confidentiality, and integrity of personal information through an assessment focusing on employee training, information systems, and potential system failures;

(3) Design and implement reasonable safeguards to identified risks; and,

(4) Evaluation and adjustments of system according to assessment, and material changes in business

D. Third Party Audit: Within 180 days after service of order and thereafter biannually for ten years, Tower Records must obtain an assessment and report from an independent, third party that:

(1) Sets forth the specific safeguards implemented and maintained by Tower Records;

(2) Explains how such safeguards are appropriate for the size and complexity of Tower Records, the nature and scope of Tower Records' activities and the sensitivity of the information;

(3) Explains how the safeguards meet or exceed the protections required above; and,

(4) Certifies that Tower-Records' security program is operating with sufficient effectiveness to provide reasonable assurances that consumer information is protected.

E. Maintenance of Relevant Documents: For a period of five years, Tower Records shall provide upon request:

(1) A copy of each representation made to consumers regarding the collection, use, and security of collected information;

(2) Any documents that indicates that Tower Records is not complying with the order.

(3) For a period of three years retain a copy of all plans, reports, studies, reviews, audits, policies, training materials, and assessments.

F. Delivery of Order: Tower Records shall deliver a copy of the FTC order to all current and future principals, officers, directors, and managers and to all other employees with managerial responsibility over the subject matter.

G. Reporting: Tower Records shall notify the FTC at least 30 days prior to any corporate change that may affect compliance with the order. Within 180 days after service of order and thereafter as requested, file a report with the FTC setting forth Tower Records' compliance with the order.

Duration of the FTC Order and Penalties for Violations
Except as otherwise indicated in the final order, the final order terminates in twenty years. Each violation of the final order may result in a civil penalty of $11,000.

Fine Imposed
None

Training, Awareness and Communication of Privacy Policy

Each organization staff member who interacts with personally identifiable information should receive training and resources that help to establish a thorough understanding of the organization's privacy policy. If the organization is very large and/or the PII will be transferred through many departments or across country borders, a training program to inform all staff, regardless of their interaction with the data is absolutely essential.

The method by which an organization's privacy policy is communicated to the general public (e.g. those whose personal information may be collected, used or disclosed) is equally essential. Effective communication of policy can increase a company's reputation with its customers as being a safe and secure place in which to do business. Ineffective posting and communication of policy could negatively impact a company's reputation and invite litigation in the event of a breach.

The following steps should be taken in determining how to communicate with both of these audiences (e.g. persons internal and external to the organization). In many cases, the best means of communicating with your audience will be through utilizing all three methods:

(1) *Post the policy on location*

Clearly post the organization's privacy policy at the location of business in the area of highest customer traffic and in legible form. Organization staff also should have ready access to copies of the up-to-date company privacy policy in case a customer wishes to obtain a copy for review.

(2) *Publish the policy annually*

After publishing the initial notice of privacy policies and practices, the organization should notify customers of the privacy policy annually irrespective of any revisions—

but especially in the event of any revision to the policy. The organization should clearly state in this notice that the customer may opt-out at any time as the customer may be unaware of or forgotten his/her rights after the initial notice was posted.

(3) *Make the policy accessible online*

If the organization maintains a Web site, use this location to post the privacy policy. The policy should be conspicuously displayed for general view as well as at each point across the Web site where PII may be obtained by the organization.

(4) *Ensure that CSRs are knowledgeable about the policy*

If your organization uses a call center, you should develop a summary statement or script for customer service representatives (CSRs) to reference that describes your privacy policy in detail and anticipates common questions with prepared answers. CSRs should have a full copy of the privacy policy in their standard reference material as well as have the ability to send or direct callers to a copy of your privacy policy that they can review in detail.

Policy Requirements under Gramm-Leach- Bliley

As first described under Chapter Two, the Gramm-Leach-Bliley Act sets forth certain requirements and standards that financial institutions must meet when handling non-public information (NPI), the variety of personal information that is subject to the Act. These requirements include the availability of the privacy policy, its location, the frequency of publishing the policy and the means for distributing the policy.

Under the GLBA, "customer" and "consumer" are two distinct concepts. A consumer is a person "who obtains or has obtained a financial product or service from a financial institution that is to be used primarily for personal, family, or household purposes, or that individual's legal representative."[471] A customer is "a consumer who has a 'customer relationship' with a financial institution. A 'customer relationship is a continuing relationship with a consumer."[472] Depending on whether the person is a customer or a consumer, he will require different notice.

The GLBA requires that financial institutions provide consumers with privacy notices before disclosing their personally identifiable information. These firms must provide customers with a privacy notice when first establishing a customer relationship—if not sooner. However, posting the privacy policy on location is not, itself, sufficient to constitute an "annual notice." Customers must be provided with a form that can be retained or accessed at a later time.[473] Such forms should be readily available at all locations in which the company does business with customers.

The annual notices provided by financial institutions do not have to be given every twelve months from the exact date at which the customer relationship began. Rather, annual notice may be given at a point the company determines is convenient, so long as the first annual notice is given within twelve months of the start of the customer relationship.[474] The chosen twelve-month period must be applied consistently to the customer after it is first employed.

For example, a customer who opens an investment account with a securities firm in December, 2006 should receive his first annual notice from the firm by no later than January, 2007 and should continue to send the annual notice to the customer in January of each subsequent year. Note that simply posting an annual notice to an organization's Web site does not comply with the annual notice requirement of GLBA.

In this example, account holders who carry investments in their own names are considered both consumers of the fund and customers of the securities firm. As a result, these shareholders must receive an annual notice of the organization's privacy policies.

Annual privacy notices may be given to customers via the Internet, but only if the customer agrees to this means:

For customers who use the organization's Web site for electronic financial transactions—and who have agreed to receive the annual notice at the Web site—the privacy notice should be clearly and conspicuously posted and updated regularly so that the most current version is always the one posted.

If the organization maintains a Web site on which consumers can conduct transactions electronically, the notice may be posted to the screen corresponding to such a transaction. The consumer should be required to give acknowledgement of receipt of the notice before he can complete his transaction.[475]

Policy Version Control

An organization's privacy policy will invariably need to be updated as its information collection, use and transfer needs evolve and change. As such changes occur, a new version of the privacy policy must be drafted to replace the older version. Replacement of the policy must occur across all areas of posting (physical and electronic) and be stored in an available manner for the purpose of customer usage.

The policy document should clearly note across all public notices both the date of policy revision date and the version number of the policy. Also, carefully save and store the older versions for later reference. A prudent company should maintain the ability to roll back to previous versions and track the usage of the policy within all versions.

Both employees and customers should be aware of the varieties of personal data an organization collects. They can be provided a hard copy or other company-proscribed means along with detailed description of the types of personal data in storage or use. The following types of information are particularly important to this disclosure:

Name and Address: Customer names and addresses are highly personal, and many customers may be sensitive to their collection. The organization should clearly delineate the circumstances in which these information types collected. Generally, they should not be collected unless entirely necessary for a defined business purpose.

Cookies: As defined under Chapter Five, a "cookie" is a piece of computer code that a Web site saves to a computer's hard drive when connected to the Internet through the means of a browser. Cookie files may contain various types of information, including user preferences, other Web sites the user has visited, and log-in or registration data.[476]

Though it remains a topic of continued debate among privacy professionals and privacy advocates, information obtained from a cookie installed on a computer may be considered PII. Consumers should be informed if the use of certain portions of a Web site will install cookies on the user's computer. The organization's Web site should not refuse customers that choose not to download a particular cookie. The organization's cookie handling practices should be clearly described to the consumer as well as the means for opting out of such usage.

Financial Information: Customers must be notified if an organization plans to collect personal financial information from them. Collected financial information is subject to the protections of relevant laws—such as Gramm-Leach-Bliley in the United States—and the organization must be sure to comply with all the attendant restrictions. Before engaging in financial information collection, be sure to determine whether the information is absolutely necessary and if it is, carefully review the procedures required under the law.

Disclosure of Types of Use

Each customer must be made aware of how his/her personal information will be used. A privacy policy is not complete unless and until the various data usage scenarios are described.

Personal information may be used for many different internal purposes within an organization. However, the organization may prefer not to narrow the data usage statement to specify and explain the specific internal purposes—unless these are absolutely certain.

If your organization contemplates multiple uses of personal information, without setting these out in advance, consider describing the uses broadly enough to cover any variations in internal practice and use. For example, if a customer's name and address are only going to be used for purposes of order confirmation and/or product delivery, this may be noted. If the information will be used for various reasons (eg. marketing, market research), you will not want to state such a narrow internal purpose and run the risk of violating your privacy policy.

Further, if your organization acquires profile information from marketing companies to amend the information you have about your customers that should be disclosed also.

Organizations should notify customers when collected information will be used to send materials to them, be it through general mail or email. Email in particular may be one use in which an organization wishes to give customers the option to opt-in rather than opt-out. Otherwise, the organization may risk annoying or alienating its customers with a barrage of unexpected email. This is covered in greater detail below under, "User Preference Strategy."

Collected personal data can be particularly useful for analysis of customer interests in order to develop new products, long-term goals and growth plans for the organization. Accordingly, the organization's privacy policy should explain that the information will be used to analyze and develop future business goals and should list the types of information that will be used to do so.

Customers should be informed of the processing their personal information will undergo. The organization should note if a third party entity will be involved in the processing of the information and if that party is located in another country . Customers should also be notified if their information will be given to unrelated third parties and on what terms this will occur. Finally, the privacy policy should delineate the measures an organization uses to ensure that the processing of data is secure.

Whenever information is collected and processed, the potential for error remains in the content of data. As a result, the individual about whom the information relates should be provided both access to the contents of the PII and the ability to correct any errors present in this information. The organization needs to determine among its various functions or divisions that such information access can be readily provided; if not, to develop the capability to provide personal data access and correction.

User Preference Strategy

Different uses of personal data require different means of obtaining consent from customers. Some information may be collected without general customer concern. The collection of other information may concern customers and discourage them from doing business with your company. Much of this difference may simply arise from what customers are accustomed to sharing as opposed to keeping private. Reviewing the practices of companies similar to your own may highlight how your customers may prefer their data to be collected. A company's preference management strategy is closely linked to its marketing and sales strategy, and they should be developed in a coordinated fashion.

An organization may choose the means by which it requires its customers to opt-out of its data sharing processes.[477] If the customer chooses an unspecified means to opt-out, the company may refuse this selection until the customer uses the correct or feasible method. However, the opt-out method must be within reason for the customer.

When a customer makes an opt-in or opt-out preference selection, this selection must be applied to the use of the data by the organization concerned. The following methods of applying customer preferences should be considered when creating the opt-out and/or opt-in alternatives:

Opt-out by account number, phone number, name, email address, household or opt-out of ALL

The organization should determine the best category by which a customer may opt-out. For instance, if the organization collects data based on a customer's name or email address, it may wish to allow the person to opt-out under one of these two. If the organization has very large databases, it should be aware that both data items may be required to ensure (authenticate) that the correct person is being opted-out. If the organization collects broader information pertaining to entire households, it may be more reasonable to allow a customer to opt-out for the entire household.

Other options in this category include: opting out by account number, phone number or of all means by which a company collects information. Providing multiple options to opt-out is a very customer-friendly method of applying preferences.

Opt-out by division or entire organization

The choice to opt-out could be specific to a division or unit of an organization or may be generally applied to the entire organization. To determine which method is best, consider how the data from each division will be used, how often customers overlap between divisions, how often data is shared between divisions, and the unique nature of each division. The pre-existence of multiple privacy policies at an organization also suggests the need for different opt-out processes by division. Last but not least, consider what customers are likely to prefer. For example, a customer may no longer wish to do business with a company that requires an opt-out of data collection each time the customer engages with a different part of the company.

No-opt

No-opt disallows the customer any choice of opting in or out of information collection, use or sharing. This mechanism is employed very rarely, if at all, and any organization considering such an option should weigh its significant impact on customer relations. Not providing a means to opt out of data collection/sharing outside may alienate customers from the organization as well as harm its reputation overall.

The no-opt is not an available alternative under many of the current privacy laws, including HIPAA and the GLBA in the U.S. These laws require an organization to provide its customers with the ability to opt-out of having their information collected or shared. Before using this option, organizations should explore all the applicable federal and state laws which may require that customers be provided with a means of choosing not to share their information.

Methods for Customer Preference Notification

Once a customer has notified an organization that he/she wishes to opt out of data use, the company should provide that individual with a confirmation that the request has been received and processed. This will help to avoid customers sending multiple opt-out choices in order to ensure they have notified the company.

Consumers should retain the ability to change their preferences to opt-out of data collection at any time. The steps to changing a preference should be easy to follow and reasonable in their terms.

Written Request: An organization should not require that its customers write their own letters-of-request as the only option to opt out.[478] This is not a reasonable means for the customer. On the other hand, a company may require that a customer return a detachable form which already contains the company's mailing information.

Verbal Request: Oral means for communicating preferences should also be available to the consumer. For example, the U.S. Securities and Exchange Commission ("SEC") has suggested a toll-free telephone number as an efficient means to allow customers to opt-out.

Electronic Request: An online form offers an easy and expedient method to change a customer's preference. Many customers will appreciate the availability of such a form. Other customers may not wish to use an online form due to the lack of an Internet connection or a secure computer. Thus, an organization that wishes to use an online opt-out process should also offer a toll-free telephone number as an alternate means to reach the organization.

Once a customer has chosen to opt out, the choice should be honored in a timely manner. Depending upon the means of data collection, this may be instantaneous or may be within a time period that is most practical for both parties (the organization and the consumer).

There should be a defined time period in which the customer's choice will be applied. Organizations should analyze the process which the preference election will have to undergo and determine the earliest feasible deadline to apply the choice. The process should avoid all unnecessary delays and make it a priority to employ the customer's choice as soon as possible. In the United States, the CAN-SPAM Act and Telemarketing Sales Rules mandate specific time periods for processing customer preferences and organizations must meet these legal requirements.

The time period in which a preference may be applied is often dependent upon the means of communication chosen. An email will be received by the company in a much shorter time than a letter. Be certain to consider these technical issues when defining the time period by which a preference will be applied.

The handling of preferences should be reviewed to ensure that they are being received and processed in a timely and secure manner. Your company may wish to minimize the amount of staff that must handle preferences in order to avoid unnecessary losses.

Regulatory Exceptions to Opt-out: HIPAA

Entities covered by HIPAA may disclose personal health information ("PHI") to public health authorities *without* giving notice or opportunity to opt-out.[479] The public health authority must be legally authorized to collect such information "for the purpose of preventing or controlling disease, injury, or disability."[480] A covered entity also may disclose PHI data to foreign government agencies if the entity is directed to do so by the public health authority.[481]

Public health authorities include a state and local health departments, the U.S. Food and Drug Administration ("FDC"), and the U.S. Centers for Disease Control ("CDC"). Also included in public health activities are those that indirectly affect the public health. These include, but are not limited to:

- Child abuse or neglect,

- Quality, safety and effectiveness of a product or activity regulated by the FDA, and,

- Workplace medical surveillance.[482]

If a public authority requests PHI data from your organization and you are uncertain whether the authority falls within this HIPAA exception, be sure to consult a privacy official or attorney before sharing the information.

HIPAA also mandates notification requirements for third parties acting on behalf of others with regard to health matters. A personal representative for an individual must be provided with the information he requests about the individual to the extent such information is relevant to the representation.[483] The scope of the personal representative's authority depends upon the applicable law which allows the representative to make medical decisions for the individual.[484] State or other applicable laws should be consulted to determine the scope of the representative's authority and thus the amount of information he may be given.

Regulatory Exceptions to Opt-out: GLBA

As first outlined in Chapter Two, the Gramm-Leach-Bliley Act provides a special set of requirements—and exceptions—around joint marketing agreements. These are situations where a financial institution has contracted with a third-party in order to provide services for or to the financial institution.

Under a standard marketing agreement, a third-party service provider may selectively market some of the financial institution's products and/or services. A joint marketing agreement between a financial institution and one or more other financial institutions allows a third-party service provider to market *all* of the institutions' products and services.

GLBA requires that the financial institution must give notice when any non-public information (NPI) is released to a third party in connection with a joint marketing activity. However, GLBA also provides that the financial institution does not have to offer the right to opt out. To take advantage of this exception, the financial institution must:

- Provide the initial notice required to consumers and customers; and ,

- Contract with the third party service provider or financial institution to prohibit disclosure or use of the information other than for the purpose for which it was disclosed.[485]

A customer does not have the right to opt-out of the sharing of information with companies outside his financial institution if those companies provide essential services to the financial institution. Essential services include such things as data processing or servicing of accounts.[486]

Customer preferences should be honored at all times, including in joint marketing agreements, when sharing information with affiliates or subsidiaries, and between different product lines, business functions or services. Federal and state laws should be reviewed regularly to ensure that your company is complying with all regulations pertaining to the honoring of customer preferences.

Regulatory Exceptions to Opt-out: Law Enforcement or Court Order (U.S.)

GLBA also provides that a financial institution must disclose a customer's NPI upon request by law enforcement. The organization is not required to provide notice of such disclosure to the customer. It is also not required to extend the customer an opt-out in of this situation.

A court order that compels the disclosure of personal information is also considered a valid legal requirement. In this situation, the financial institution must comply with the order and disclose the personal information. Customers do not have the choice to opt-out and the organization is not compelled to provide notice of such disclosure.

Acquiring Preferences from Third Parties

Customer preferences should be honored in all instances—even those where the organization responsible for preference management did not collect the information directly. An organization has the legal and practical obligations of acquiring, preserving and maintaining the customer preferences which pertain to the data it owns. This includes information obtained from a company's affiliates, subsidiaries and/or vendors.

All pre-existing customer preference elections should be obtained from third parties. These preferences should be honored at all times. The organization should not assume that it has already been notified of all customer preferences given to an affiliate or subsidiary. Rather, each affiliate and subsidiary should be required to provide your company with the customer preferences it has obtained.

Ensuring the integrity of customer lists is integral to any customer preference management effort. Your organization should review a third party's means of allowing its customers' to opt-out of data collection and the processing and honoring of those preferences. A written agreement stating the means by which preferences were collected and processed may be obtained from the third party to guarantee the list's integrity.

Maintaining Customer Preferences

Personal information acquired from third parties, including subsidiaries or affiliates of the organization, may change as the third party receives changes in customer preference choices. The organization is obligated to both obtain and apply these changes to the personal information that has been gathered from the third party.

Despite the legal and practical obligations, organizations do retain some flexibility as to how customer preferences should be categorized and maintained over time. For example, customer references may be stored according to the product line, business function or service to which they pertain. The best method of managing these preferences depends upon the nature of your organization, the nature of the customer preference and the infrastructure that is in place to track customer preferences.

Customer Access and Redress

As stated earlier in this chapter, customers should be provided with a means to access the personal information collected on them as well as review the information, and correct or delete any incorrect information. This process is known holistically as customer access and redress.

An organization's access and redress program begins with a clear process disclosure. The organization should readily disclose the process necessary for customers to access information and correct any errors. An appropriate place for the instructions of how to access information is within the company's privacy policy.

Under the E.U. Directive, all individuals must be allowed access to the personal data collected on them from organizations that operate internationally within E.U. jurisdiction. These customers also must be given a reasonable form of redress to amend any errors found within that information.

When a customer makes a change to their personal information held within one company or one division of a company, all other companies or divisions that are also using that personal information should be notified of the error. The notification must include any correction or deletion provided by the customer.

The security of information during and after its transfer from your company to a third party can be difficult to maintain. At various steps in the process, the data may be lost or stolen. To ensure the efficient and effective transfer of information, the following issues must be addressed. Accountability for the secure transfer of personal information is the responsibility of your company and the third party entity.

Contract and Vendor Management

Personal information collection and analysis can be a complicated and time consuming process. Many organizations will elect to outsource these efforts to an outside vendor or (in the United States especially) will choose to sell the collected information to a third party. Specific precautions must be taken if your company plans to share personal data with an affiliate or third party.

A company is responsible for the actions of vendors it contracts with to collect, analyze, catalog or otherwise provide data management services for personal data on the company's behalf. Thus, the claims in your privacy policy should hold true for any third parties that are also working with data you collect or use. To ensure the responsibility and security of data once it is in the hands of a contractor or vendor, the following precautions should be taken.

(1) *Confidentiality Provision*

All contractors and vendors involved in personal information collection for an organization—or with whom an organization shares data—should be required to sign a contract containing a confidentiality provision before engaging in business that uses the information.

(2) *Further Use of Shared Information*

The contract with the vendor managing personal information on the organization's behalf should specify that the data be used only for the purposes contracted. Further use of the shared data beyond the terms in the contract should be strictly forbidden.

(3) *Use of Sub-Contractors*

Should the vendor intend to use sub-contractors in the collection or use of personal information, the contractor organization should require that all sub-contractors follow the privacy protection terms in the vendor's contract (which, in turn, should be consistent with the organization's own privacy protection terms).

(4) *Requirement to Notify and to Disclose Breach*

An organization should require immediate notification in the event of a breach of contract through the misuse of personal data by a vendor or contractor. The exact nature of the breach should be disclosed immediately and in full detail.

(5) *Background Checks*

In order to ensure privacy policy and security obligations in the vendor contract are met, all service providers and employees who will have access to and interact with personal data should undergo a thorough background check before beginning their employment. This check should include contacting the references of a potential employee. If a potential employee has a record of criminal activity, particularly activity involving fraudulent acts, the company should deny employment.

Note that this background check requirement applies equally to domestic employees as well as employees who are stationed internationally. With the increasing globalization of information and the availability of internet, personal information lost, stolen or leaked out in another country can easily impact an individual in the United States, causing harm to that individual, along with harming a company's reputation.

(6) *Background Checks of Service Providers and Employees*

Similar to the requirement above, an organization should require that firms who provide data management services using compiled data also utilize background checks on the employees involved in the use of such data.

Vendor Due Diligence

Choosing a vendor can be a difficult process not the least because an organization is liable if a vendor breaches the organization's privacy policy. Several steps should be taken to meet due diligence in choosing a responsible, reliable vendor in all engagements—but particularly those involving the handling or processing of personal information.

The procuring organization may have specific standards and processes for vendor selection. The prospective vendor should be thoroughly evaluated against these standards before an organization enters into a business relationship with the vendor. These standards include business reputation, financial condition, insurance policy, information security controls and secure point of transit in addition to verifiable processes for document destruction and effective privacy training and awareness programs for vendor employees.

Reputation: A vendor's reputation with other companies can be a valuable gauge of the vendor's appropriate collection and use of personal data. An organization should require references from the vendor that can attest to the vendor's care in privacy and security procedures. The references provided should always be contacted.

Financial condition: The vendor's finances should be reviewed to ensure the vendor has sufficient resources in the case of breach of security and subsequent litigation. If the review reveals any inconsistencies in finances or a lack of sufficient resources, your company should deny business with the potential vendor.

Insurance: The vendor company should carry a current and comprehensive insurance policy that covers a potential security breach. Such insurance will protect both the vendor and the contracting company.

Information security controls: A service provider should have sufficient security controls in place to ensure the data is not lost or stolen. The following are common security controls that vendors ought to have in place and that should be reviewed by the contracting organnization before entering into a contract. The contracting organization's information security department can further assist with assessment of these controls.

- *Access* of the vendor's staff to customers' personal information should be limited to only those staff members who must work with the information. These same staff members should be the most familiar with, and capable of, complying with the organization's privacy procedures. The personal information should not be readily available to all staff members for any reason.

- *Physical security.* The same security principles described in Chapter Three apply in equal measure to external entities such as vendor companies and other third parties that may be engaged by an organization. Personal information should be stored in a secure place, such as electronically locked data centers, secure consoles, locked file cabinets or locked offices and located away from any potential hazards, such as fires, floods or other emergencies. Sensitive information should not be stored in an area where the general public has access or where there is regular traffic of individuals who are not authorized to view such information. The contract with a vendor should guarantee the secure storage of personal data and be specific to the type of data being stored and the required security protections.

- *Firewalls.* If data is to be stored in computer systems and databases, the company network infrastructure, individual computers and application databases should utilize firewall protections to deter hacking into computer files. Have your information security department review the adequacy of the firewall protections of the vendor company.

- *Audit procedures* should be required to ensure that personal information is not improperly disclosed or stolen. The vendor's previous audits may be reviewed to indicate areas in which the vendor is lacking sufficient security measures.

- *Intrusion detection.* The vendor company should employ means by which audits will detect intrusions upon the data for which it is responsible. The FTC has suggested that customer lists be supplemented with at least one data element (such as an account number or address) that the company controls.[487] The company can then monitor use of this data element to detect all unauthorized contacts or charges.

- *Incident response:* The vendor company should provide its employees with a detailed description of how to appropriately respond in the event of a breach of security affecting personal information for which that vendor is responsible. Such response to breach should include immediately notifying the contracting company and, where appropriate, notifying law enforcement officials.

- *Disaster recovery / Business contingency plan:* As addressed in length under Chapter Three, information security is maintained in the event of a disaster or emergency through an effective continuance plan. A vendor company or service provider should have an established plan of how to respond in the event of a disaster and how to resume business afterwards. Your organization should review this policy to determine if it fits your organization's privacy policy and provides the protections necessary for the data you are sharing. If the plan is not sufficient, the contracting company should require increased protections and a more comprehensive recovery and resumption plan before entering into a business relationship.

The point of transfer is the threshold at which information is highly susceptible to theft or breach. This point, whether electronic or physical, should be reviewed carefully and a process of secure transfer should be developed and maintained.

Disposal of information: Appropriate document destruction is a key component information management—both for the contracting the organization and its vendors. Common methods to ensure proper disposal of secure personal information include:

(1) Hiring or designating a records retention manager to supervise the disposal of records containing personal information—in accordance with your privacy policy;

(2) Shredding customer information recorded on paper;

(3) Erasing all data when disposing of computers, diskettes, magnetic tapes, hard drives or any other electronic media that contain customer information; including use of industry standard technologies to fully erase personal data from storage devices;

(4) Effectively recycling or destroying the hardware used to retain sensitive information; and,

(5) Promptly disposing of outdated customer information per the above.[488]

Employee training and user awareness: The vendor should have an established system to train its employees about its responsibilities in managing personal or sensitive information. The contracting organization must review this system in light of duties to its customers. If the vendor does not have such a system—or, or has one that does not meet the organization's core requirements—then it must provide further training of vendor employees to meet the policy requirements before data is transferred to or from the vendor.

Vendor Data

An organization may wish to share employee data with a third party in a service provider arrangement for reasons not specifically related to employment such as marketing or promoting products or services to the employee. The E.U. Directive carries specific requirements for these scenarios if the information meets the definition of "personally identifiable" to the employee. If this is the case, the organization should notify the employee of its intent and provide the employee with an opportunity to choose before the information is shared.

Conversely, an organization need not provide both notice and choice if it wishes to use employment data for statistical reporting or other uses in which the data is not personally identifiable. "Reporting relying on aggregate employment data and/or the use of anonymized or pseudonymized data does not raise privacy concerns" under the E.U. Directive.[489] Data is not personally identifiable if it does not require accessing or transferring specific individual records. Organizations may choose to provide notice only in these circumstances, or if required by a Works Council or related labor agreement.

Aligning Privacy Policy with Vendor Contracts

Before an organization shares personal information with a third party, the business and policy decision of what information to share and with whom must undergo an approval process by the privacy officer within the company. The privacy officer should consider the following issues when determining if the information should be shared, with whom, and how it will be shared.

The very act of sharing personal information with an outside party as part of a business process may be inconsistent with your organization's core privacy policy. Certainly, your organization has a duty to comply with this policy or follow certain measures to change the policy in order to accommodate the information sharing activity. If transferring new information, the same factors need to be considered. Your organization should also consider these problems when drafting privacy policy and subsequent versions.

As a general practice, organizations should only share personal information based on well defined business needs and measurable benefit to the company. If customers believe their information is being shared by an organization—or its affiliated third parties—without regard to their expressed preferences, they may not do business or engage with that organization again.

International Data Transfers

In today's global economy, organizations are likely to establish business relationships with affiliates, partners or vendors that are located across the world. If an organization engages in business activities that requires the transfer of personal information outside of the native country, extra security and safety measures must be taken to ensure that the organization complies with all the applicable national and international laws within each jurisdiction, along with ensuring customer satisfaction and protection throughout the process.

Organizations are encouraged to develop and understand an international privacy vocabulary in order to navigate through the practical and legal challenges inherent in global information transfers. Many of these common terms have been cited earlier in this volume within the context of various international privacy laws (most notably the E.U. Directive). They include the following:

- *Data Subject* refers to the individual that is the subject of personal data.[490]

- *Data Controller* is an organization that wishes to hold or already holds personal data. This entity controls the use of personal data by determining its purposes and the manner in which the data will be processed.[491] The data controller may be an individual or an organization that is legally treated as an individual, such as a corporation or partnership.

- *Data Processor* is any individual or organization that processes data on behalf of the data controller. A higher duty of care is required of data controllers when personal data is processed by a data processor rather than by the controller itself.[492]

- *Personal Data* may also be referred to as personal information. This data is defined similarly to Personally Identifiable Information in the U.S. Personal data is any data that may be used to identify or locate a living individual. Such information includes data that may be used to directly identify a person or that may be used to do so with additional information that the third party has or is likely to have or come into possession of.[493] Both factual information and opinions expressed about an individual are personal data

Each country in which an organization operates or engages in business may have specific differences or exceptions to the organization's general global policy of data protection. For example, the E.U. Directive recognizes that some personal freedoms may be stifled in an effort to protect privacy and allows countries to establish laws protecting personal freedoms, such as freedom of the press and media.[494] National laws also may exempt companies from the E.U. Directive's obligation to publicize data processing operations or exempt companies that are processing data merely for scientific or statistical purposes.[495]

Because these exceptions are specific to each country, an organization must thoroughly review the laws of the country in which it is doing business to establish what exceptions there may be to a global policy. For more detail on these exceptions, please review the international privacy laws covered within Chapters Two and Three of this text.

The Safe Harbor Agreement and Framework

Some U.S.-based organizations may elect to work with vendors or affiliates that are located overseas or outsource their data processing to companies based overseas. This collaboration between U.S. companies conducting business internationally or global multinationals creates extra responsibilities that must be meet to meet the privacy obligations they have committed to in their policy, with a special emphasis on protecting the security of data during and after its transfer.

As originally discussed under Chapter Two, the E.U. Data Protection Directive prohibits the transfer of personal data to countries outside of the E.U. unless those countries have met the adequacy standards established by the E.U.[496] Because the U.S. and the E.U. have very different approaches to data protection, a "Safe Harbor" framework has been established and approved by the E.U. in order for businesses in the U.S. and E.U. to work together.[497]

A company that plans to transfer data to or from a country in the E.U. to the U.S. should obtain Safe Harbor self-certification before engaging in such an act and should renew the self-certification annually. Participation in the Safe Harbor is a voluntary self-certification process that involves agreeing to follow seven privacy principles deemed compatible (but not exactly equivalent) to E.U. Directive requirements, commitment to a training and compliance program, cooperation with the FTC and/or E.U. Data Protection Authorities and certain other requirements. Commitment to the Safe Harbor includes publishing that in the company privacy policy.[498] A U.S. company self-certifies with the U.S. Department of Commerce.[499] The self-certification indicates to the E.U. that the company has established adequate safety measures to protect data privacy and allows a company to avoid interruptions in E.U.-US business dealings and prosecution under E.U. privacy laws.[500] Safe Harbor applies only to data flows from the E.U. to the US.

Standard Model Clauses, Consent and Notification

Organizations that plan to transfer data to or from a country in the E.U. other than the U.S., must meet standard "adequacy" requirements defined under the E.U. Directive. As of this writing, only two countries outside the E.U. meet such standards—Canada and Argentina.

> ***Standard model clauses:*** *Contractual agreements defined by the E.U. and the Article 29 Working Party for the purpose of meeting the adequacy standards defined under the E.U. Data Protection Directive. Standard model clauses contain extensive data protection commitments and company liability requirements that some companies may find difficult to accept.*

In the absence of formal adequacy standard or Safe Harbor, organizations are encouraged to implement Standard Model Clauses. Organizations must be willing to implement the Standard Model Clauses for each business process or personal data flow leaving an E.U. country for a non-adequate country. These contractual agreements help to ensure that an organization can avoid interruptions in global business dealings and prosecution, related to E.U. countries.

Other national data protection laws may have similar cross-border data flows as those found in the E.U.: Japan and Australia, for example. Please consult Chapter Two for further details on international privacy laws and their data flow provisions.

Under the E.U. Directive, customers' personal data may not be processed unless they have given express consent to its use or transfer outside the country.[501] This differs from the typical opt-out method used within the U.S. Before engaging in data collection in another country, a company must review the applicable laws and determine what procedures must be followed. Some data protection authorities are may be reluctant to accept consent as valid for employee personal data transfers.

Some country's privacy authorities (DPAs) may need to be notified before a company begins transferring personal data to or from the country. The requirements of the country in which your company wishes to do business should be reviewed before engaging in transfer. All relevant authorities should be notified of the business's activities as laws and regulations require. These notifications may need to be reviewed or amended on an annual or periodic basis.

Conducting business overseas requires different strategies, processes and infrastructure to manage and safeguard personal information. This goes beyond the more straightforward focus on simply transferring information overseas. When a company employs staff outside of the U.S., a wholly different set of laws and regulations will apply.

Employee Information vs. Customer Information

Chapter Three outlined the many ways that U.S. privacy laws differ in the treatment of employee information from customer information—and how international laws often do not make any distinctions between the two. For example, under the E.U. Directive, European countries tend to limit the secondary use of customer or employee data to a greater extent than the U.S. Organizations that have elected to participate in the Safe Harbor program are protected under this self-certification, when they chose to cover "HR personal data", when transporting employee data from an E.U. country.[502] A company transferring information out of an E.U. country must still follow that country's laws restricting the information that is transferred.

As a general rule, organizations should treat employee data with the same care and security that they treat customer data. Country-specific implementations of the E.U. Directive are quite specific about the high level of protection required for employee personal data. The notice and choice principles of the E.U. Directive should be honored for all employee data. This means that an employee should be given notice of the company's intent to share the information and give the employee the choice not to share this information. The same level of choice may not be available or required for employees in U.S. or other countries. Under no circumstances should a choice be used to restrict employment or promotion.[503]

Before engaging in any multi-country transport of employee data, a company must review all the applicable U.S. and other country's laws to determine what specific conditions or restrictions apply. In addition, regional groups of countries may have regulations like the E.U. Directive that must be complied with.

Under the E.U. Directive, employee directories or phone lists, information, benefits and payroll are all considered employee data which may be subject to provisions of the Directive. An organization should put in place methods to manage privacy obligations to its employees. These methods may include the initial employment contract, Works Council or other labor agreements or specific privacy preferences a particular employee program. Organizations should be aware that many E.U. country DPAs no longer recognize employee choice (or consent) as a valid means of supporting personal data use or transport.

Notice and choice should not hinder an organization's business processes, and an organization need not apply employee preferences to areas that may inhibit or prevent proper functioning of the organizations operations. For example, employee information may be used for legitimate company interests, such as making promotions and appointments, without offering employees prior notice and choice. In some situations such as system usage or some performance reporting, individual employees do not need to be visible, instead the information can be aggregated. In other instances, access to the data may be restricted or anonymized.[504]

International Privacy Policies

As discussed earlier in this chapter, development and approval of an organization's privacy policy is ultimately a strategic decision. The same process applies whether considering multiple lines of business or multiple countries of operation. Because international laws may vary greatly from those in the U.S., one alternative an organization should consider is employing different policies within the U.S. and outside of the U.S. If the organization maintains a vast network outside of the U.S., it may be prudent to create policies tailored to each of those international markets in which the company functions. This approach may require a complex data management and policy governance framework.

Another option for large international organizations with many customers in the U.S. and around the world is to adopt a global policy based on the most common, if not most stringent, requirements from all the countries in which the organization does business. This approach allows an organization the simplicity of maintaining one privacy policy and one data management framework. It may provide consistency in managing global business processes and IT infrastructures. The attempt to meet all laws in one policy may be too difficult or restricting for most companies to achieve though. In addition, countries may have diametrically opposed privacy policies in which this approach will not work.

International Marketing Issues

Marketing privacy is a discipline unique to geography. Unlike the U.S. regulatory system which typically stipulates an opt-out provision from companies using personal data, the international community (particularly the E.U.) often requires organizations to use an opt-in provision. Before an organization engages in overseas marketing that relies upon collected personal data, the organization should review each country's laws pertaining to opt-in or opt-out requirements particularly as these relate to marketing products or services.

Customer preference elections must be maintained and honored when marketing overseas. In countries that generally use an opt-in (consent-based) method, if a customer has not consented by opting in to the receipt of marketing information, a company must not market to that person. Otherwise, a company risks violating international laws and alienating customers that expect opt-in method of marketing.

Privacy Program Oversight and Governance

The establishment of a privacy policy and a logical process of analyzing, sharing and transferring personal information are crucial steps in maintaining information privacy and security both within an organization and through its various outside partnerships and contracting agreements. This policy-and-process combination must be continually maintained through an established system of oversight and governance. As a privacy professional, your responsibility will be to assess and provide guidance to your organization's management and lines of business to maintain standard practices or apply better practices where necessary.

Once an organization has established its privacy policy and begun conducting business using personal information under the policy, the organization must continue to monitor and update customer preferences as they change over time. The ongoing disclosure of personal information also must be monitored to ensure compliance with the company privacy policy and customer preference elections.

Self Assessments and Third Party Audits

As a best practice, an organization should complete a self assessment of its data storage and processing methods on a regular basis. Particular attention should be paid to whether information privacy and security procedures are fully compliant—to published policy as well as applicable laws and regulations. These assessments may be conducted by privacy staff, a compliance department or an internal audit department. Assessment results should be analyzed and action plans developed to remediate any policy deficiencies with the affected line of business. The results of assessments should be also analyzed in light of any new changes in regulations and laws, and policy or practices adjusted accordingly. The assessment should also take into account changing business strategies or expectations of the company from customers and clients.

Some organizations may prefer to have a complete assessment conducted by an authorized third party auditor. A privacy policy audit conducted by a third party is an effective means of assessing compliance to the policy and locating areas that need better security measures. An audit may also provide information useful for streamlining the data sharing or transfer processes. Large companies in particular may find a third party audit useful in reviewing what may be a very complicated policy and data management infrastructures, personal data security and sharing processes. Third party auditors can leverage additional experience or expertise from the industry in which the audited organization operates—and share industry standards and best practices that may serve to benefit the audited organization.

Employee Training and Awareness

All organization staff that deals with personal information collected by the organization should thoroughly understand the company privacy policy. Employees directly involved with handling or accessing the personal information of customers or employees should receive formal training. The training should include a plan of action if a breach or mistake occurs along with providing information on data storage and security. Your organization may wish to consider some basic level of company-wide training for privacy policies and practices.

Just as with customers and vendors, employees and privacy staff who interact with personal information must also be informed as the privacy policy is updated and changed. If the policy or procedures change significantly, staff should receive updated training. New employees should always receive training when they begin working with the company.

Privacy Certification

Lastly, privacy professionals, compliance managers, security professionals, general counsel and any other individuals associated with information management at an organization ought to consider professional certification. The certification process will train professionals as to the best methods for information privacy program development, structure and management in relation to major domestic and international regulatory requirements and industry-standard best practices. The certification designation identifies the individual as having achieved a fundamental understanding of information privacy laws, concepts, technologies and practices that are integral to information management as established by reputable, third party organizations.

The leading information security credentials include Certified Information Systems Auditor (CISA) and Certified Information Systems Manager (CISM), both offered by the Information Systems Audit and Control Association (ISACA) and the Certified Information Systems Security Professional (CISSP) offered by the International Information Systems Security Certification Consortium (ISC²).

IAPP continues to offer the leading credential in information privacy, the Certified Information Privacy Professional (CIPP) as well as certifications for U.S. government privacy (CIPP/G) and Canadian privacy (CIPP/C) with additional certifications forthcoming for European privacy (CIPP/E.U.) and privacy in the Asia Pacific region (CIPP/AP).

Conclusion

Public concern continues to grow over how much personally identifiable information is collected, transported and used around the globe electronically—making responsible information management one of the most fundamentally important aspects of a privacy professional's role in an organization.

Understanding your information assets and data flows is critical to creating a workable, sustainable privacy program within your organization. This program must incorporate methods for policy development, customer preference management, vendor relations, employee training and privacy certification. Such a program will create better accountability and responsibility for information management and ensure that the inevitable customer issues, data breaches or other incidents are kept to a manageable minimum. The result assures that an organization's brand trust and customer relations will remain intact.

END NOTES

[1] Samuel Warren & Louis Brandeis, *The Right to Privacy*, 4 HARV. L. REV. 193 (1890), www.lawrence.edu/fast/boardmaw/Privacy_brand_warr2.html. As an aside there are numerous sources of legal privacy, including tort privacy (Warren and Brandeis's original conception), Fourth Amendment privacy, First Amendment privacy, fundamental-decision privacy, and state constitutional privacy. Ken Gormley, *One Hundred Years of Privacy*, 1992 WIS. L. REV. 1335 (1992).

[2] *The Australian Privacy Charter*, Australian Privacy Charter Group (University of New South Wales Law School 1994).

[3] Alan F. Westin, *Privacy and Freedom* (New York: Atheneum, 1967).

[4] Edward Bloustein, *Privacy as an Aspect of Human Dignity*, 39 N.Y.U. L. REV. 971 (1964).

[5] Ruth Gavison, *Privacy and the Limits of Law*, 89 YALE L.J. 421, 428 (1980).

[6] *Report of the Committee on Privacy and Related Matters*, Cm. 1102, Calcutt Committee (1997) (Chairman David Calcutt).

[7] *Global Trends* at 6.

[7] *Id.*

[7] *Id.*

[7] *Id.*

[7] *Id.*

[7] *Id.* at 8.

[8] *Id.*

[9] *Id.*

[10] *Colloquium on Privacy & Security*, Transcript, Gary M. Schober, Moderator, 50 BUFFALO L. REV. 703, 726 (2002); *Privacy and Human Rights: An International Survey of Privacy Laws and Developments*, Electronic Privacy Information Center & Privacy International (2002) ("Privacy and Human Rights").

[11] an-Noor 24:27-28 (Yusufali); al-Hujraat 49:11-12 (Yusufali).

[12] *Privacy and Human Rights* at 5.

[13] *Id.*

[14] *Fiftieth Anniversary of the Universal Declaration of Human Rights*, United Nations, www.un.org/rights/50/decla.htm.

[15] *Id.* at Article 12.

[16] *American Declaration of the Rights and Duties of Man*, April 1948, Conference of American States, www.cidh.org/Basicos/basic2.htm.

[17] *Id.* at Article V.

[18] *Convention for the Protection of Human Rights and Fundamental Freedoms*, April 11, 1950, Council of Europe, http://conventions.coe.int/Treaty/Commun/QueVoulez Vous.asp?NT=005&CM=8&DF=18/07/2005& CL=ENG.

[19] *Id.* at Article 8.

[20] *Id.* at 8.

[21] *Id.*

[22] *Id.*

[23] *Id.*

[24] *Id.* Judgment of June 16, 1858, Trib. pr. inst. de la Seine, 1858 D.P. III 62 (Fr.) (affaire Rachel); *see also* Jeanne M. Hauch, *Protecting Private Facts in France: The Warren & Brandeis Tort is Alive and Well and Flourishing in Paris*, 68 TUL. L. REV. 1219 (1994).

[25] *See Privacy and Human Rights 2003: Norway*, Privacy International (2003), www.privacy-international.org/survey/phr2003/countries/norway.htm.

[26] *Id.*

[27] *Global Trends* at 13.

[28] *Id.* at 14.

[29] *Global Trends* at 11.

[30] *Global Trends* at 14.

[31] *Id.*

[32] *Id.* at 13-14.

[33] *Id.*

[34] www.privacyalliance.org/.

[35] Major R. Ken Pippin, *Consumer Privacy on the Internet: It's "Surfer Beware"*, 47 A.F. L. REV. 125, 131 (1999) ("Surfer Beware").

[36] *Commentary to the Mission Statement and Guidelines*, Nov. 19, 1998, Online Privacy Alliance, www.privacyalliance.org/news/12031998-4.shtml.

[37] *Id.* at 132.

[38] *Id.*

[39] *Id. See also Self-Regulation and Online Privacy: A Report to Congress* at 6, July 1, 1999, Federal Trade Commission, www.ftc.gov/opa/1999/9907/report1999.htm.

[40] www.truste.org/.

[41] www.bbbonline.org/.

[42] *Surfer Beware* at 133.

[43] www.cpawebtrust.org/.

[44] *Id.*

[45] *Global Trends* at 14.

[46] *Id.*

[47] *Data Protection Directive* at Article 2(b).

[48] *Data Protection Directive* at Article 25.

[49] L. Richard Fischer & Ivan J. Flores, *Privacy Recommendations for Compliance with California Law*, Morrison & Foerster, www.privacylawreport.com/privacylawreport/article.htm.

[50] *Id.* at 15.

[51] *Emerging Trends* at 96.

[52] *Id.*

[53] *Id.*

[54] *Id.*

[55] *Id.* at 93.

[56] U.S. Dep't. of Health, Education and Welfare, Secretary's Advisory Committee on Automated Personal Data Systems, Records, computers, and the Rights of Citiznes viii (1973).

[57] Center for Democracy and technology, "Privacy Basics: Generic Principles of Fair Information Practices" (www.cdt.org/privacy/guide/basic/generic.html); for a slightly different drafting of the principles see Federal Trade Commission, "Fair Information Principles" (www.ftc.gov/reports/privacy3/fairinfo.htm).

58 *Guidelines Governing the Protection of Privacy and Transborder Data Flows of Personal Data,* Sept. 23, 1980, Organization for Economic Cooperation and Development ("OECD Guidelines"). An important distinction between the OECD and the COE is the involvement and support of the United States government. For more information, see www.oecd.org/about/general/member-countries.htm.

59 Blanke, *"Safe Harbor" and the European Union's Directive on Data Protection.*

60 *Convention for the Protection of Individuals with Regard to the Automatic Processing of Personal Data,* Jan. 8, 1981, Council of Europe, http://conventions.coe.int/treaty/EN/cadreprincipal.htm.

61 *Global Trends* at 11. See also *Emerging Trends* at 91-92.

62 *Emerging Trends* at 91.

63 *Global Trends* at 11.

464 *Emerging Trends* at 92.

65 *Id.*

66 *Data Protection Directive* at Article 2(d).

67 *Id.* at Article 2(e).

68 *Id.* at Article 2(g).

69 *Id.* at Article 25. See also *Council Directive* 95/46/EC of 15 June 2001 on standard contractual clauses for the transfer of personal data to third countries, Council of Europe, http://europa.eu.int/eur-lex/pri/en/oj/dat/2001/l_181/l_18120010704en00190031.pdf.

70 Gramm-Leach-Bliley Act, Pub L. No. 106-102 (1999) (codified as amended in scattered sections of 12 U.S.C. and 15 U.S.C.), www.ftc.gov/privacy/glbact/.

71 15 U.S.C. §§ 1601 et. cet.

72 15 U.S.C. § 6802.

73 Health Insurance Portability and Accountability Act of 1996, Pub. L. No. 104-191 (1996), http://aspe.hhs.gov/admnsimp/pl104191.htm.

74 Steve Fox & Rebekah A.Z. Monson, *And Then There Were Four—HIPAA Covered Entities, That Is,* HIPAAdvisory (June 2004), www.hipaadvisory.com/action/legalqa/law/Legal48.htm.

75 Ryan S. Johnson, *Joined at the HIPAA: Covered Entities and Their Business Associates,* Fredrikson & Byron (2001), www.fredlaw.com/articles/health/heal_sp01_rsj.html.

76 See, e.g., the Gramm-Leach-Bliley Financial Services Modernization Act (15 U.S.C. § 6801-6809), including the Privacy Rule and Safeguards Rule; the Children's Online Privacy Protection Act and implementing regulations (15 U.S.C. §§ 6501-6506) and the FTC's COPPA Regulation (64 Fed. Reg. 212),;the Fair Credit Reporting Act and the

Fair and Accurate Credit Transactions Act (15 U.S.C. §§ 1681-1681u), along with FTC regulations and guidance; the Telemarketing and Consumer Fraud Abuse Prevention Act (codified in relevant part at 15 U.S.C. §§ 6101-6108), including the Federal Trade Commission's regulations (the Telemarketing Sales Rule at 16 C.F.R. Part 310); and the CAN SPAM Act of 2003 (15 U.S.C §§ 7701-7713). Copies of all laws and regulations enforced by the FTC can be found online at: www.ftc.gov/ogc/stat3.htm.

[77] "Enforcing Privacy Promises: Enforcement: Cases," Federal Trade Commission, www.ftc.gov/privacy/privacyinitiatives/promises_enf.html

[78] U.S. Constitution, Tenth Amendment

[80] CITE [no need for cite; not a law review]

[81] "Enforcement Activity," Privacy Exchange, www.privacyexchange.org/legal/enforcement.html

[82] "Privacy Enforcement Actions, Office of the Attorney General, State of Washington, www.atg.wa.gov/consumer/idprivacy/priv_enforcement.shtml

[83] "Privacy Law Enforcement Efforts," Office of the Attorney General, State of Minnesota, www.ag.state.mn.us/consumer/privacy/Privacy_Law.htm

[84] A system of laws originated and developed in England and followed in the United States, based on court decisions, on the doctrines implicit in those decisions, and on customs and usages rather than on codified written laws. "Common law," Answers.com, www.answers.com/topic/common-law

[85] Many of these cases have their foundation in protecting private sexual conduct,[40] Some cases include: *Griswold v. Connecticut* (1965) (voiding a state statute preventing the use of contraceptives); *Roe v. Wade* (1973) (overturning state law that barred abortion); *Lawrence v. Texas* (2003) (striking down anti-sodomy laws)

[86] *Black's Law Dictionary*

[87] *Ohio Art Consent Decree*, April, 2004, www.ftc.gov/os/2002/04/ohioartconsent.htm; "FTC Protecting Children's Privacy Online," Federal Trade Commission Press Release, April 22, 2002, www.ftc.gov/opa/2002/04/coppaanniv.htm

[88] *April 8, 2002 Letter From J. Howard Beales, Director, Bureau of Consumer Protection, to the American Bar Association*, Privacy: Gramm-Leach-Bliley Act and Privacy Rule Staff Opinions, www.ftc.gov/os/2002/04/hirshon-beales020408.pdf

[89] "Welcome to the Safe Harbor," Export Portal, U.S. Dept. of Commerce, www.export.gov/safeharbor/index.html

[90] Sherrie Bennett, "Contract Basics," LexisNexis/Martindale-Hubbell, www.lawyers.com/lawyers/A~1001072~LDS/CONTRACTS.html

[91] "Tort law—an overview," legal information institute, www.law.cornell.edu/topics/torts.html

[92] "The Privacy Torts," Privacilla, www.privacilla.org/business/privacytorts.html

[93] "Subject Matter Jurisdiction," www.lectlaw.com/def2/s188.htm

[94] "Personal Jurisdiction in Cyberspace," Joe Kesan, University of Illinois at Urbana-Champaign, College of Law, www.cyberspacelaw.org/kesan/kesan1.html

[95] U.S. Constitution, Article VI (The Supremacy Clause)

[96] www.truste.org

[97] www.dmaconsumers.org/privacy.html

[98] www.bbbonline.org/ and www.caru.org/

[99] Samuel Warren & Louis Brandeis, *The Right to Privacy*, 4 HARV. L. REV. 193 (1890); available online at www.lawrence.edu/fast/boardmaw/Privacy_brand_warr2.html

[100] Convention for the Protection of Human Rights and Fundamental Freedoms, April 11, 1950, Council of E.U.rope, Art. 8 http://conventions.coe.int/treaty/en/Treaties/Html/005.htm

[101] E.U. Data Protection webpage, http://E.U.ropa.E.U..int/comm/internal_market/ privacy/index_en.htm; Directive 95/46/EC of the E.U.ropean Parliament and of the Council of 24 October 1995 on the protection of individuals with regard to the processing of personal data and on the free movement of such data, Official Journal of the E.U.ropean Communities of 23 November 1995 No L. 281 p. 31.

[102] Courts have found privacy protections in 1st, 4th, 5th, and 14th Amendments. See generally http://netsecurity.about.com/od/newsandeditorial1/a/aaprivacyrights.htm

[103] Samuel Warren & Louis Brandeis, *The Right to Privacy*, 4 HARV. L. REV. 193, 215 (1890).

[104] William Prosser, Privacy, 48 Cal.L.Rev. 383 (1960)

[105] Restatement (Second) of Torts at §§ 652A-652I (1977).

[106] Griswold v. Connecticut. 381 US 479 (1965)

[107] Roe v. Wade, 410 US 113 (1973)

[108] Lawrence and Garner v. Texas. 539 US 558 (2003)

[109] Federal Trade Commission, Financial Privacy, The Gramm-Leach-Bliley Act (www.ftc.gov/privacy/glbact/)

[110] Federal Trade Commission, The Fair Credit Reporting Act (www.ftc.gov/os/statutes/fcra.htm)

[111] U.S. Dep't. of Health, Education and Welfare, Secretary's Advisory Committee on Automated Personal Data Systems, Records, computers, and the Rights of Citiznes viii (1973).

[112] Center for Democracy and technology, "Privacy Basics: Generic Principles of Fair Information Practices" (www.cdt.org/privacy/guide/basic/generic.html); for a slightly different drafting of the principles see Federal Trade Commission, "Fair Information Principles" (www.ftc.gov/reports/privacy3/fairinfo.htm)

[113] Ibid

[114] EPIC, The Fair Credit Reporting Act (FCRA) and the Privacy of Your Credit Report (www.epic.org/privacy/fcra/)

[115] White House Fact Sheet: President Bush Signs the Fair and Accurate Credit Transactions Act of 2003, Dec. 4, 2003 (http://www.whitehouse.gov/news/releases/2003/12/20031204-3.html); also see National Consumer Law Center, Analysis of the Fair and Accurate Credit Transactions Act of 2003, Pub. L. No. 108-159 (2003): Summary of FACTA Changes to the FCRA (www.consumerlaw.org/initiatives/facta/nclc_analysis.shtml#1)

[116] Fair Credit Reporting Act (FCRA), 15 U.S.C. § 1681d(1) (www.ftc.gov/os/statutes/fcra.htm#603)

[117] FTC's NOTICE TO USERS OF CONSUMER REPORTS: OBLIGATIONS OF USERS UNDER THE FCRA

[118] A Health Care Clearinghouse means a public or private entity, including a billing service, repricing company, community health management information system or community health information system, and "value-added" networks and switches, that does either of the following functions:

- Processes or facilitates the processing of health information received from another entity in a nonstandard format or containing nonstandard data content into standard data elements or a standard transaction.

- Receives a standard transaction from another entity and processes or facilitates the processing of health information into nonstandard format or nonstandard data content for the receiving entity.

[119] This HIPAA statute, Transaction Rule, Privacy Rule (with all the amendments), Security Rule, and published guidance can be found online at www.hhs.gov/ocr/hipaa/.

[120] OCR Guidance Explaining Significant Aspects of the Privacy Rule—DISCLOSURES FOR PUBLIC HEALTH ACTIVITIES, page 28; see also 45 CFR 164.512(b)(1)(i) and (iii)

[121] Health Insurance Portability and Accountability Act of 1996, 45 CFR 164.502(b) and 164.514(d) (1996)

[122] Please note that, in order to be a "business associate" under HIPAA, the person or organization must process PHI. Entities that do not process PHI (or whose access to be PHI is truly incidental) are not business associates. Covered entities can themselves be business associates of other cover entities.

[123] HHS has indicated that it is considering extending the Security Rule to non-electronic PHI, so that the provisions mirror the scope of protection offered by the Privacy Rule.,(Please note that the financial services counterpart, the Gramm-Leach-Bliley Act, does not limit applicability of its Safeguards Rule to electronic data. For health insurers subject to be HIPAA and GLBA, the security program must encompass paper as well as electronic records.)

[124] Gramm-Leach-Bliley Act, 15 USC, Subchapter I, Sec. 6801-6809 (1999); Also see FTC, "In Brief: The Financial Privacy Requirements of the Gramm-Leach-Bliley Act" (www.ftc.gov/bcp/conline/pubs/buspubs/glbshort.htm)

[125] In Vermont, the State's Department of Banking, Insurance, Securities, and Health Care Administration adopted opt-in provisions for information sharing. To comply with the regulation, some companies have treated all Vermont residents as having opted-out under GLBA.

[126] Providing a toll-free telephone number or a detachable form with a pre-printed address is, requiring someone to write a letter as the only way to opt out is not.

[127] The GLBA does not give consumers the right to opt out when the financial institution shares other information with its affiliates. Consumers have this right under the FCRA Act.

[128] Gramm-Leach-Bliley Act, 15 U.S.C. § 6801(b)

[129] 16 C.F.R. § 314.1(a).

[130] *Id.*

[131] 16 C.F.R. § 314.3(a).

[132] 16 C.F.R. § 314.4.

[133] Children's Online Privacy Protection Act of 2000, 15 USC 6501

[134] FTC, Privacy Online: A Report to Congress, 1998 (www.ftc.gov/reports/privacy3/index.htm)

[135] FTC, UMG Recordings, Inc. to Pay $400,000, Bonzi Software, Inc. To Pay $75,000 to Settle COPPA Civil Penalty Charges, Feb. 18, 2004 (www.ftc.gov/opa/2004/02/bonziumg.htm)

[136] See: www.ftc.gov/privacy/coppafaqs.htm#consent

[137] *Id.* www.ftc.gov/privacy/coppafaqs.htm#consent

[138] FTC, UMG Recordings, Inc. to Pay $400,000, Bonzi Software, Inc. To Pay $75,000 to

Settle COPPA Civil Penalty Charges, Feb. 18, 2004
(www.ftc.gov/opa/2004/02/bonziumg.htm)

[139] Privicilla, History of the Driver's Privacy Protection Act
(www.privacilla.org/government/dppahistory.html)

[140] Reno v. Condon, 528 U.S. 141 (2000).

[141] A list of permissible uses for personal information under the DPPA is found here:
https://dhr.ky.gov/DHRWeb/permissiblE.U.ses.jsp

[142] *Reno v Condon*, United States Supreme Court, 98-1464, January 2000. The Court unanimously determined that the DPPA as amended by the Shelby Amendment did not violate the 10th or 11th Amendments. Of note, the Court determined that personal information in DMV files was itself an article of interstate commerce.

[143] Ex: The Directive on Privacy and Electronic Communications (Directive 2002/58/EC) (http://E.U.ropa.E.U..int/information_society/topics/ecomm/useful_information/library/legislation/index_en.htm#dir_2002_58_ec)

[144] Material terms may include: cost, quantity, restrictions, limitations, conditions, no-refund policies, etc…

[145] Upselling is the sale of a product or service in addition to the product or service the customer has purchased

[146] Intrastate calls are covered by the Federal Communications Commissions regulations under the Telephone Consumer Protection Act (TCPA) (47 U.S.C. § 227). These rules are similar to the TSR rules described herein.

[147] not all telemarketing activities are covered by the TSR. For example, most business-to-business calls are excluded for the Rule. Additionally, the TSR only applies to entities subject to FTC jurisdiction, with other entities (such as banks) covered solely by the TCPA referenced in footnote one. Finally, some types of calls are partially exempt from the Rule. As discussed below, calls to existing customers are exempt from the Do-Not-Call Registry provisions. In-bound calls from customers are also excluded, although up-selling during the call will bring it back within the scope of the Rule with regard to disclosures, payment provisions, etc. If you have any questions about the scope of coverage of the TSR, please let me know.

[148] FTC, The Amended TSR at a Glance
(www.ftc.gov/bcp/conline/pubs/buspubs/tsrcomp.htm#glance)

[149] At the beginning of the call, prior to delivery of any sales content.

[150] Online at: www.ftc.gov/bcp/conline/pubs/buspubs/tsrcomp.htm

[151] Please note that the TSR differs from the Federal Communication Commission's rules with regard to pre-recorded messages and call abandonment. The FCC's call abandonment rules have a exception that permits companies to use pre-recorded messages for

marketing to individuals with whom they have an existing business relationship. In November 2004, the FTC issued a notice of proposed rule-making to add this exception (and harmonize the rules). Consumer groups have opposed the change, and the FTC has not yet taken any further action. Accordingly, for companies subject to FTC jurisdiction, marketing calls may not be made to consumers using pre-recorded messages.

[152] Including a sales message would violate the Federal Communication Commission's rules under the Telephone Consumer Protection Act (47 U.S.C. § 227) and FCC regulations at 47 C.F.R. Part 64.1200.

[153] Private individuals have to meet certain damage requirements to bring suit.

[154] The Direct Marketing Association (DMA) a members-only list of state telemarketing legislation summaries at www.the-dma.org/cgi/member/privacy/statetelephone.shtml.

[155] DMA, Where Marketers Can Obtain State Do-Not-Call Lists (www.the-dma.org/government/donotcalllists.shtml)

[156] The CAN-SPAM Act of 2003 (Public Law 108-187) (www.spamlaws.com/federal/can-spam.shtml)

[157] Telephone Consumer Protection Act (TCPA), 47 USC 227 (1991) (http://straylight.law.cornell.edu/uscode/html/uscode47/usc_sec_47_00000227----000-.html); also see FCC, Telemarketing Policy (www.fcc.gov/cgb/policy/telemarketing.html)

[158] In 2003, the FCC approved a $5.3 million fine against Fax.com for violations of the act (http://hraunfoss.fcc.gov/edocs_public/attachmatch/DOC-242654A1.pdf); in 2001 a Hooters of Augusta (Ga.) was found to have violated the act and had to pay out over $1 million in a class action suit.

[159] Cal. Civ. Code §§ 1798.80 et seq.

[160] FTC, Guide to the Federal Trade Commission (www.ftc.gov/bcp/conline/pubs/general/guidetoftc.htm#bcp)

[161] Ex: New York Consumer Protection Board, False Advertising and Deceptive Trade Practices (www.consumer.state.ny.us/clahm/clahm-falseadvertising.htm)

[162] Federal Trade Commission Act, 15 U.S.C. § 45(a)(1)

[163] Federal Trade Commission Act, 15 U.S.C. § 45(a)(2)

[164] "Gateway Learning Settles FTC Privacy Charges," FTC Press Release, July 7, 2004 (www.ftc.gov/opa/2004/07/gateway.htm)

[165] See: www.ftc.gov/privacy/privacyinitiatives/promises.html

[166] Financial Recordkeeping and Reporting of Currency and Foreign Transactions Act of 1970, 31 USC 1051

[167] In addition to the federal Bank Secrecy Act and other regulations that require reporting to the U.S. government, many states also provide for the disclosure of banking records and financial transaction data to state and local law enforcement agencies.

[168] See 31 CFR 103.33; 31 CFR 103.34; 31 CFR 103.38

[169] See 12 CFR 21.11; 12 CFR 208.62; 12 CFR 353.3

[170] (1 CFR 5321

[171] "Uniting and Strengthening America by Providing Appropriate Tools Required to Intercept and Obstruct Terrorism (USA Patriot Act) Act of 2001," Public Law No: 107-56 (2001)

[172] For more also see: Ronald R. Glancz, Wallace E. Christner and Samuel A. Ozeck , USA PATRIOT Act, 2002 (www.venable.com/publication.cfm?publication_type_ID=2&publication_ID=489)

[173] Communications Assistance to Law Enforcement Act of 1994, 47 U.S.C. §§ 1001-1021 (1994)

[174] See www.askcalea.net/

[175] U.S.C. Title 21, Chapter 9

[176] See www.osha.gov

[177] See www.cdc.gov

[178] OCR Guidance Explaining Significant Aspects of the Privacy Rule— DISCLOSURES FOR PUBLIC HEALTH ACTIVITIES, page 28; see also 45 CFR 164.512(b)(1)(i) and (iii)

[179] For an excellent summary of FOIA, see EPIC.org www.epic.org/open_gov/rights.html

[180] *Id.* Epic Summary: www.epic.org/open_gov/rights.html

[181] *Id.* Epic Summary: www.epic.org/open_gov/rights.html

[182] http://laws.justice.gc.ca/en/p-8.6/93196.html

[183] The types of data elements commonly found on a business card are excluded from coverage of the Act.

[184] Canadian Dept. of Justice, "Privacy provisions highlights" (http://canada.justice.gc.ca/en/news/nr/1998/attback2.html)

[185] Office of the Privacy Commissioner of Canada (www.privcom.gc.ca/incidents/index_e.asp)

[186] Provincial / Territorial Privacy Laws, Oversight Offices and Government Organizations (www.privcom.gc.ca/information/comms_e.asp)

[187] http://E.U.ropa.E.U..int/information_society/topics/ecomm/all_about/todays_framework/privacy_protection/index_en.htm

[188] http://E.U.ropa.E.U..int/comm/justice_home/fsj/privacy/workinggroup/index_ en.htm

[189] www.cdt.org/privacy/E.U.directive/EU_Directive_.html#HD_NM_6

[190] http://E.U.ropa.E.U..int/comm/justice_home/fsj/privacy/law/implementation_en.htm

[191] The 25 current E.U. member states are: Belgium, Czech Republic, Denmark, Germany Estonia, Greece, Spain, France, Ireland, Italy Cyrus, Latvia, Lithuania, Luxembourg, Hungary, Malta, The Netherlands, Austria, Poland, Portugal, Slovenia, Slovakia, Finland, Sweden, and the United Kingdom.

[192] For example, the E-Privacy Directive, 2002/58/EC, the E-Commerce Directive, 2000/31/EC, Telecommunications Privacy Directive, 97/66/EC, the Distance Contracts Directive, 97/7/EC as well as guidance from the Article 29 Working Party

[193] Article 25.1 of the Directive 95/46/EC provides: "the transfer to a third country of personal data which are undergoing processing or are intended for processing after transfer may take place only if … the third country in question ensures an adequate level of data protection."

[194] In addition to the countries listed in the next paragraph above, additional adequacy determinations have been made for transfers to the United States within the Safe Harbor framework (discussed below), pursuant to certain model contracts (also discussed below) and within the Air Passenger Name Record data agreement.

[195] The Framework documents and related materials are online at www.export.gov/safe-harbor/

[196] This enforcement scheme has resulted in certain U.S. industries being ineligible for Safe Harbor certification. For example, because the FTC and DOT do not have jurisdiction to regulate banks and other financial institutions, these types of entities are not eligible for the Safe Harbor. (These entities are exclusively regulated by other Federal and state regulators, who have not agreed to enforce Safe Harbor promises.)

[197] www.export.gov/safeharbor/sh_overview.html

[198] E.U., Model Contracts for the transfer of personal data to third countries (http://E.U.ropa.E.U..int/comm/justice_home/fsj/privacy/modelcontracts/index_en.ht m)

[199] Transfer contracts are specifically permitted by Article 26 of the Directive, and are therefore occasionally referred to as "Article 26 contracts."

[200] Please note that even model contacts are subject to national laws and process require-ments, such as requirements that international data transfer agreements be deposited with the national DPAs.

[201] These principles are (1) the purpose limitation principle; (2) the data quality and pro-portionality principle; (3) the transparency principle; (4) security and confidentiality

requirements; (5) rights of access, rectification, deletion and objection, as provided for in Article 12 of the Directive; (6) restrictions on onward transfer; and (7) additional measures with respect to sensitive data, direct marketing processing and automated individual decisions. These principles must be interpreted in the sense as provided in the EC Data Protection Working Group's Opinion 12/98.

[203] The minimum information to be provided to data subjects in this case must include (1) the purposes of the onward transfer; (2) the identification of the data exporter established in the EC; (3) the categories of further recipients of the data and the countries of destination; and (4) an explanation that, after the onward transfer, the data may be processed by a controller established in a country where there is not an adequate level of protection of the privacy of individuals.

[204] Parties must also agree to permit the data subject to rely on ADR mechanisms, provided that the parties are established in a country that has ratified the NY Convention on enforcement of arbitration awards; and that the available options do not prejudice the data subject's substantive or procedural rights to seek remedies in accordance with other provisions of national or international law.

[205] 97/66/EC of the European Parliament and of the Council of 15 December 1997 concerning the processing of personal data and the protection of privacy in the telecommunications sector.

[206] Traditional (manual) telemarketing remained subject to the general Data Protection Directive's notice and opt-out provisions.

[207] 2002/58/EC, Directive of the European Parliament of the Council of 12 July 2002 concerning the processing of personal data and the protection of privacy in the electronic communications sector.

[207] http://E.U.ropa.E.U..int/information_society/topics/ecomm/useful_information/library/legislation/index_en.htm#dir_2002_58_ec

[208] http://secretariat.efta.int/Web/E.U.ropeanEconomicArea/introduction

[209] www.edsb.ch/e/gesetz/schweiz/background.htm

[210] The member economies consist of Australia, Brunei Darussalam, Canada, Chile, the People's Republic of China, Hong Kong China, Indonesia, Japan, the Republic of Korea, Malaysia, Mexico, New Zealand, Papua New Guinea, Peru, Philippines, Russia, Singapore, Chinese Taipei, Thailand, the United States, and Viet Nam.

[211] Online: www.apec.org/apec/news_media/2004_media_releases/201104_apecmin-sendorseprivacyfrmwk.html

[212] Implementing guidelines are issued by the Ministry of Economy, Trade and Industry (METI), the Ministry of Health, Labor and Welfare (MHLW), the Financial Services Agency (FSA), the Ministry of Finance, the Ministry of Internal Affairs and

Communications, the Ministry of Land, Infrastructure and Transport, and the Ministry of Justice.

[213] For example, databases with fewer than 5,000 records are not covered by the Law.

[214] Transfers to mere data processors or delegates are not subject to these requirements, as the obligations proper handling of the Personal Information and supervision of the delegates remains with the Business Handling Personal Information.

[215] A few narrow exceptions exist, such as for transfers made pursuant to a law or ordinance or as necessary for the protection of human life, safety, or property, and when it is difficult to obtain the consent of the Principal.

[216] See, *e.g.*, FSA Guidelines, Art. 13.5.

[217] To see the 11 Information Privacy Principles go to: www.privacy.gov.au/publications/ipps.html

[218] Available online at www.privacy.gov.au/act/privacyact/index.html

[219] To see the 10 National Privacy Principles go to: www.privacy.gov.au/publications/npps01.html

[220] www.derechos.org/nizkor/arg/eng.html

[221] Article 43, Constitucion de la Nacion Argentina (1994) (www.constitution.org/cons/argentin.htm) (in Spanish); (www.oefre.unibe.ch/law/icl/ar00000_.html - translation).

[222] www.privacyinternational.org/countries/argentina/argentine-dpa.html

[223] See, *e.g.*, the Brazilian Consumer Protection Law (Federal Law No. 8,078, Article 43, September 11, 1990), and the Mexican Consumer Protection Law (cited below).

[224] *Ley Federal de Protecci_n al Consumidor*

[225] New article 76 took effect in May 2004 which provides (among other things) that subject companies shall not be able to transfer information provided by consumers to third parties, unless there is express consent from the consumer or a requirement from a public authority.

[226] Cal. Civ. Code §§ 1798.80 *et seq.*

[227] Civil Rights Act of 1964, Title VII, 42 U.S.C. §§ 2000e-2000e-17 (2005).

[228] Pregnancy Discrimination Act, Title VII, 42 U.S.C. §§200e-2000e-17 (2005).

[229] Americans with Disabilities Act, 42 U.S.C. §§ 12101-12213 (2005).

[230] Age Discrimination in Employment Act, 29 U.S.C. §§ 621-634 (2005).

[231] Equal Pay Act of 1963, 29 U.S.C. §§ 206(d), 209, 211, 213, 215-219, 255, 256, 259, 260, 262 (2005).

[232] Health Insurance Portability and Accountability Act (HIPAA), 42. U.S.C. §§ 300gg-300gg-2 (2005).

[233] Consolidated Omnibus Budget Reconciliation Act (COBRA) of 1986, 42 U.S.C. §§ 300bb-1-300bb-8 (2005).

[234] Employee Retirement Income Security Act (ERISA) of 1974, 29 U.S.C. §§ 1001-1461 (2005).

[235] Family Medical Leave Act (FMLA) of 1993, 29 U.S.C. §§ 2601-2654 (2005).

[236] Fair Credit Reporting Act (FCRA), 15 U.S.C. §§1681-1681v (2005).

[237] Fair Labor Standards Act (FLSA) of 1938, 29 U.S.C. §§ 201-219 (2005).

[238] Occupational Safety and Health Act (OSH Act) of 1970, 29 U.S.C. §§ 651-678 (2005).

[239] Whistleblower Protection Act of 1989, Public Law No. 101-12, 5 U.S.C. §§ 1201 et seq.

[240] National Labor Relations Act (NLRA), 29 U.S.C. §§ 151-159 (2005).

[241] Immigration Reform and Control Act (IRCA) of 1986, 8 U.S.C. §§ 1324a-b (2005).

[242] Privacy Act of 1974, 5 U.S.C. § 552a (2005).

[243] U.S. Const. amend. IV (2005).

[244] California Constitution, Art. 1, § 1.

[245] See, e.g., Cal Gov't Code 12940; N.Y. Exec. Law § 296; Del. Code Ann. Tit. 19, § 711.

[246] See, e.g., Illinois Right to Privacy in the Workplace Act, 820 I.L.C.S. § 55.

[247] Department of Labor, *Our Mission*; available from www.dol.gov/opa/aboutdol/mission.htm.

[248] See Fair Credit Reporting Act (FCRA), 15 U.S.C. §§ 1681 et seq., and the FTC's FCRA guidance for Employers, found at www.ftc.gov/privacy/privacyinitiatives/credit_bus.html

[249] Donald C. Dowling, "Preparing to Resolve U.S.-Based Employers' Disputes Under Europe's New Data Privacy Law," *ALSB International Business Law Journal* 1 (2000): 39; available from www.wsu.edu:8080/~legal/ijrnl/dowling/.

[250] *E.U. Directive 95/46/EC of the European Parliament and the Council of 24 October 1995 on the Protection of Individuals with Regard to the Processing of Personal Data and the Free Movement of Such Data;* available from www.cdt.org/privacy/eudirective/EU_Directive_.html.

[251] Janice R. Bellace, "The European Works Council Directive: Transnational Information and Consultation in the European Union," *Comparative Labor Law Journal* 18 (1997): 325.

[252] Ibid., 342. Contrast this to the American system where the union must ask for information to activate a disclosure obligation.

[253] Philip M. Berkowitz, *The European Works Councils*; available from www.lawinternational.com/articles/euroworks.html.

[254] Congress Youth, *European Collective Bargaining*; available from www.ictu.ie/html/services/eubarg.html

[255] U.S. Department of Labor, *Foreign Labor Trends- European Union;* available from www.dol.gov/ILAB/media/reports/flt/european-union-2003.htm#d04.

[256] See www.apec.org/apec/apec_groups/som_special_task_groups/electronic_ commerce.html

[257] Privacy Rights Clearinghouse, *Employment Background Checks: A Jobseeker's Guide*; available from www.privacyrights.org.

[258] Privacy Rights Clearinghouse, *Employment Background Checks: A Jobseeker's Guide*; available from www.privacyrights.org

[259] 15 U.S.C. § 1581a.

[260] Investigative Consumer Reporting Agencies Act, 1.6A Cal. Civ. Code §§ 1786-1786.60 (2005).

[261] *California Law Is Amended*; available from www.mccoyinvestigations.com/CALIFORNIAUPDATE.html.

[262] Employee Polygraph Protection Act, 29 U.S.C. §§ 2001-2009 (2005).

[263] Paul F. Gerhart, "Employee Privacy Rights in the United States," *Comparative Labor Law Journal* 17 (1995): 195.

[264] Ibid.

[265] Ibid.

[266] Equal Employment Opportunity Commission, *Disability Discrimination*, available from www.eeoc.gov/types/ada.html.

[267] Ibid.

[268] Ibid.

[269] Ibid.

[270] Gerhart, 196.

[271] Ibid.

[272] ISK Task Force on Privacy and Protection of Personal Data, *ICC report on binding corporate rules for international transfers of personal data*, 4; available from www.iccwbo.org/home/ebitt/FINAL_ICC_BCRs_report.pdf#search='ICC%20report %20on%20binding%20corporate%20rules%20for%20international%20transfers%20of%2 0personal%20data'.

273 Graham Greenleaf, "The European Privacy Directive-Completed," *Privacy Law and Policy Report* 2 (1995); available from http://austlii.edu.au/~graham/PLPR_EU_1.html.

274 Directive 95/46/EC, Article 1; available from http://www.cdt.org/privacy/eudirective/EU_Directive_.html.

275 Ibid., Article 10,11.

276 Ibid., Article 7.

277 Ibid., Article 8.

278 Ibid., Article 25.

279 Ibid., Article 26.

280 United States Department of Labor, *Alphabetical List of Major Laws*; available from www.dol.gov/dol/compliance/compliance-majorlaw.htm#alphabet.

281 Fair Labor Standards Act (FLSA), 29 U.S.C. § 211(c) (2005).

282 U.S. Department of Labor, Fair Labor Standards Act of 1938, as amended, 27; available from www.dol.gov/esa/regs/statutes/whd/FairLaborStandAct.pdf.

283 Occupational Health and Safety Act (OSH Act), 29 U.S.C. § 657(c)(2) (2005).

284 Ibid.

285 Ibid., § 657(c)(3).

286 Employee Retirement Income Security Act (ERISA), 29 U.S.C. § 1059(a) (2005).

287 Ibid., § 1059(a)(1).

288 Securities and Exchange Commission, *Introduction: The SEC- Who We Are, What We Do*; available from www.sec.gov/about/whatwedo.shtml.

289 Securities and Exchange Commission, *The Laws That Govern The Securities Industry*; available from www.sec.gov/about/whatwedo.shtml#laws.

290 Securities and Exchange Commission, *The Laws That Govern the Securities Industry: Securities Act of 1933*; available from www.sec.gov/about/whatwedo.shtml#laws.

291 Ibid.

292 Ibid.

293 Ibid.

294 Ibid.

295 Ibid.

296 Ibid.

297 Ibid.

298 Ibid.

[299] Ibid.

[300] Ibid.

[301] Equal Employment Opportunity Commission, *Laws Enforced by the EEOC*; available from www.eeoc.gov/policy/laws.html.

[302] Civil Rights Act of 1964, Title VII, 42 U.S.C. § 2000e-8(c) (2005).

[303] Ibid.

[304] Equal Pay Act of 1963, 29 U.S.C. § 211(c) (2005).

[305] Ibid.

[306] Centers for Medicare & Medicaid Services, *Covered Entity Decision Tools: Background*; available from www.cms.hhs.gov/hipaa/hipaa2/support/tools/decisionsupport/default.asp.

[307] HIPAA Employer, *HIPAA as An HR Issue*; available from www.bairdholm.com/issues/hipaa/print/hipaaemployer.htm.

[308] HIPAA Employer, *HIPAA as An HR Issue*; available from www.bairdholm.com/issues/hipaa/print/hipaaemployer.htm.

[309] Ibid.

[310] Ibid.

[311] Ibid.

[312] Ibid.

[313] Ibid.

[314] Ibid.

[315] Ibid.

[316] Ibid.

[317] Ibid.

[318] Ibid.

[319] Ibid.

[320] Peter J. Kok & Marcus W. Campbell, *Undercover Employee Misconduct Investigations: The 'Vail' has Just Been Removed*; available from www.hrgofwestmichigan.org/legal%20updates/apr04_update.html.

[321] Ibid.

[322] Ibid.

[323] Ibid.

[324] Ibid.

[325] See 1.8 Cal. Civ. Code §1798.29 (2005).

[326] Ibid., Recitals § 30.

[327] Ibid., Recitals § 33.

[328] Ibid., Article 8 § 1.

[329] Ibid., Article 8 § 2(a).

[330] Ibid., Article 8 § 2(b).

[331] Ibid., Article 8 § 2(c), § 4.

[332] Ibid., Article 8 § 3.

[333] Ibid., Article 8 § 5.

[334] Safety and Security Information Center, *Workplace Surveillance*; available from www.securityworld.com/library/workplacetech/workplacesurveillance.html

[335] Ibid.

[336] Risk Control, Inc.; available from http://rciutah.com/why.htm.

[337] Ibid.

[338] Ibid.

[339] Ibid.

[340] Securonce, *The New Spam Onslaught: A Cat and Mouse Game*; available from www.securence.net/resources/White_Paper_The_New_Spam_Onslaught.htm

[341] Declan McCullagh, "Porn spam--legal minefield for employers," *News.com*; available from http://news.com.com/2100-1032-995658.html

[342] See, e.g., 18 U.S.C. §§1700, 1701, 1702 & 1703

[343] Online Spying, *Monitoring Employees: Security Beings From Within*; available from www.online-spying.com/monitoring-employees.html.

[344] Jaime Cowper, *Why Businesses Need To Manage And Monitor Employee Email Usage*; available from www.toptensoft.com/monitoring_software/support/Why_Businesses_Need_To_Manage_And_Monitor_Employee_Email_Usage.htm

[345] FLG Networking Sevices, *Monitoring Internet Usage in the Workplace;* available from www.flgnetworking.com/article1.html.

[346] See, *e.g.*, Del Code Ann. tit. §19-7-705 and Conn. Gen. Stat. 31-48d(3)

[347] U.S. Department of Labor, *Workplace Violence*; available from www.osha.gov/SLTC/workplaceviolence/.

[348] Norman D. Bates, "Workplace Violence and Employer Liability," *Victim Advocate*; available from www.liabilityconsultants.com/article.htm.

[349] Ibid.

[350] Ibid.

[351] Timothy E. McKenna, *Recovering Damages*; available from www.timmckennalaw.com/article.jsp?practArea=42&articleIndex=3.

[352] U.S. Department of Labor, *General Duties Clause*; available from www.osha.gov/pls/oshaweb/owadisp.show_document?p_table=OSHACT&p_id=3359.

[353] 18 U.S.C §2510(5)(a)(1)

[354] 18 U.S.C §2511(2)(d)

[355] 18 U.S.C. § 2701(c)(1).

[356] 18 U.S.C. § 2701(c)(1)).

[357] Frank J. Cavico, "Invasion of Privacy in the Private Employment Sector: Tortious and Ethical Aspects," *Houston Law Review* 30 (1993): 1304-1306.

[358] Ibid., Article 8.

[359] Ibid., Article 25.

[360] Ibid., Article 26.

[361] Ibid., Article 6.

[362] Ibid., Article 12.

[363] Ibid., Article 6.

[364] Ibid., Article 17.

[365] Ibid., Article 17.

[366] Ibid., Article 15.

[367] Ibid., Article 14.

[368] Ibid., Article 12.

[369] Twelfth Meeting of European Labour Court Judges, *Protection of Worker's Privacy Questionnaire*; available from www.ilo.org/public/english/dialogue/ifpdial/downloads/lc_05/ireland_2.pdf#search='Directive%2095/46/EC%20and%20Background%20Checks

[370] ?

[371] Advisory Consulting and Publishing, LLC, *Documentation of Poor Employee Performance or Employee Misconduct*; available from www.advisorypublishing.com/employee_documen-tation.shtml.

[372] Peter J. Kok & Marcus W. Campbell, *Undercover Employee Misconduct Investigations: The 'Vail' has Just Been Removed*; available from www.hrgofwestmichigan.org/legal%20updates/apr04_update.html.

[373] Ibid.

[374] Ibid.

[375] Ibid.

[376] There are various tools available to assist in mapping out systems on your network. This can be helpful because it gives you the same perspective on the network as someone trying to infiltrate it. Be careful in downloaded software from these sites as it is a common practice to code back-door exploits into the software. Some of these tools are available at www.treachery.net/tools. A popular tool, both for network and security administrators and hackers a like, is n-map, a network-mapping tool available at www.insecure.org (note: the tool is available for Windows but is much more robust for Linux).

[377] A fairly comprehensive database of whitepapers on auditing best practices is available at www.sans.org/rr/whitepapers/auditing.

[378] For more information on system logging system, see, Seham Mohamed GadAllah, *The Importance of Logging and Traffic Monitoring for Information Security*, Dec. 2003, at www.sans.org/rr/whitepapers/logging/1379.php.

[379] For more information about digital signatures see, Minnesota State Colleges and Universities, *A Brief Introduction to Digital Signatures and Public Key Encryption*, at www.hr.mnscu.edu/faq/pke.html.

[380] For more information on securing centralized data backups, see, Scott M. Parrish, *Security Considerations for Enterprise Level Backups*, 2002, www.sans.org/rr/whitepapers/backup/515.php.

[381] For more information on the importance of physical security for network and data integrity see, B. Fraser, RFC 2196—*Site Security Handbook*, Sept. 1997, at www.faqs.org/rfcs/rfc2196.html.

[382] For more information on the security threat posed by ipods, see, Simon Dawson, *Information Theft*, May 19, 2005, at http://www.legalit.net/PrintItem.asp?id=24195.

[383] Some are beginning to explore the risks to data security posed by camera phones and blue-tooth phones. See, Russell Robinson, *Surviving The Camera Phone Phenomenon: An Analysis of Personal & Corporate Security*, Feb. 2004, at www.sans.org/rr/whitepapers/privacy/1387.php.

[384] See, Daniel Oxenhandler, *Designing a Secure Local Area Network*, 2003, at www.sans.org/rr/whitepapers/bestprac/853.php.

[385] For one example of how to mitigate extranet risks, see, *Business Partner VPN: Needed Now*, 2003, at www.sans.org/rr/whitepapers/vpns/880.php.

[386] See, Michael Stines, *Remote Access VPN—Security Concerns and Policy Enforcement*, 2003, at www.sans.org/rr/whitepapers/vpns/881.php.

[387] For more information about digital signatures see, Minnesota State Colleges and Universities, *A Brief Introduction to Digital Signatures and Public Key Encryption*, at www.hr.mnscu.edu/faq/pke.html.

[388] See, Keith MacLeod, *Patch Management and the Need for Metrics*, Jul. 2004, at http://www.sans.org/rr/whitepapers/bestprac/1461.php.

[389] This includes an understanding that information is not only vulnerable on computers, but that paper must also be secured as well, especially since it is difficult to secure paper centrally.

[390] For more information on the types of threats internal users pose and ways of mitigating those risks, see, Charles Rhodes, *The Internal Threat to Security Or Users Can Really Mess Things Up*, 2003, at www.sans.org/rr/whitepapers/bestprac/856.php.

[391] Janne Saarikko, *The Threat from Within—Challenges of Managing Internal Information Security Risks*, May 2004, at http://securitysa.com/article.asp?pklArticleID =2967&pklIssueID=487&pklCategoryID=106.

[392] This follows the principle of least privilege, a concept popularized by the NSA. For information on implementing this principle, see, Jeff Langford, *Implementing Least Privilege at your Enterprise*, Jul. 5, 2003, at www.sans.org/rr/whitepapers/bestprac/1188.php.

[393] For more information on the importance of incorporating end users into data security models and the threats posed to end user sytems, see Andrew Conry-Murray, *Securing End Users from Attack*, Oct. 5, 2002, at www.networkmagazine.com/shared/printableArticle.jhtml?articleID=8703428.

[394] For a short overview of legal issues to consider in creating a data retention policy, see, Barbara Weil Gall, *Document Retention Policies: Legal Reasons to Keep Email, Web Pages and Other Records*, Sept. 2000, at www.gigalaw.com/articles/2000-all/gall-2000-09-all.html.

[395] Paul Fest and Lisa Bowman, *Computers Hinder Paper Shredders*, Feb. 4, 2002, at news.com.com/2100-1023-829004.html.

[396] Justin Pope, *Haunted By Ghosts Of Hard Drives Past*, Jan. 16, 2003, at www.cbsnews.com/stories/2003/01/16/tech/main536774.shtml.

[397] For an example of how one company maintained security over outsourced IT, see, Leslie Martinez, *Retain Control of Security (Even in the Wake of an IT Outsource)*, Feb. 2003, at www.sans.org/rr/whitepapers/casestudies/1244.php.

[398] Christopher Koch, *Don't Maroon Security*, CIO Magazine, May 15, 2005 at www.cio.com/archive/051505/security.html

[399] For a more complete introduction to PKI see, ArticSoft, *Introduction to Public Key Infrastructure*, Feb 2, 2003, at www.articsoft.com/wp_pki_intro.htm

[400] For more detailed information on PKI, see, Duncan Wood, *PKI, The What, The Why, and The How*, 2002, at www.sans.org/rr/whitepapers/vpns/764.php

401 For information on public key encryption generally, and one of its most popular implementations, PGP (Pretty Good Privacy), see, *How PGP Works*, 1999, at www.pgpi.org/doc/pgpintro.

402 Visa. "USA Cardholder Information Security Program: Overview." (2005). Available from World Wide Web: www.usa.visa.com/download/business/accepting_visa/support_center/cisp_overview.pdf?it=c|/business/accepting_visa/ops_risk_management/cisp%2Ehtml|CISP%20Overview.

403 For more information on vectoring or perimeter-based virus protection, see, Daniel Boyd, *Scanning for Viruses*, Feb. 2003, at www.sans.org/rr/whitepapers/firewalls/995.php.

404 Microsoft, Monitoring Reliability and Availability of Windows 2000 based Server Systems (2000), Available from www.microsoft.com/windows2000/docs/MonitorRel.doc.

405 The National Strategy to Secure Cyberspace, *supra* note 21, at 45.

406 Technology Assessment, *supra* note 18, at 66.

407 *Id.*, at 24.

408 Information Security, *supra* note 25, at 6.

409 *Id.*

410 Pam Cocca, Email Security Threats 3 (Sept. 20, 2004), Available from www.sans.org. See also, Larry Bridwell, ICSA Labs 9th Annual Computer Virus Prevalence Survey (2004), Available from www.trusecure.com/cgi-bin/download.cgi?file=wp_vps2003_report.pdf&ESCD=w0169.

411 Larry Bridwell, ICSA Labs 9th Annual Computer Virus Prevalence Survey (2004), Available from www.trusecure.com/cgi-bin/download.cgi?file=wp_vps2003_report.pdf&ESCD=w0169.

412 *Id.*

413 *Id.*

414 Pam Cocca, Email Security Threats 4 (Sept. 20, 2004), Available from www.sans.org.

415 Janne Saarikko, *The Threat from Within—Challenges of Managing Internal Information Security Risks*, May 2004, at www.securitysa.com/article.asp?pklArticleID=2967&pklIssueID=487&pklCategoryID=106.

416 See, Andrew Conry-Murray, Application-Layer Protection, Jul 5, 2004, at www.networkmagazine.com/shared/article/showArticle.jhtml?articleId=22103705&classroom=.

417 Tripwire is a perennial favorite for this task. The program is available in open source format from http://surceforge.net/projects/tripwire or together with commercial services and add-on features from companies like Tripwire Inc. at www.tripwire.com.

[418] See, Nathaniel Hall, *Creating A Secure Linux Logging System*, Oct. 2004, at www.sans.org/rr/whitepapers/logging/1529.php, or Gregory Lalla, *Centralizing Event Logs on Windows 2000*, Feb. 2003, at www.sans.org/rr/whitepapers/logging/902.php.

[419] GAO. Statement of Jack L. Brock, Jr. and Keith A. Rhodes before the Permanent Subcommittee on Investigations, Committee on Governmental Affairs, U.S. Senate, Information Security: Computer Hacker Information Available on the Internet (June 5, 1996). Available from: (www.gao.gov/archive/1996/ai96108t.pdf).

[420] NASA. "NASA World Wide Web Best Practices Version 2.0: 7.0 Site Search." Available from: (http://nasa-wbp.larc.nasa.gov/7.0/)

[421] GAO. "Technology Assessment: Cybersecurity for Critical Infrastructure Protection." (May 2004):151. Available from: (http://161.203.16.2/new.items/d04321.pdf) (hereafter: Technology Assessment).

[422] ICANN controls the creation of Top Level Domains. (The application can be viewed at ICANN's Web site. Available from: (www.icann.org).

[423] WiredSafety.org. "Thinking Outside the "Porn" Box ...separating the sexual content debate from issues relating to marketing, commercial practices and child exploitation: Finding a Workable Solution to Privacy, Security, Consumer Fraud and Child-Exploitation Issues Relating to Adult Websites." 5. Available from: (www.wiredsafety.org/resources/documents/xxx_whitepaper.doc).

[424] Network Advertising Initiative (NAI). "Self-Regulatory Principles for Online Preference Marketing by Network Advertisers." 22. Available from: (www.networkadvertising.org).

[425] The National Strategy to Secure Cyberspace. (Feb. 2003): 38. Available from: (www.whitehouse.gov/pcipb/cyberspace_strategy.pdf).

[426] *Id.*

[427] *Id.*

[428] Federal Trade Commission. "Children's Online Privacy Protection Rule—Comment, P994504, Comments of the Center for Democracy and Technology." (June 11, 1999). Available from: (www.ftc.gov/privacy/comments/cdt.htm).

[429] Children's Online Privacy Protection Rule. 16 C.F.R. Part 312 (Apr. 21, 2000). Available from: (www.ftc.gov/os/1999/10/childrensprivacy.pdf).

[430] Freier, Alan O. and Philip Karlton and Paul C. Kocher. "The SSL Protocol Version 3.0." (November 1999). Available from: (www.mozilla.org/projects/security/pki/nss/ssl/draft302.txt).

[431] *Id.*

[432] MIT Libraries Web Advisory Group. "Javascript." Available from: (http://macfadden.mit.edu/webgroup/guidelines/javascript.html). Javascript should be used sparingly to allow for a broader audience.

[433] Bear, David. "Glossary.": (www.public.asu.edu/~iddwb/writeups/glossary.html).

[434] McGraw-Hill/Osborne. "JavaScript Security." JavaScript. (Oct. 4, 2004). Available from: (www.devarticles.com/c/a/JavaScript/JavaScript-Security/).

[435] Staniford, Stuart, Vern Paxson, and Nicholas Weaver. "How to Own the Internet in Your Spare Time." Proceedings of the 11th USENIX Security Symposium. (May 21, 2002). Available from: (www.icir.org/vern/papers/cdc-usenix-sec02/cdc.web.pdf).

[436] *Id.*

[437] McDaniel, Patrick. "Computer and Network Authentication." 10. Available from: (www.patrickmcdaniel.org/pubs/mcdaniel-netauth.pdf).

[438] "RealNetworks Patches Media-Player Vulnerabilities: After confirming three flaws uncovered in U.K.." *TechBuilder.org* (Feb. 6, 2004). Available from: (www.techbuilder.org/news/59201488).

[439] GAO. "Information Security: Weak Controls Place Interior's Financial and Other Data at Risk." (July 3, 2001): 14. Available from: (www.iwar.org.uk/comsec/resources/gao/d01615.pdf) (Hereafter Information Security).

[440] Shiftlett, Chris. "PHP Security." (Nov. 14, 2004): 14. Available from: (http://shiftlett.org).

[441] *Id.*

[442] Technology Assessment, *supra* note 18, at 118.

[443] Online Personal Privacy Act, S. 2201, Report of the Committee on Commerce, Science, and Transportation (Aug. 1, 2002). Available from: (http://thomas.loc.gov/cgi-bin/cpquery/T?&report=sr240&dbname=cp107&).

[444] FTC, Final Report of the FTC Advisory Committee on Online Access and Security (May 15, 2000), Available from: (www.ftc.gov/acoas/papers/finalreport.htm).

[445] *Id.*

[446] *Id.*

[447] FTC, ACOAS Draft Advisory Committee Report (April 26, 2000), Available from: (www.ftc.gov/acoas/papers/draft_advisory_committee_report_body.htm).

[448] *Id.*

[449] *Id.*

[450] *Id.* See also, BBB *OnLine*, European Union/U.S. Safe Harbor Compliance, at www.bbbonline.org/privacy/eu.asp (last visited June 30, 2005). *See also*, U.S. Department of Commerce, Safe Harbor Overview, Available from:

(www.export.gov/safeharbor/sh_overview.html). *See also*, European Union, Directive 2002/58/EC (July 12, 2002), Available from: (http://europa.eu.int/eur-lex/pri/en/oj/dat/2002/l_201/l_20120020731en00370047.pdf).

[451] FTC, Final Report of the FTC Advisory Committee on Online Access and Security (May 15, 2000), Available from: (www.ftc.gov/acoas/papers/finalreport.htm).

[452] *Id.*

[453] TRUSTe. "TRUSTe Guidance on Website Disclosures." Available from: (www.truste.org/docs/Model_ Privacy_Policy_Disclosures.doc).

[454] Goldman, Janlori. Health Privacy Project. "Testimony before the U.S. House of Representatives Subcommittee on Government Management, Information, and Technology of the Committee on Government Reform and Oversight on "The Consumer Protection and Medical Record Confidentiality Act of 1998" Discussion Draft 5/14/98, Authored by Congressman Chris Shays (R-CT)." (May 14, 1998): 6. Available from: (www.healthprivacy.org/usr_doc/33815.pdf).

[455] The Privacy Act of 1974. 5 U.S.C. §552a. (1974). Available from: (www.usdoj.gov/foia/privstat.htm).

[456] Larson, Annelise. "Privacy Laws and Best Practices." *IIMA March 2003 Newsletter* (March 2003). Available from: (www.iimaonline.org/newsletter/newsletter-march-03.html).

[457] NAI. Available from: (www.networkadvertising.org).

[458] Berman, Jerry. CDT. Before The Senate Committee On Commerce, Science, And Transportation Subcommittee on Communications On The SPY BLOCK Act (March 23, 2004). Available from: (www.cdt.org/testimony/20040323berman.shtml).

[459] FTC v. Seismic Entm't Prods., 2004 U.S. Dist. LEXIS 22788, n.4 (Oct. 21, 2004). ("Instead, the court concluded that the plaintiff was not likely to succeed on its constitutional challenge to that part of the law which prohibits unauthorized installations of software on computers but that the prohibition against all pop-up ads and a protocol for authorization and consent would likely violate the *Commerce Clause*.")

[460] WhatIs.Com. Available from: (http://whatis.techtarget.com/definition/0,,sid9_gci887624,00.html). ("A drive-by download is a program that is automatically downloaded to your computer, often without your consent or even your knowledge…")

[461] Leyden, John. "One Third of Email is Now Spam." (April 2004). Available from: (www.theregister.co.uk/2004/04/20/idc_spam_survey/).

[462] Gaur, Nalneesh. "Hooked." *Information Security*. Available from: (http://infosecuritymag.techtarget.com/ss/0,295796,sid6_iss426_art874,00.html).

[463] Cocca, Pam. "Email Security Threats." (Sept. 20, 2004):3. Available from: (www.sans.org/).

[464] GAO, 01-424 "Internet Privacy: Implementation of Federal Guidance for Agency Use of "Cookies." (Apr. 2001). Available from: (www.gao.gov/new.items/d01424.pdf).

[465] Network Advertising Initiative (NAI). "Self-Regulatory Principles for Online Preference Marketing by Network Advertisers." Available from: (www.networkadvertising.org).

[466] Ghosts, *supra* note 55, at 14.

[467] *Id.*

[468] Cocca, Pam. "Email Security Threats. *Sans* (Sept. 20, 2004): 3. Available from : (www.sans.org/).

[469] *Id.*

[470] Robert G. Bagnall, *Investment Company Regulation and Compliance Conference: Privacy*, SJ095 ALI-ABA 209 (2004).

[471] *Supra* note 6.

[472] *Id.*

[473] *Id.*

[474] Privacy of Consumer Financial Information (Regulation S-P), 17 C.F.R. Part 248 (2000), at www.sec.gov/rules/final/34-42974.htm#P225_87089.

[475] *Supra* note 6.

[476] Center for Democracy and Technology, *CDT's Guide to Online Privacy Protection: Existing Privacy Protections*, at www.cdt.org/privacy/guide/protect/ (last viewed June 26, 2005).

[477] *Supra* note 13.

[478] *Supra* note 6.

[479] U.S. Dep't of Health and Human Services, *OCR HIPAA Privacy: Disclosures for Public Health Activities* (April 3, 2003), at www.hhs.gov/ocr/hipaa/publichealth.pdf.pdf.

[480] *Id.*

[481] *Id.; see also* 45 C.F.R. 164.512(b)(1)(i).

[482] *Supra* note 18.

[483] U.S. Dep't of Health and Human Services, *OCR HIPAA Privacy: Personal Representatives* (April 3, 2003), *at* www.hhs.gov/ocr/hipaa/guidelines/personalrepresentatives.pdf.

[484] *Id.*

[485] *Supra* note 6.

[486] Federal Trade Commission, *In Brief: The Financial Privacy Requirements of the Gramm-Leach Bliley Act*, at www.ftc.gov/bcp/conline/pubs/buspubs/glbshort.htm (last viewed June 26, 2005).

[487] Federal Trade Commission, *Financial Institutions and Customer Data: Complying with the Safeguards Rule,* at www.ftc.gov/bcp/conline/pubs/buspubs/safeguards.htm (last viewed June 26, 2005).

[488] *Id.*

[489] *Id.*

[490] Charity Commission for England and Wales, *Operational Guide: Data Protection Act 1998 Series Glossary of Terms*, at www.charity-commission.gov.uk/supportingcharities/ogs/g058g001.asp#datac (last updated Feb. 14, 2002).

[491] *Id.*

[492] *Id.*

[493] *Id.*

[494] Directorate-General for Justice, Freedom, and Security of the European Commission, *Data Protection in the European Union* 9, http://europa.eu.int/comm/justice_home/fsj/privacy/docs/guide/guide-ukingdom_en.pdf (last viewed June 26, 2005).

[495] *Id.*

[496] U.S. Dep't of Commerce, *Safe Harbor Overview*, at www.export.gov/safeharbor/sh_overview.html (last viewed June 26, 2005).

[497] *Id.*

[498] *Id.*

[499] For further information on obtaining Safe Harbor certification and being listed as a Safe Harbor business, visit the Dep't of Commerce Web site at www.export.gov/safe-harbor/index.html.

[500] *Supra* note 35.

[501] *Supra* note 33.

[502] U.S. Dep't of Commerce, *Frequently Asked Questions: Human Resources*, available at www.export.gov/safeharbor/FAQ9HumanResFINAL.htm (last viewed June 27, 2005).

[503] *Id.*

[504] *Id.* (listing methods to comply with employee preferences without affecting how the business functions).

INDEX

A

Access
    by the customer, 243
    controls as monitoring devices, 146
    to information, definition of, 3
    roles-based controls, 177
    root-level, 173
    Web, 217
Accountability principle,
    under the OECD guidelines, 12,
    under the code of fair information practices, 28
    under the APEC privacy principles, 100
Acquiring user preferences from third parties, 242-243
ADA, *see* Americans with Disabilities Act
Advance Research Projects Agency
    ARPANet, 199
    definition of, 199
Adware, 191, 211
Aligning privacy policy with vendor contracts, 248-249
American Declaration of the Rights and Duties of Man, 3
Americans with Disabilities Act, 133
Anti-privacy laws, *see* Laws that compel disclosure of personal information
Anti-virus applications, 146, 186-189
APEC, *see* Asia Pacific Economic Cooperation
Application-layer attacks, 192

C

F

I

R

S

Safe harbor
   definition under the E.U. Directive, 91, 250
   definition under U.S. Department of Commerce framework, 250
SB-1386 (California), 69-70
   disclosures, 69
   exceptions to, 69
   personal information, definition of, 69
SEC, *see* Security and Exchange Commission
Secure Sockets Layer, 201, 219-220
Securities Act of 1933 (U.S.), 137
Securities Exchange Act of 1934 (U.S.), 137
Security
   breach notification laws, 69-70
   logs, 188-189
   monitoring, 187
   safeguards principle, 12, 27, 99
   Web, 217
Security and Exchange Commission, 136, 239
Self-assessment, 253
Self-regulatory regime, *see* Network Advertising Initiative
Shelby amendment, *see* Drivers Privacy Protection Act of 1994
Short notice, *see* Layered privacy notices
Smart-card, 182
Sources of law, 21-23
Spam email, 62-66, 211
Spyware, 190, 209-210
SSL, *see* Secure Sockets Layer
Standard model clauses, 250-251
Subpoenas and court orders, 77-78
Syndicated content, 205
System logs, *see* Logs

T

TCP, *see* Transmission Control Protocol
TCPA, *see* Telephone Consumer Protection Act of 1991
TCP/IP, *see* Transmission Control Protocol
Telemarketing rules, U.S. state, 62

X